| | |
|---|---|
| | |
| Bertrams | 11/10/2018 |
| J912.42 | |
| DG | 02358456 |

# MAPS
## OF THE
# UNITED
# KINGDOM

written by
### RACHEL DIXON

illustrated by
### LIVI GOSLING

## WIDE EYED EDITIONS

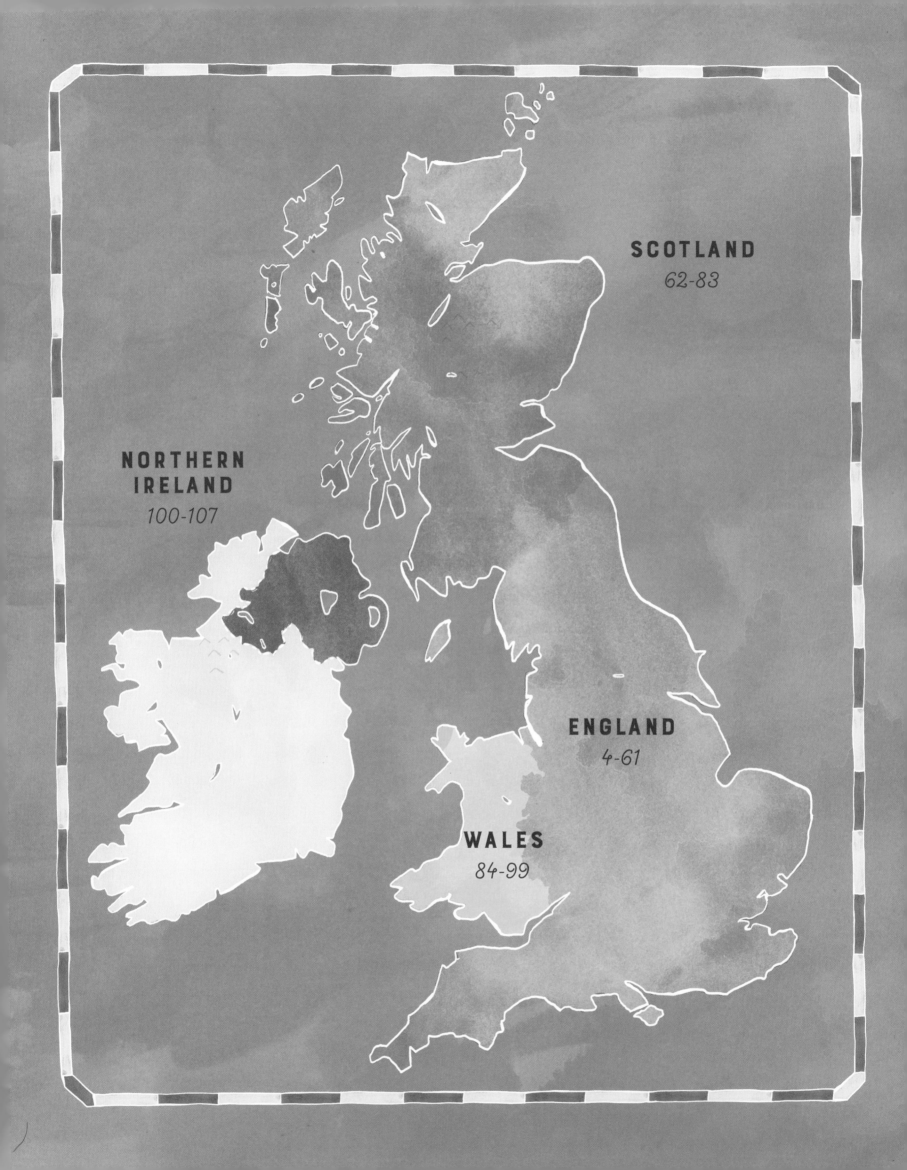

SCOTLAND
62-83

NORTHERN
IRELAND
100-107

ENGLAND
4-61

WALES
84-99

# WELCOME TO THE UNITED KINGDOM

## Your adventure starts here!

Although it might be relatively small in size, the United Kingdom is crammed with diverse experiences to delight any traveller. It's impossible to include everything from its long and rich history, wild and varied countryside, and cosmopolitan, diverse cities in one book, but this compendium of maps offers a gateway to explore the four countries that make this nation truly unique.

While tourists from all four corners of the globe flock to explore its ancient monuments, world-leading culture and pristine countryside, what really makes the United Kingdom special are the people that live here. We've included more than 300 movers and shakers from the past and present in this book, but whether you're queuing for fish and chips, scaling a mountain or hopping on a big red bus, be sure to say hello to the everyday people on the street. Each one will have their own story to tell, and their own ideas about what puts the "great" into Great Britain and Northern Ireland.

## How to use this book

Each of the 48 maps contained in this book gives some particular information about either one county, or a small group of neighbouring counties.

### MAP NAME
Highlighted in bold type in a corner of each map.

### COUNTY NAME
Noted in a bevel-edged label matching the colour of the map name.

### BORDERING COUNTIES
Noted in a box-shaped label in a contrasting colour.

### 5 BIGGEST CITIES
Noted in coloured type.

### FAMOUS PEOPLE
Seven famous people are included in each map.

### COUNTY BOUNDARIES
Demarcated by a white dotted line. Neighbouring counties are shown with a contrasting background colour.

### COUNTRY BOUNDARIES
Demarcated by a continuous grey line. Neighbouring countries are shown in a shaded background colour.

# ENGLAND

## *Enjoy this green and pleasant land!*

England as we know it has existed since the 10th century, and its long history spans the Battle of Hastings, the Wars of the Roses, the English Civil War, the Industrial Revolution and two world wars. These momentous events have left their mark in the form of monuments and museums, while other sites are even older... Stonehenge dates back to 3000BC! The red-and-white flag flying at football matches is the symbol of patron saint St. George, while other emblems include the red rose and the three lions. England's vast cultural contribution ranges from William Shakespeare to The Beatles; its systems of law and government have been adopted by many other countries; and it was the first industrialised nation in the world. The poet William Blake despaired at these "dark Satanic mills" but praised the country's "green and pleasant land", which today is protected in ten spellbinding national parks. From fish and chips by the seaside to the bright lights of London, England has something for everyone!

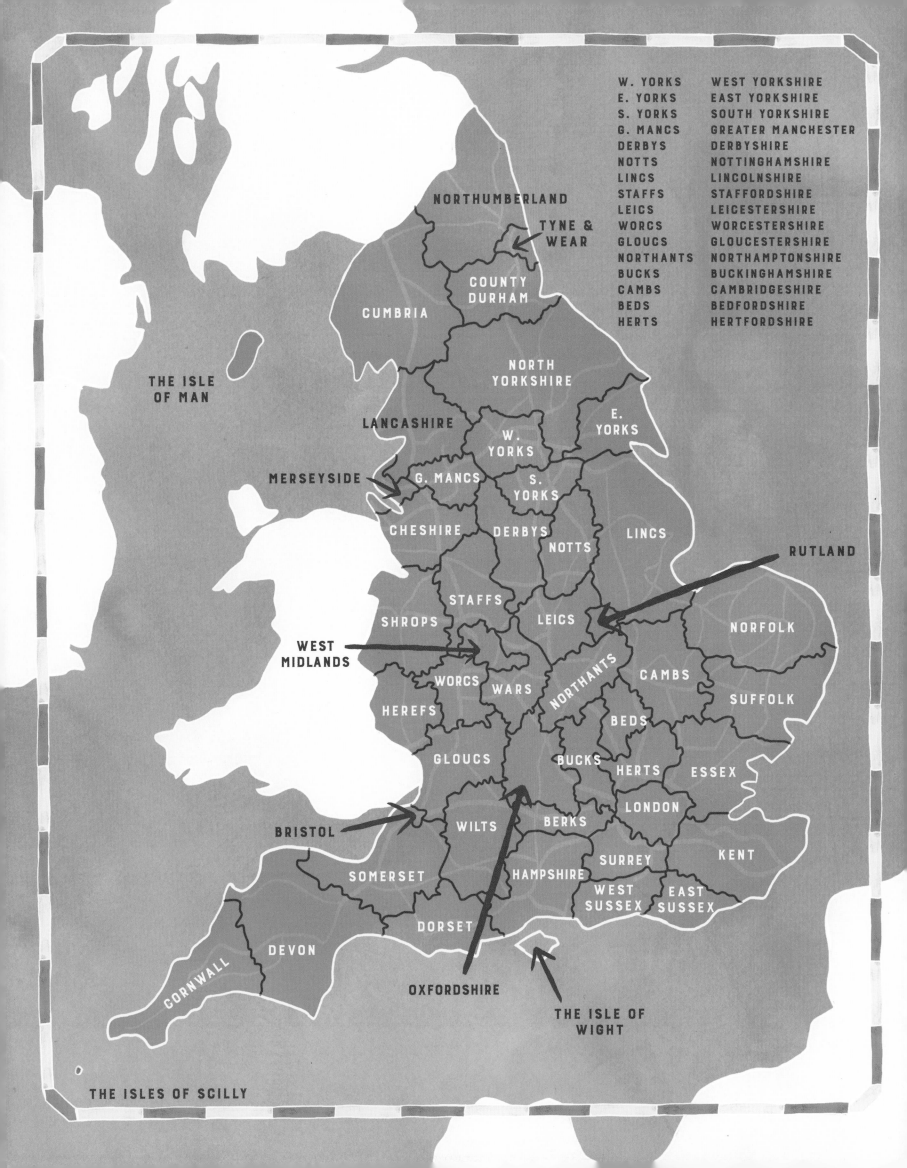

## Come to see the king of the castles!

You've reached the far north of England: next stop, Scotland. Wild, remote Northumberland is the most sparsely populated county in England, with only 62 people per square kilometre. But what it lacks in population, it makes up for with castles; it has more than any other English county, including the mighty Bamburgh. Other sights include Hadrian's Wall, the great Roman frontier (you can walk its length, stopping off at ancient forts) and Northumberland National Park, which covers a quarter of the county and has some of the darkest skies in England, making it a top spot for stargazing by night. By day, discover its wonderful wildlife: the Farne Islands are famed for their puffins, while the cows at Chillingham Park are rarer than giant pandas. All in all, a county fit for a king!

### BORDER BALLADS
Songs about battles have been sung since medieval times – one of the most famous is the Ballad of Chevy Chase.

### FOOTBALL FACT
Northumberland has the only English club to play in the Scottish football league: Berwick Rangers FC.

### BATTLE ROYAL
King James IV was killed at the Battle of Flodden between England and Scotland in 1513, the last British monarch to die on the battlefield.

### STARRY NIGHT
Northumberland Dark Sky Park is one of the best places for stargazing in the world – try it at Kielder Observatory.

**SCOTLAND**

### PETAL POWER
The county flower is the Bloody Cranesbill (Geranium sanguineum), which has bright pinky-purple flowers in summer.

### GLORIOUS GROUSE
80% of the UK's black grouse live in the North Pennines, a vast area of heather moors, meadows and waterfalls.

### BIRD WATCH
The curlew, a moorland bird with a haunting cry, is the emblem of the Northumberland national park.

**GRACE DARLING**
1815–1842
The lighthouse keeper's daughter helped rescue nine people from the shipwrecked *Forfarshire* in 1838.

**LANCELOT 'CAPABILITY' BROWN**
1716–1783
'England's greatest gardener' was born in the hamlet of Kirkharle. He designed over 170 parks across the country.

**JACK AND BOBBY CHARLTON**
B.1935; B.1937
The footballing brothers who won the World Cup in 1966 were born in Ashington.

**WILLIAM ARMSTRONG**
1810–1900
The industrialist and inventor built Cragside, the first house in the world to be powered by hydro-electricity in 1878.

### CENTRE POINT
The small town of Haltwhistle claims to be the exact geographic centre of Great Britain.

**ST HILDA**
C.614–680
The seventh-century saint was a key figure in the conversion of England to Christianity.

**GEORGE STEPHENSON**
1781–1848
The 'father of the railway' and inventor of the Rocket locomotive was born in Wylam in 1781.

**JOSEPHINE BUTLER**
1828–1906
The feminist and social reformer was born in Milfield and campaigned for women's rights.

**CUMBRIA**

# AND

**HOLY ISLAND**
A monastary was built on the island of Lindisfarne in the 7th century. The beautiful Lindisfarne Gospels were made here.

**SEAL SPOT**
You can dive with seals around the rocky Farne Islands, and watch razorbills, guillemots, eider ducks and puffins.

**NORTH POLE**
Marshall Meadows Bay is the northernmost point of England, and further north than a swathe of Scotland.

ONE TICKET
ONE TICKET

**BY THE SEASIDE**
Fishing village Seahouses is a great place to play crazy golf, spend pocket money in the arcades and eat fish and chips.

**CASTLE COUNT**
There are more castles here than any other English county. They include Bamburgh, Alnwick, Warkworth, Chillingham and Lindisfarne.

**HISTORY LESSON**
Prehistory is alive! Visit the iron-age hillfort Yeavering Bell, see some stone circles at Duddo Five Stones, or search for neolithic rock art across the county.

**CLONED COWS**
The fierce Chillingham wild cattle at Chillingham Park are natural clones, and rarer than giant pandas.

**FISHY BUSINESS**
Craster claims to be the birthplace of the kipper: herring smoked in oak barrels and eaten for breakfast.

**HIGH LIFE**
The Cheviot is the highest peak in the county, at 815 metres. The view isn't brilliant from the top, so look around on your way up and down.

**BARTER BOOKS**
Step into this old Victorian station and swap your books instead of buying them.

**TEATIME**
Prime Minister Charles Grey lived in Howick Hall, and Earl Grey tea was first blended here – taste it in the Tea House.

**MINI MUSEUM**
The Ferryman's Hut by Alnmouth harbour is thought to be the smallest museum in the country.

**CAUGHT ON CAMERA**
Watch live CCTV footage of roseate terns – one of the UK's most endangered seabirds – at the Northumberland Seabird Centre in Amble.

**FIRE AND WATER**
Linhope Spout is a spectacular waterfall in the Cheviot Hills, which are made from lava that cooled millions of years ago.

**ON LOCATION**
Alnwick (rhymes with 'panic') Castle doubled as Hogwarts in the first two Harry Potter films.

**FESTIVAL FEVER**
Rothbury holds a traditional music festival every July, with pipe music, dancing and storytelling.

**PLAYTIME**
The Northumberland national park is one big adventure playground, with rock-climbing, horse-riding, mountain-biking and kayaking.

## NORTHUMBERLAND

**PUFFIN FESTIVAL**
Every May, Amble celebrates the 36,000 puffins and baby pufflings that nest on Coquet Island.

MORPETH

**ENCHANTED FOREST**
Kielder Water & Forest Park has the largest man-made lake in northern Europe, the biggest forest in England, and 50% of England's red squirrels.

**PIPE DREAMS**
Morpeth has a Bagpipe Museum devoted to small Northumbrian pipes – different to Scottish bagpipes.

**MINING MUSEUM**
Woodhorn Museum near Ashington, once the largest coal-mining village in the world, tells the story of the dark and dangerous pits.

ASHINGTON

NORTH SEA

BLYTH

BEDLINGTON

**LADY OF THE NORTH**
Northumberlandia is a huge earthwork sculpture of a reclining woman, 30 metres high and 400 metres long.

**TOP OF THE TREE**
Wallington Hall's 14-metre high Nootka Cypress was named the best tree to climb in Britain by the National Trust.

CRAMLINGTON

**HADRIAN'S WALL**
This mighty wall was the northern frontier of the Roman Empire – and inspired George RR Martin's Wall in Game of Thrones.

**ROMAN FORTS**
Roman Forts line Hadrian's wall: visit a Roman toilet at Housesteads; see live excavations at Vindolanda; and step into a Roman bath house at Chesters.

**ADVENTURE ALERT**
The Northumberland coastline is ideal for stand-up paddleboarding, kitesurfing and coasteering.

**TAR BARLE**
In Allendale, revellers called 'guisers' celebrate dangerously at New Year: by carrying whisky barrels full of blazing tar on their heads.

**BORDER REIVERS**
Hexham Old Gaol tells how the Scottish clans and English families raided each other's land from the late 13th century to the 17th century.

TYNE AND WEAR

COUNTY DURHAM

7

# TYNE & WEAR & COUNTY DURHAM

## Go to toon by the Tyne!

Tyneside includes the city of Newcastle upon Tyne and the town of Gateshead – they are joined by seven bridges across the River Tyne. The area, is bursting with galleries, but Tyne & Wear's most famous artwork is too big to fit inside four walls: the Angel of the North, whose wingspan measures 54 metres, holds Gateshead in her broad embrace and is one of the most popular public artworks of all time.

Over the boarder in County Durham stands an equally impressive landmark: Durham Cathedral, which together with the city of Durham's castle has been deemed a UNESCO World Heritage Site. Standing on the banks of the River Wear, the castle is now home to Durham University.

**NORTHUMBERLAND**

### ROWAN ATKINSON
**B.1955**
The actor and comedian was born in Consett and has starred in *Mr Bean*, *Blackadder* and *Johnny English*.

### TYNESIDE TILT
Gateshead and Newcastle are joined by seven bridges across the River Tyne – including the tilting Gateshead Millennium Bridge, opened in 2001.

### FOOTBALL FACT
The first Tyne-Wear derby between Newcastle United and Sunderland was in 1883, but their rivalry dates back to 1642, when they were on opposing sides in the English Civil War.

### LOCAL FOOD

A saveloy dip is a sausage sandwich with gravy, pease pudding (split-pea paste), stuffing and mustard; a stotty is a round, flat loaf; panackelty is a corned beef and root vegetable casserole; and a singing hinny is a sort of scone.

### THE VENERABLE BEDE
**C.673-735**
The monk and scholar is considered the father of British history – he lived in monasteries in Wearmouth and Jarrow, and Jarrow Hall is now a Bede museum.

### ANT AND DEC
**B.1975**
The presenter duo, were born in Newcastle and met on children's TV drama *Byker Grove* – they now present *Britain's Got Talent*, *I'm a Celebrity...* and *Ant and Dec's Saturday Night Takeaway*.

### GERTRUDE BELL
**1868-1926**
The explorer, mountaineer, archaeologist and writer was born in Durham. She travelled extensively in the Middle East, and drew the boundaries of the country that is now Iraq.

**COUNTY DURHAM**

### FULL STEAM AHEAD
Heritage railways include Tanfield and Weardale; the National Railway Museum is in Shildon; and Causey Arch, built in 1726, is the world's oldest single-arch railway bridge.

### ENCHANTED FOREST
Hamsterley Forest in the Durham Dales is one of the best places for walking, biking and horse-riding, and has lots of picnic spots and play areas.

**CUMBRIA**

### CHERYL
**B.1983**
The singer, born Cheryl Tweedy, is from Newcastle. She was in Girls Aloud and has been a judge on *The X Factor*.

### CATHERINE COOKSON
**1906-1998**
The writer was born in South Shields and many of her (almost 100) novels are set in South Tyneside. She has sold more than 120 million copies.

### ANTHONY EDEN
**1897-1977**
Born near Rushyford, he became UK foreign secretary and then Prime Minister – he resigned two months after the 1956 Suez Crisis.

### WATER WORLD
High Force on the River Tees is one of the biggest waterfalls in England – walkers can visit the nearby Low Force falls and Cauldron Snout cascade, too.

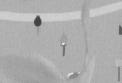

## BIG CITY
Newcastle upon Tyne's sights include a castle, a cathedral, Grey's Monument and lots of Victorian buildings, plus the Life Science Centre, Discovery Museum and Laing Gallery.

## ROMAN REMAINS
Segedunum Roman Fort, Baths and Museum is in Wallsend on Hadrian's Wall, and Arbeia Roman Fort and Museum is in South Shields.

## STORY TIME
Seven Stories, the National Centre for Children's Books, is in the Ouseburn Valley, and The Word, the National Centre for the Written Word, is in South Shields.

## MULTICULTURAL BRITAIN
There has been a Yemeni community in the seaside town of South Shields since the 1890s – boxer Muhammad Ali had his marriage blessed at the local mosque in 1977.

## DESERT ISLAND
You can walk to St Mary's Island at low tide to climb the lighthouse, go rockpooling or play on the beach.

## BUCKETS & SPADES
There are lots of sandy beaches, including Tynemouth Longsands, Seaburn, Roker and Marsden, where you can see the Marsden Rock sea stack.

## JARROW MARCH
In 1936, 200 men marched 468 kilometres from Jarrow to London to protest against unemployment and poverty.

**NEWCASTLE UPON TYNE**

**GATESHEAD**

**TYNE & WEAR**

## LEADING LIGHT
Souter Lighthouse, which opened in 1871, was the first lighthouse in the world built to use electricity. Climb the tower, and visit the engine room and keeper's house.

## MODERN ARTWORK
The Angel of the North is an enormous sculpture of an angel by Antony Gormley. It is 20 metres tall and 54 metres wide, and made from 200 metric tons of steel.

## PRESIDENT'S HOUSE
Washington Old Hall is the ancestral home of George Washington, the first US president.

## ANIMAL MAGIC
At Washington Wetland Centre you can feed the world's rarest goose, called a nene, visit a family of otters and see a flock of Chilean flamingos.

**SUNDERLAND**

## SEASIDE CITY
Sunderland was once a shipbuilding and glassmaking centre, and is now home to the National Glass Centre and the Sunderland Museum (don't miss the 250-million-year-old gliding reptile).

## MUSEUM TIME
The Beamish Museum recreates the 1820s, 1910s and 1940s; the Great North Museum showcases natural history and ancient civilisations; and Killhope is a lead-mining museum.

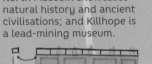

## SPORTS REPORT
Durham County Cricket Club play at the Riverside Ground in Chester-le-Street, which also hosts international matches, including the 2013 Ashes.

## CATHEDRAL CITY
Durham's cathedral and castle is a world heritage site. Its Open Treasure exhibition reveals the Monks' Dormitory, The Great Kitchen and 7th-century Treasures of St Cuthbert.

## TREASURE HUNT
You can collect sea glass at Blast Beach, Seaham: waste glass from the bottle factory was dumped in the sea and, 100 years on, smooth beads are still washed up by every tide.

## LOOKOUT POINT
The Penshaw Monument, built on top of Penshaw Hill in 1844, is a replica of the Temple of Hephaestus in Athens, Greece – you can climb one of the pillars to the top.

**NORTH SEA**

**HARTLEPOOL**

## ROWING RACES
The Durham Regatta dates back to 1834, predating the more famous Henley Regatta by five years, and takes place each June.

## MINERS' MEETING
The Durham Miners' Gala has been held since 1871 – the political gathering is a celebration of the area's coal-mining heritage, and coincides with the Durham Brass Festival in July.

## SHIP SHAPE
Hartlepool's Historic Quay is a reconstructed 18th-century seaport that berths HMS Trincomalee, Europe's oldest floating warship, which was launched in 1817.

## CASTLE COUNT
Castles open to visitors include Tynemouth, Hylton, Raby and Auckland; Lumley Castle is now a hotel.

## NORTH-EAST NICKNAMES
Geordies are from Newcastle and Tyneside, Mackems are from Sunderland, Sandancers are from South Shields and Monkey Hangers are from Hartlepool.

## SWANNING AROUND
Barnard Castle, a town named after its medieval castle, is home to the Bowes Museum: visit at 2pm to see its 18th-century silver swan automaton preening and catching a fish.

## TRAIN TOWN
Darlington is the birthplace of the railways – the first steam-powered railway opened here in 1825 – and its Head of Steam Museum displays the first locomotive.

**DARLINGTON**

## BRIGHT SPARK
Stockton-on-Tees has the widest high street in the UK (Marlborough in Wiltshire comes second), and chemist John Walker invented the friction match here in 1826.

**NORTH YORKSHIRE**

SCOTLAND

### WINTER WOOLIES
Herdwick sheep are native to the Lake District and are extremely hardy – they are said to survive for days under snow drifts by eating their own wool.

## Plunge into the Lake District!

This region of Cumbria is full of fells (mountains) and lakes, including the highest mountain and the deepest – and biggest – lakes in England. And there's a reason why Lakeland came into being here: it rains a lot, so pack your umbrella, especially if you plan to visit Seathwaite, which is officially the wettest place in England. Rain or shine, Cumbria's beauty sparkles through the greyest of rainclouds, and the county has inspired many of the U.K.'s most celebrated writers, including William Wordsworth, Arthur Ransome and Beatrix Potter. Peter Rabbit fans can visit the World of Beatrix Potter in Bowness, and if you feel a sonnet coming on yourself, the Cumberland Pencil Museum is a fine destination for any budding writer. Just remember to take a brolly with you!

### FOOTBALL FACT
Uppies and Downies, a kind of medieval football, is played every Easter in Workington – there are said to be no rules!

### HOUND TRAILING
From March to October, dog races take place on the fells: the hounds follow a scent trail at speeds of up to 12km/h.

MAP NYC

### OLD NEW YORK
Thanks to its layout of planned streets on a right-angled grid, many historians think the town of Whitehaven was the blueprint for New York City.

WORKINGTON

WHITEHAVEN

#### CATHERINE PARR
**1512-1548**
The Queen Consort of England and Ireland was the last of Henry VIII's six wives and outlived him. Her father was lord of the manor of Kendal, where it is thought she was born.

#### WILLIAM WORDSWORTH
**1770-1850**
The Romantic poet was born in Cockermouth and was one of the Lake Poets, a group who lived in and were inspired by the Lake District – his home, Dove Cottage, is now a museum.

#### JOHN KENT
**1795-1886**
Britain's first black police officer was a constable with the Carlisle City Police from 1837-1845 – the next known black British policeman didn't join the force until 1964.

### COAST TO COAST
St Bees is a lovely red sand and shingle beach at the start of the Coast to Coast walk to Robin Hood's Bay in North Yorkshire.

#### ARTHUR RANSOME
**1884-1967**
The writer is buried in Rusland and is best known for his Swallows and Amazons children's books set in the Lake District. Take a boat cruise on Coniston Water where the film of the book was shot in 2016.

#### BEATRIX POTTER
**1866-1943**
The children's writer and illustrator lived in the Lake District and wrote tales about the wildlife she saw, such as Peter Rabbit and Mrs Tiggy-winkle. Visit the World of Beatrix Potter in Bowness.

#### NELLA LAST
**1889-1968**
The housewife lived in Barrow-in-Furness and wrote a fascinating diary from 1939 to 1966 for Mass Observation, which was set up to record ordinary people's lives.

### FUNNY FACES
The Egremont Crab Fair – dating back to 1267 – is home to the Gurning World Championships, where competitors compete to pull the ugliest face.

### TALKATIVE TOADS
Sandscale Haws nature reserve is home to a fifth of Britain's noisy natterjack toads; you can hear their cacophonous mating calls between April and June.

### TREASURE TROVE
Furness Abbey was founded in c. 1125 by Count Stephen, later King of England. A hoard of medieval treasure was found there in 2012.

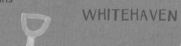

**BIRD WATCHING**
Ospreys chicks hatched in Cumbria in 2001 – the first time these birds of prey had nested successfully in England in more than 150 years.

## NORTHUMBERLAND

**CASTLE COUNT**
Impressive castles include Carlisle Castle (above), Muncaster and Sizergh, and the ruins of Brougham and Brough.

**WESTERN WALL**
The longest continuous remaining stretch of Hadrian's Wall – built by the Romans in 120AD – is in Cumbria and can be seen from Birdoswald Roman Fort.

**ENCHANTED FOREST**
Grizedale and Whinlatter forests have high ropes courses and mountain bike tracks; Grizedale also has a sculpture trail and Whinlatter has a WildPlay route.

BASSENTHWAITE

CARLISLE

**PENCIL IT IN**
The first pencil factory opened in Keswick in 1832, and the Cumberland Pencil Museum boasts the biggest colouring pencil in the world.

**GREAT LAKES**
Cumbria has both the deepest and the largest lakes in England: Wastwater is 79 metres deep, and Windermere is 14.8 square kilometres, with 18 islands.

**LAKELAND**
The Lake District is a beautiful region of fells (mountains) and glacial lakes, although Bassenthwaite is the only 'official' lake – all the others are called meres or waters.

CUMBRIA

**LADY OF THE LAKE**
Lady of the Lake, a pleasure boat on Ullswater, was launched in 1877 and is believed to be the oldest working passenger vessel in the world.

**HORSING AROUND**
The Appleby Horse Fair in June is one of the largest gatherings of Gypsies and Travellers, with up to 15,000 people attending.

**MIGHTY MINE**
At Honister Slate Mine, daredevils can climb to the top of the mountain, go down a mine or a take a sky walk across the UK's longest infinity bridge.

**WETLAND**
Seathwaite in Borrowdale is the wettest inhabited place in England, with a sopping 3,552mm of rain per year.

**SPORTS DAY**
Cumberland and Westmorland wrestling may have been brought over by the Vikings and still takes place at county summer shows.

**PANTS ON FIRE**
The World's Biggest Liar competition is held every November at the Bridge Inn, Santon Bridge – competitors have five minutes each to tell the tallest tale.

**HIGH GROUND**
Cumbria contains all the land in England over 910 metres, including Scafell Pike, the highest English mountain at 978 metres.

**ALL AFLOAT**
Windermere Jetty has 50 vessels telling the story of boating on the lake from 1870 to today, including the UK's oldest sailing yacht and Beatrix Potter's rowing boat.

COUNTY DURHAM

**TOP GEAR**
Hardknott Pass is the joint steepest road in England, along with Rosedale Chimney Bank, Yorkshire – both have a gradient of one in three.

30%

**LOCAL FOOD**
Food from Cumbria includes Kendal Mint Cake, which was eaten by Edmund Hillary on the first successful ascent of Everest; coiled, peppery Cumberland sausages; and tasty Grasmere gingerbread.

KENDAL

**FULL STEAM AHEAD**
The Ravenglass and Eskdale Railway is one of the oldest and longest narrow gauge railways in England.

**ROYAL SERVICE**
Piel Island has its own castle and king – the reigning monarch also doubles as the pub landlord at the Ship Inn.

**STAN LAUREL**
**1890-1965**
The comic actor was born in Ulverston and appeared in 107 films with his comedy partner, Oliver Hardy. There is a Laurel and Hardy Museum in his home town.

BARROW-IN-FURNESS

**OTTER SPOTTER**
Walk through an underwater otter tunnel and meet some friendly rays at the Lakes Aquarium, Windermere.

LANCASHIRE

NORTH YORKSHIRE

### NICK PARK
**B.1958**
The animator was born in Preston and is the creator of Wallace and Gromit and Shaun the Sheep.

### BIGGEST BAY
Morecambe Bay is a huge tidal estuary where locals catch cockles and shrimps. It is known for its dangerously fast tides and quicksand.

### BACK TO NATURE
Watch for water birds in the reed beds at RSPB Leighton Moss, such as juvenile bearded tits.

### SKY DANCER
The endangered hen harrier is the symbol of the Forest of Bowland, which is the bird's most important breeding site. It is known for its 'sky-dancing' and its 'yikkering' call.

### ENCHANTED FOREST
The Forest of Bowland is said to have inspired Middle-earth in *The Hobbit* and *The Lord of the Rings*. You can walk the J.R.R. Tolkien trail there.

### CASTLE COUNT
There are medieval castles at Lancaster and Clitheroe, and other historic buildings include Whalley Abbey and Hoghton Tower.

### COUNTY TOWN
Lancaster is one of England's heritage cities, which means it has lots of historic buildings, including a castle, a priory and the Aston Memorial.

### RELIGIOUS ROOTS
George Fox had a vision on Pendle Hill in 1652, which led him to found the Religious Society of Friends, better known as the Quakers.

### ALL ABOARD
At Heysham, you can board ferries for Douglas on the Isle of Man and Belfast in Northern Ireland.

Fleetwood Museum

### FISHY BUSINESS
Fleetwood was once a big fishing port. You can learn all about it at the Fleetwood Museum or board an old trawler, Jacinta, on open days.

### CENTRE POINT
The Whitendale Hanging Stones near Dunsop Bridge are the centre of the British Isles, depending on how it's measured; Haltwhistle in Northumberland also claims the title.

### FAIRTRADE TOWN
Garstang became the world's first Fairtrade town in 2000: the council, schools and businesses use fairly traded products.

BLACKPOOL

### FOOTBALL FACT
Preston North End FC were the first team to win the football league followed by the FA Cup the same year (in 1889).

### TOP TOWER
Blackpool is famous for its Tower, long sandy beaches, theme park and Illuminations.

### ANIMAL MAGIC
Visit the rescued horses at Penny Farm in Blackpool, explore the Bowland Wild Boar Park and see the birds of prey at Turbury Woods Owl and Bird Sanctuary.

### SANDY SHORELINE
There are lots of sandy beaches on the Fylde coast, including St Annes, Blackpool, Cleveleys and Fleetwood.

PRESTON

BAMBER BRIDGE    BLACKBURN

### MUSEUM TIME
Unusual museums include the British in India museum in Nelson and the Lytham Windmill Museum.

### BLACKBURN BRIDGE
The Wainwright Bridge in Blackburn is named after Alfred Wainwright, a fell walker who wrote guidebooks about the Lake District.

### ROAD WORKS
Preston has one of Europe's biggest bus stations, built in the 1960s' brutalist style.

### BEST VIEW
From Darwen Tower on Darwen Hill, built in 1898, you can see Morecambe Bay, Blackpool Tower and the Isle of Man, on a clear day.

### LOCAL FOOD
Lancashire hotpot – a mutton stew – and Chorley cakes (flat, fruit-filled pastries eaten with Lancashire cheese) are popular fare in the county.

### MOVING THE BOUNDARIES
Lancashire County Cricket Club has played at Old Trafford in Manchester since 1864, but in 1974 the ground became part of the new county of 'Greater Manchester'.

### JENNA COLEMAN
**B.1986**
The actor was born in Blackpool and is best known for playing Clara Oswald, the Doctor's companion in Doctor Who.

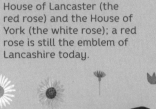
NORTH YORKSHIRE

### WARS OF THE ROSES
Wars were fought from 1455 to 1487 between the House of Lancaster (the red rose) and the House of York (the white rose); a red rose is still the emblem of Lancashire today.

### TAP DANCE
Clog dancing originated in Lancashire cotton mills, where workers wore wooden shoes and danced at lunchtime – Charlie Chaplin was a clog dancer before becoming a film star.

**ANDREW FLINTOFF**
**B.1977**
Talented all-rounder "Freddie" Flintoff was a stalwart of Lancashire County Cricket Club and briefly served as England captain, before becoming a popular television personality.

**EDITH RIGBY**
**1872-1948**
The activist was born in Preston and became a suffragette and an advocate of workers' rights, universal education and protecting the environment.

### WITCH HUNT
The Pendle witch trials of 1612 are among the most famous in English history – you can learn about them at the Pendle Heritage Centre and follow the trail to Lancaster Castle.

**IAN MCKELLEN**
**B.1939**
The actor was born in Burnley and played Gandalf in *The Lord of the Rings* and *The Hobbit*, and Magneto in the *X-Men* films; he is also a classical theatre actor.

**BRIAN COX**
**B.1968**
Oldham-born professor of particle physics at Manchester University, Brian is best known as a presenter of science shows on the BBC.

**MAHATMA GANDHI**
**1869-1948**
A Hindu believer in non-violent protest, this campaigner for Indian independence and the rights of the poor visited mill workers in Darwen in 1931.

BURNLEY

### SINGING TREE
The Singing Ringing Tree on Crown Point, overlooking Burnley, is a sound sculpture made from steel pipes, which produce a low, tuneful sound in the wind.

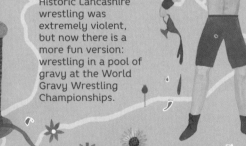

### GRAVY WRESTLING
Historic Lancashire wrestling was extremely violent, but now there is a more fun version: wrestling in a pool of gravy at the World Gravy Wrestling Championships.

### TEXTILE MILLS
During the industrial revolution, Lancashire had lots of mill towns producing cotton cloth.

WEST YORKSHIRE

## Run wild in the Red Rose County!

If you're tempted by a traditional British seaside holiday then you could do no better than to head for Blackpool, Lancashire's glitzy seaside resort. Blackpool is famous for its beaches, its ballroom and the Big One – the UK's tallest rollercoaster, which you'll find at the Pleasure Beach. This amusement park has been delighting visitors dating back more than one hundred years, when the mill towns of Blackburn, Preston and Burnley were in their heyday, producing and shipping cotton all over the world. While its industry is world-renowned, Lancashire's countryside is equally celebrated – take a walk in the ancient Forest of Bowland (said to have inspired the writer JRR Tolkien) and you'll discover why – so it's fitting that Lancaster's Red Rose serves as the county's emblem.

# LANCASHIRE

## Scare yourself silly in haunted Britain!

York was founded by the Romans in 71AD and is said to be the most haunted city in Europe, if not the entire world! Are you brave enough to go on a night-time ghost walk around the dark, narrow streets? You'll hear stories of ghoulish goings-on while hunting for the Lost Boy and listening out for the Lonely Piper. The fishing town of Whitby is almost as spooky – this is where Dracula landed in Bram Stoker's novel. The Dracula Experience is a scream, but beware the huge black dog that prowls around the abbey …

Ghost stories aside, there is plenty more to leave you breathless in this region – starting with the beautiful Yorkshire Dales and North York Moors. Don't be scared to get out and explore!

COUNTY DURHAM

### CAPTAIN COOK
**1728-1779**
Explorer and navigator James Cook was born in Marton and mapped the Pacific, New Zealand and Australia – there is a museum devoted to him at his birthplace.

### CASTLE COUNT
Richmond Castle was built in 1071 and is one of the oldest stone fortresses in England; other castles include Skipton, Bolton, Middleham and Helmsley.

### THE DALES
In the Yorkshire Dales national park, you can climb the Yorkshire Three Peaks and walk to Malham Cove and Gordale Scar.

### COUNTY TOWN
Northallerton is the county town of North Yorkshire and is an area known as "Herriot Country", named after the All Creatures Great and Small books.

### FUN AND GAMES
The Ultimate at Lightwater Valley is one of the world's longest roller coasters; Flamingo Land is a theme park and zoo.

CUMBRIA

### AMY JOHNSON
**1903-1941**
The aviator, born in Hull, was the first female pilot to fly solo from Britain to Australia – learn more at the museum at Sewerby Hall.

### BEN KINGSLEY
**B.1943**
The actor was born in Snainton – he won an Oscar for *Gandhi* in 1982, and voiced Bagheera the panther in the 2016 film *The Jungle Book*.

**NORTH YORKSHIRE**

### GOING UNDERGROUND
There are 2,500 caves in the Yorkshire Dales, including the 89km-long Three Counties; Gaping Gill, which could hold St Paul's Cathedral; and show caves such as Ingleborough.

### HORNBLOWER
Ripon's cathedral dates back to 672 and its town charter was granted by Alfred the Great in 886: since then, a horn has sounded in the market square at 9pm every single night.

### ANCIENT ABBEY
Fountains Abbey in Studley Royal Park is one of England's biggest and best preserved Cistercian monasteries.

### BALANCING ACT
Explore the amazing rock formations at Brimham Rocks such as the Dancing Bear, the Eagle and the Gorilla.

HARROGATE

LANCASHIRE

### STEVIE SMITH
**1902-1971**
The poet and novelist was born in Hull and is best known for her poem "Not Waving But Drowning".

### JUDI DENCH
**B.1934**
The Oscar-winning actor was born in Heworth – recently she has played M in the James Bond films.

### LOCAL FOOD
Try Yorkshire puddings with roast beef; Wallace and Gromit's favourite, Wensleydale cheese; or Yorkshire curd tarts at one of Bettys tearooms.

WEST YORKSHIRE

### SPA BREAK
Harrogate is a Victorian spa town famous for its water containing iron, sulphur and salt – today the Royal Pump Room is a museum.

# NORTH & EAST YORKSHIRE

MIDDLESBROUGH

## FOSSIL HUNT
This coastline is known as the Dinosaur Coast – hunt for fossils, and see the finds at the Rotunda Museum in Scarborough.

## COUNT DRACULA
Whitby's landmarks include a ruined abbey and whalebone arch; part of Bram Stoker's *Dracula* was set here – visit the Dracula Experience!

### WILLIAM WILBERFORCE
**1759-1833**
The politician was born in Hull and led the anti-slavery movement – Wilberforce House tells the story of his life-long campaign.

## THE MOORS
The heather-covered North York Moors national park has hiking trails including the Cleveland Way and the Lyke Wake Walk.

## FULL STEAM AHEAD
The North Yorkshire Moors Railway chugs from Pickering to Whitby – one station, Goathland, was used as Hogsmeade Station in the Harry Potter films.

## SMUGGLERS' HAUNT
Robin Hood's Bay is an old smuggling village with tiny streets and secret passages; walk to Boggle Hole at low tide or go rockpooling.

## BY THE SEASIDE
Scarborough is the biggest holiday resort on the Yorkshire coast, with surfing spots, a Sea Life centre and the Alpamare waterpark.

## RELIGIOUS RELICS
The dissolution of the monasteries by Henry VIII in the 1530s led to the ruin of Rievaulx, Bolton and Byland abbeys, and Gisborough, Kirkham and Mount Grace priories.

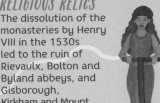

## ENCHANTED FOREST
Try Dalby Forest's mountain biking trails; 'Go Ape' at the tree-top and segway courses, or visit the centre for stargazing.

SCARBOROUGH

## PREHISTORIC HOUSE
The remains of Britain's oldest house were discovered at Star Carr, a Mesolithic site, alongside 10,000-year-old deer skull headdresses.

### GUY FAWKES
**1570-1606**
"Guido" was born in York and was a member of the failed Gunpowder Plot to assassinate King James in 1605 – his effigy is still burned on Bonfire Night.

## SPOOKY CITY
York is a 2,000-year-old walled city famous for its minster, castle, Shambles and Snickelways (medieval streets) – visit York Dungeon or go on a ghost walk.

## MUSEUM TIME
Eden Camp housed Italian and German prisoners during the Second World War – now it is a modern history museum.

## GHOST VILLAGE
Wharram Percy is one of 3,000 deserted medieval villages in Britain – visit the ruined church and trace the outlines of the houses abandoned in c.1500.

## MEGA MONOLITH
The Rudston Monolith is the tallest standing stone in Britain at 7.6m – it is thought to date to the Late Neolithic period (over 4,500 years ago).

## BUCKETS AND SPADES
Bridlington is a traditional seaside town with sandy beaches, a funfair, amusement arcades and donkey rides.

YORK

## VIKING INVASION
Walk down reconstructed Viking Age streets at the Jorvik Viking Centre, and visit the York Viking Festival each February.

## BATTLE OF STAMFORD BRIDGE
King Harold II of England defeated King Harald Hardrada of Norway in 1066, marking the end of the Viking Age.

## BEVERLEY BEAVERS
The town of Beverley is named after the beavers that used to live there; Beverly in Massachusetts and Beverly Hills in California were named after it.

## LOOKOUT POINT
Climb Withernsea Lighthouse's 144 steps for views over East Yorkshire and the Humber Bridge.

## CHOC'S AWAY
Chocolate companies Terry's and Rowntree's were founded in York in 1767 and 1862; take a tour at York's Chocolate Story.

## SPORTS REPORT
The Kiplingcotes Derby is the oldest annual horse race in England, said to have begun in 1519.

**EAST YORKSHIRE**

KINGSTON UPON HULL

## MARITIME CITY
In Hull, visit aquarium The Deep's loggerhead turtles; see a whale skeleton at the Maritime Museum; and climb aboard the Arctic Corsair trawler and the Spurn Lightship.

## BED RACE
Great Knaresborough boasts a Bed Race (teams push beds along a 3.9km course) and England's oldest paid attraction: Mother Shipton's cave and well, opened in 1630.

## BUILDING BRIDGES
The Humber Bridge, which spans the River Humber, was the world's longest single-span suspension bridge when it opened in 1981.

## BACK TO NATURE
Spurn, a narrow sand spit, is a national nature reserve and one of the UK's bird migration hotspots – see the wildlife on a Spurn Safari.

**NORTH SEA**

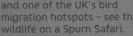

## LANCASHIRE

### TWIN TOWNS
Keighley and Poix-du-Nord, France, were the first recorded twin towns, in 1920.

### ART ATTACK
Saltaire model village is a UNESCO world heritage site and includes Salts Mill, which displays paintings by local artist David Hockney.

## NORTH YORKSHIRE

### PARK LIFE
Roundhay Park in Leeds is one of the biggest city parks in Europe and contains Tropical World, an indoor wildlife park.

### LOCAL FOOD
Parkin is a gingerbread cake made with oatmeal and black treacle, traditionally eaten on Bonfire Night.

### JESSICA ENNIS-HILL
B.1986
The heptathlete was born in Sheffield – she is the 2012 Olympic champion and a three-time world champion.

### WELCOME TO HOLLYWOOD
Bradford is a Unesco City of Film: the National Science and Media Museum shows the world's first moving pictures, and there is a Family Film Festival in August.

BRADFORD

### WAR AND PEACE
There is a Peace Museum in Bradford, and a Royal Armouries Museum in Leeds, displaying the national collection of arms.

LEEDS

### FULL STEAM AHEAD
Middleton Railway is the world's oldest continually working public railway – you can ride a steam train there.

## WEST YORKSHIRE

### CHILD'S PLAY
Halifax is home to Eureka! The National Children's Museum, which has more than 400 interactive exhibits.

### PRIDE OF YORKSHIRE
Hebden Bridge is known as the lesbian capital of the UK and holds an annual Happy Valley Pride festival.

### GET ACTIVE
Calderdale's activity centres include Roktface, the UK's highest outdoor climbing wall; Another World Adventure Centre; and the Halifax Ski and Snowboard Centre.

### PRINCE OF THIEVES
Robin Hood's grave is in the grounds of Kirklees Hall.

### GOING UNDERGROUND
Coal mining was a major industry in Yorkshire until the 1980s – tour a former mine at the National Coal Mining Museum.

### RHUBARB RULES
The Rhubarb Triangle is an area between Wakefield, Morley and Rothwell where forced rhubarb is grown – there is a rhubarb festival in Wakefield each February.

HUDDERSFIELD

### SIGN OF SPRING
Marsden celebrates the cuckoo, a herald of spring, at an annual festival in April, with a procession headed by a giant cuckoo.

### LEAGUE LEADER
Huddersfield was the birthplace of rugby league in 1895; the town's most famous landmark is Victoria Tower on top of Castle Hill.

### CULTURE VULTURE
The Yorkshire Sculpture Park has work by local artists Henry Moore and Barbara Hepworth.

### BRASSED OFF
Barnsley is known for its colliery brass bands, the Barnsley chop (a kind of lamb chop), and for having the first bottle bank to recycle glass, in 1977.

### BACK TO NATURE
The Dearne Valley has several RSPB nature reserves – the main one is Old Moor, a wetland where you can see kingfishers.

### THE BRONTË SISTERS
CHARLOTTE 1816-1855
EMILY 1818-1848
ANNE 1820-1849
The sisters were writers from Haworth whose books include *Jane Eyre*, *Wuthering Heights* and *The Tenant of Wildfell Hall*; their home is now the Bronte Parsonage Museum.

## GREATER MANCHESTER

### HIGH LIFE
Emley Moor mast is the tallest freestanding structure in the UK at 330.4m – 20m taller than the Shard in London.

### SEVEN HILLS
Sheffield is built on seven hills, like Rome – its landmarks include the Winter Garden, the Crucible Theatre and the Millennium Gallery.

### BRIDGE CHAPEL
Chapels were once built on town bridges so travellers could pray for a safe journey – only four remain, and the one on Rotherham Bridge, from 1483, is the best preserved.

SHEFFIELD

### FOOTBALL FACT
Sheffield United and Sheffield Wednesday contest the Steel City derby, and United are nicknamed the Blades, because Sheffield was once the UK's steel capital.

### ZAYN MALIK
B.1993
The singer was born in Bradford and became famous with One Direction – he left the band in 2015 and is now a solo artist.

DERBYSHIRE

### MUSEUM TIME
There are lots of industrial museums including Abbeydale Industrial Hamlet; other museums include the Thackray Medical Museum and the Magna Science Adventure Centre.

# SOUTH & WEST YORKSHIRE

### SHAGGY DOG STORY
The Yorkshire terrier was bred in the 19th century to catch rats in mills – Huddersfield Ben, a famous dog in the 1860s, is the father of the breed.

**EAST YORKSHIRE**

### SWEET TOOTH
Liquorice has been grown in Pontefract since at least the 17th century, Pontefract cakes (liquorice sweets) are still made there, and there is a liquorice festival in July.

**SOUTH YORKSHIRE**

### HELEN SHARMAN
### B.1963
The chemist was born in Grenoside and became the first British astronaut in 1991 (24 years before Tim Peake!), and the first woman to visit the Mir space station.

**LINCOLNSHIRE**

### STARTER'S ORDERS
Horse races have been held in Doncaster since the 16th century – the St Leger Stakes was first run in 1776 and is the UK's oldest classic horse race.

**DONCASTER**

### CASTLE COUNT
Conisbrough Castle has a 12th-century "great tower"; Richard II is thought to have died at Pontefract Castle; Sandal is a ruined medieval castle.

### MIGHTY MONUMENTS
Roche Abbey and Kirkstall Abbey are ruined Cistercian monasteries, both founded in the 12th century, and now good places for a picnic.

### ANIMAL MAGIC
The Yorkshire Wildlife Park is home to more than 80 species including polar bears, lions and tigers; Tropical Butterfly House has lemurs, meerkats and otters as well as butterflies.

## Steel yourself for Sheffield's hills!

Sheffield is known as the Steel City because of the metal made there in the 19th and 20th centuries – today there are many steel-framed buildings, industrial museums and workshops used by modern makers. The Steel City has something in common with the Eternal City, Rome: they are both built on seven hills. Perhaps surprisingly, Sheffield is also one of Britain's greenest cities, with hundreds of parks and millions of trees.

There are lots of other sterling cities and towns to visit in this region, including Leeds, Bradford, Huddersfield, Doncaster and Halifax. The latter also has a link with Italy – its recently renovated Piece Hall looks like St Mark's Square in Venice! Instead of gelato, the sweet treats in these parts include parkin and liquorice.

**NOTTINGHAMSHIRE**

### NICOLA ADAMS
### B.1982
The boxer was born in Leeds and became the first female Olympic boxing champion in 2012 – she won gold again in 2016 and turned professional in 2017.

### HERBERT HENRY ASQUITH
### 1852-1928
The politician was born in Morley and was Prime Minister from 1908-1916 – he is known for social reform and for taking Britain into the First World War.

### ED SHEERAN
### B.1991
The singer was born in Halifax and raised in Suffolk – in January 2017, he became the first artist to debut two songs in the US top 10 in the same week.

# MERSEYSIDE

## Take a look around Liverpool!

Liverpool, the biggest city in Merseyside, is perhaps most famous as the birthplace of the Beatles, but the Fab Four aren't the only chart-topping things about Merseyside: this is one of the country's sporting hubs, home to the Grand National at Aintree and two world-famous Premiership football teams, Liverpool FC and Everton. In-between fixtures, why not make a magical mystery tour of the city or take a trip on the Mersey Ferry? From the water, you can spot two birds perched atop the Liver Building – one looks across the docs and out to sea, making sure sailors make it safely back to port, while the other watches over the city, keeping its citizens safe. And once you've worked up an appetite, why not try some scouse? This stew has given Scousers their nickname – and a city of full bellies!

**IRISH SEA**

### ADVENTURE SPORT
Ainsdale Beach is the best place for kitesurfing and kite buggies, as well as windsurfing and swimming, too.

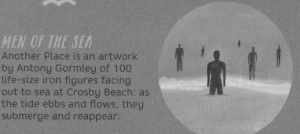

### MEN OF THE SEA
Another Place is an artwork by Antony Gormley of 100 life-size iron figures facing out to sea at Crosby Beach: as the tide ebbs and flows, they submerge and reappear.

### WILLIAM GLADSTONE
### 1809-1898
The Liberal politician from Liverpool was prime minister four times (more than anyone else) and chancellor four times.

### WAYNE ROONEY
### B.1985
The footballer from Croxteth began his career at Everton and is the all-time record goalscorer for Manchester United and England.

### LITA ROZA
### 1926-2008
The singer from Liverpool was the first woman to have a No.1 hit record in the UK, with (*How Much Is*) *That Doggie in the Window?* in 1953.

### BRIGHT IDEA
The Solar Campus in Leasowe, built in 1962, is thought to be the first building in the world heated entirely by solar power.

### MIKE MYERS
### B.1963
The Canadian-born actor's parents were from Liverpool – he is the voice of Shrek and the star of *Wayne's World* and *Austin Powers*.

### CILLA BLACK
### 1943-2015
Born Priscilla White, the singer and entertainer rose to fame during the "Swinging Sixties" alongside her friends the Beatles. She later became a popular television presenter.

### DESERT ISLAND
You can walk to Hilbre Island, at the mouth of the Dee Estuary, at low tide to visit the bird observatory and watch the grey seals on the West Hoyle sandbank.

### BEST VIEW
Bidston Hill is one of the highest points on the Wirral, and has a historic windmill, observatory and lighthouse, plus an ancient rock carving of a Sun Goddess.

### ALL SQUARE
Hamilton Square in Birkenhead has five Grade I-listed buildings, as many as Trafalgar Square in London.

**WALES**

### RIDE TO RHYL
In summer 1962, the world's first commercial passenger hovercraft briefly ran from Moreton Beach to Rhyl, north Wales – a storm soon put it out of action.

BRITISH UNITED AIRWAYS

### PARK LIFE
The Wirral Country Park was the first country park in Britain (1973). You can go camping, walking, cycling and hang gliding there.

## SEASIDE FUN
Walk along Southport's pier, visit Pleasureland, dive into Splash World waterpark or see some celeb' machines at the Lawnmower Museum!

SOUTHPORT

## WILDLIFE WATCH
The beach, dunes and woods at Formby are home to red squirrels, natterjack toads, sand lizards and great crested newts. Prehistoric human and animal footprints have also been found here.

## LOCAL FOOD
Scouse is a meat and vegetable stew served with crusty bread and beetroot or red cabbage – this is where the nickname 'Scouser' comes from.

## THE BEATLES
**JOHN LENNON 1940-1980**
**PAUL MCCARTNEY B.1942**
**GEORGE HARRISON 1943-2001**
**RINGO STARR B.1940**
The best-selling band of all time, aka The Fab Four, all come from Liverpool.

GREATER MANCHESTER

## FOOTBALL FACT
Games between Liverpool and Everton are the longest-running top-flight derby, having been played every season since 1962.

## BOOKWORM ALERT!
Liverpool Central Library is one of the biggest libraries in the UK and has a beautiful Picton Reading Room, and rare books in the Oak Room and Hornby Library.

## MULTICULTURAL CITY
Liverpool is home to Britain's oldest black community, dating back to the 1730s, and one of the oldest Chinese communities, from the early 19th century.

## STARTER'S ORDERS
Liverpool's Aintree Racecourse is home to the Grand National steeplechase, one of the most famous horse races in the world.

## BRITISH BASEBALL
Merseyside is one of the few places where teams still play British baseball – Liverpool Trojans are Britain's oldest club.

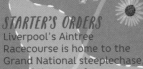

MERSEYSIDE

## TOP OF THE GLASS
St Helens made a lot of the world's glass during the Industrial Revolution. Visit the World of Glass museum and watch a glassblowing demonstration.

## MUSEUM TIME
Museums include the International Slavery Museum; Seized! The Border and Customs Uncovered; and the Merseyside Maritime Museum.

## ANIMAL MOVES
Knowsley Safari Park has an 8-kilometre drive where your car will be surrounded by a pride of lions, a crash of rhinos, a troop of baboons and other wild animals.

THE CAVERN CLUB

## FAB FOUR
Fans of the Beatles can visit The Beatles Story museum and Cavern Club, go on the Magical Mystery bus tour and stay in the Hard Day's Night hotel.

ST HELENS

## SPORTS REPORT
St Helens RFC were founded in 1873 and are one of the 22 original members of the Northern Rugby Football Union; they play at the Totally Wicked Stadium.

## CITY SIGHTS
Liverpool landmarks include the Three Graces along the river: The Port of Liverpool Building, The Royal Liver Building and The Cunard Building.

CHESHIRE

## SECRET PLACES
Speke Hall is a Tudor manor house with a 'priest hole' (to hide priests), an observation hole in a chimney and an 'eavesdrop' (for listening to visitors at the door).

WALLASEY

LIVERPOOL

## TUNNEL VISION
Three tunnels under the Mersey connect Liverpool with the Wirral; the Queensway Tunnel, which appears in *Harry Potter and the Deathly Hallows*.

## DREAM ON
*Dream* by Jaume Plensa is a 20-metre-tall, white sculpture of a girl's head with closed eyes on the site of a former colliery in Sutton.

BIRKENHEAD

## MODEL VILLAGE
Port Sunlight is a beautiful village built in Birkenhead in 1888 for workers in the nearby Sunlight Soap factory.

## ACROSS THE MERSEY
Liverpool's Mersey Ferries are world-famous. Take a cruise on the river and hop off to visit the Spaceport and U-boat Story.

FRANK HORNBY
**1863-1936**
The Liverpudlian invented popular toys including Meccano, Hornby Model Railways and Dinky Toys.

## ART ATTACK
There are excellent galleries including Tate Liverpool and the Walker Art Gallery, plus the Williamson Art Gallery in Birkenhead.

# GREATER MANCHESTER

## FRESH AIR
Greater Manchester is the second-most populous urban area in the UK after London, but it still has lovely countryside, including the South Pennines and West Pennine Moors.

## FULL STEAM AHEAD
The 19th-century East Lancashire Railway runs 20km between Heywood and Rawtenstall every weekend.

## COTTONOPOLIS
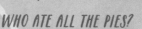
Greater Manchester was the centre of the cotton and textile trade during the 19th century: you can see mills in Ancoats and Castlefield, and visit the Bolton Steam Museum.

### BOLTON

**AMIR KHAN**
**B.1986**
Born and raised in Bolton, Amir became the youngest British Olympic boxing medallist when he won silver at the 2004 Olympics, aged 17 years.

## BY THE BOOK
George Orwell spent three weeks in Wigan researching his book *The Road to Wigan Pier*. The library where he worked is now the Museum of Wigan Life.

## WHO ATE ALL THE PIES?
Wigan hosts the World Pie-Eating Championship every year. The locals there are nicknamed 'Pie Eaters'.

## GARDEN PARTY
A huge, 156-acre RHS Garden, with an education centre where you can learn about horticulture, is due to open at Worsley New Hall in Salford in 2019.

## BEAN COUNTER
The Heinz factory in Kitt Green, Wigan, is the biggest in the world – it makes 1.5 million tins of baked beans every day!

## LOCAL FOOD
Eccles cakes – also called 'squashed fly cakes' – were first made in Eccles in 1793. The drinks Vimto and Tizer come from Manchester, too.

## INDOOR ADVENTURE
Ski the UK's longest indoor ski slope at Chill Factore, or skydive at iFly – both are in the Trafford Quays Leisure Village.

**GREATER MANCHESTER**

### MERSEYSIDE

## POP STARS
Greater Manchester has spawned many big names in music, including Oasis; the Gallagher brothers – (Wil)liam and Noel were born in Longsight.

## CANAL CRAZE
Canals were built during the Industrial Revolution: the Bridgewater Canal was the first, in 1761, and the Manchester Ship Canal was one of the last, in 1894.

**L.S. LOWRY**
**1887-1976**
The artist was born in Stretford and lived in Greater Manchester all his life; his industrial landscapes peopled with 'matchstick men' can be seen at The Lowry, named after him.

### CHESHIRE

## Go for a mooch about Manchester!

Greater Manchester is metropolitan hub, filled with exciting cities and towns, including Manchester and Salford, Bolton, Bury, Oldham, Rochdale, Stockport and Wigan. Once known as Cottonopolis thanks to its status as the world centre of the cotton industry in the 19th century, today it is celebrated for its culture and sport. The National Football Museum is in Manchester, as is SportCity, which houses the City of Manchester stadium, and Old Trafford, home to the U.K.'s most successful football club, Manchester United FC. The county also competes in the kitchen, with Wigan's World Pie-eating Championship and several local specialties to its name: black pudding from Bury, pasty-barm cakes from Bolton, curries from Rusholme, and Eccles cakes from… Eccles!

**DODIE SMITH**
**1896-1990**
The author of *The Hundred and One Dalmatians* and *I Capture the Castle* was born in Whitefield.

**MAXINE PEAKE**
**B.1974**
The actor was born in Westhoughton; she recently played Hamlet at the Royal Exchange.

**MARKET DAY**
Bury Market started in 1444 and it is still the best place to buy black pudding; at the World Black Pudding Championships in Ramsbottom, competitors hurl them at yorkshire puddings.

**MONKEY TOWN**
Heywood has been nicknamed Monkey Town since the 1850s – no one is quite sure why!

**LET'S CO-OPERATE**
The co-operative movement started in Rochdale in 1844, when tradesmen opened a shop selling good food at fair prices. The Rochdale Pioneers Museum tells the full story.

**CHIPPY TEA**
A blue plaque at Tommyfield Market in Oldham celebrates the UK's first chip shop, which opened in 1860.

**RUSH HOUR**
A rushbearing ceremony is performed in Saddleworth every August: Morris men scatter rushes in church and parade through the parish, singing and dancing.

**POWER TO THE PEOPLE**
The Working Class Movement Library in Salford documents ordinary people's lives, and the People's History Museum in Manchester tells the story of democracy.

**LOVELY LIBRARIES**
Chetham's, which was founded in 1653, is the oldest public library in the English-speaking world.

**EGG PLAYS**
Traditional Easter plays used to be performed all over England, and they still take place in Middleton, Mossley and Bury.

**PETERLOO MASSACRE**
On 16 August 1819, a peaceful rally of 60,000 pro-democracy reformers was attacked by armed cavalry, killing 15 and injuring more than 600 – a red plaque marks the spot.

OLDHAM

**SPORTY CITY**
SportCity is the biggest set of sporting venues in Europe, housing Manchester City's stadium, national centres for cycling and squash, an athletics arena, a tennis centre and the English Institute of Sport.

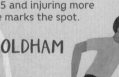

**SOAP STAR**
Coronation Street is made at MediaCity in Manchester and set in Weatherfield, a fictional local town – it is the world's longest running TV soap opera.

**MANCHESTER MUSEUMS**
There's a museum for everyone: study frogs and reptiles in the vivarium in the Manchester Museum; visit the Museum of Science and Industry in the world's first railway station; or sit in a cell in the Police Museum.

**NORMAN FOSTER**
**B.1953**
The architect was born in Reddish and grew up in Levenshulme; his famous London buildings include the Gherkin, the 'wobbly' Millennium Bridge and Wembley Stadium.

SALFORD

**GAY PRIDE**
Manchester is the UK's LGBT centre outside of London, with a gay village around Canal Street, and a huge Pride parade every August.

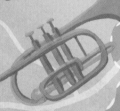

**BRASS BANDS**
Towns and villages in Saddleworth and Tameside hold brass band contests every Whit Friday; the first was in Stalybridge in 1870.

MANCHESTER

**FOOTBALL FACTS**
Manchester is home to the National Football Museum, the Hotel Football, Manchester City and Manchester United. Why not take a tour of Old Trafford?

**CULTURE VULTURE**
The recently revamped Whitworth Gallery has 55,000 artworks in its collection, many by modern artists.

STOCKPORT

**CURRY MILE**
Wilmslow Road in Rusholme is nicknamed the Curry Mile because over 70 Asian and Middle Eastern restaurants can be found there.

**ROBERT PEEL**
**1788-1850**
The statesman was born in Bury, became prime minister (twice) and founded the modern police force; His monument stands on Holcombe Hill.

**EMMELINE PANKHURST**
**1858-1928**
The leader of the suffragettes was born in Moss Side and her activism helped women win the right to vote; her former home is now the Pankhurst Centre.

**WAR WORK**
Go underground at Stockport Air Raid Shelters, tunnels built to protect people from bombs during the second world war.

**HATS OFF**
See over 250 different hats at Hat Works, and learn about Stockport's hatting industry, which used to have more than 100 factories and businesses.

**IRISH SEA**

## CASTLE COUNT
Castles include Tamworth, Stafford and Cholmondeley, as well as the ruins of Halton, which is on top of Halton Hill.

**MERSEYSIDE**

### SAMUEL JOHNSON
**1709-1784**
Dr Johnson was born in Lichfield and became an influential literary critic and lexicographer, most famous for his dictionary, which took him nine years to write.

### JOSIAH WEDGWOOD
**1730-1795**
The potter was born in Burslem and built up the pottery industry around Stoke-on-Trent, using modern methods and marketing; he also campaigned against slavery.

### WATER WORLD
Cruise along the six canals of the Cheshire Ring, visit the Anderton Boat Lift, built in 1875, and learn canal lore at the National Waterways Museum, Ellesmere Port.

### COUNTY TOWN
Chester is one of the best-preserved walled cities in Britain, famous for its Medieval two-level shopping arcades, the Rows.

**CHESHIRE**

### CHESHIRE CAT
Visit the Lewis Carroll Centre in Daresbury, where the creator of *Alice's Adventures in Wonderland* – and the Cheshire Cat – was born.

**CHESTER**

### MO CHAUDRY
**B.1960**
The multimillionaire was born in Pakistan and now lives in Newcastle-under-Lyme; he owns the Water World aqua park.

### DANIEL CRAIG
**B.1968**
The sixth James Bond was born in Chester and took over from actor Pierce Brosnan as *007* in 2005 in the film *Casino Royale*.

### SPORT OF KINGS
Chester Racecourse is the oldest one still in use in England: the first recorded race was in 1539. You can watch for free from the city walls.

### LOCAL FOOD
Cheshire cheese is moist, crumbly, mild and salty; Staffordshire oatcakes are savoury pancakes made from oatmeal.

**WALES**

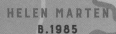

### NUCLEAR BUNKER
The Hack Green Secret Nuclear Bunker was built as the centre of regional government in the event of a nuclear war – today you can explore the huge bombproof HQ.

## *Pop along to the Potteries!*

A world-famous centre for ceramics, the Staffordshire Potteries is an area made up of six towns where pottery has been produced as far back as the 17th century. But pot-throwing isn't the only pasttime here; outdoor enthusiasts are spoilt for choice too, with the Peak District to the north, Cannock Chase to the south, and miles of canals to explore in between. While Staffordshire lends its name to a breed of dog (the Staffordshire Bull Terrier), its neighbouring county is better known for its famous (if fictional) Cheshire cat, popularised by Lewis Carroll in *Alice's Adventures in Wonderland*. The county's other namesake – Cheshire cheese – is equally celebrated – and certainly just as welcome at a tea party!

### HELEN MARTEN
**B.1985**
The artist was born in Macclesfield and works in sculpture, video and installation art; she has won the Turner Prize and the Hepworth Prize.

**SHROPSHIRE**

# CHESHIRE &
# STAFFORDSHIRE

### TOP FLIGHT
Warrington Wolves RLFC, who play at the Halliwell Jones Stadium, are the only rugby league team to have played every one of their seasons in the top flight.

### GOLDEN TRIANGLE
Lots of rich celebrities and footballers live around Wilmslow, Alderley Edge, Mottram St Andrew and Prestbury: the 'Golden Triangle'.

## WARRINGTON

### PINCH OF SALT
Salt has been made for over 2,000 years around the 'salt towns' of Natwich, Winsford, Middlewich and Northwich.

### REAL-LIFE CRANFORD

Writer Elizabeth Gaskell grew up in Knutsford, which inspired the towns of Cranford and Hollingford in her novels.

### BEST IN SHOW
The Staffordshire bull terrier was first bred as a fighting dog, but today makes an affectionate pet when properly trained.

### MAKE A WISH
If you can climb the 108 steps from Water's Green to St Michael's Church in Macclesfield while holding your breath, your wish is said to come true.

Peak National Park
**FLASH**
Highest village in Britain
1518 feet

Please drive carefully

### HIGH LIFE
Flash is the highest village in Britain – although this is disputed by towns in Dumfries and Galloway, and Cumbria.

### TOP TELESCOPE
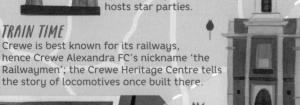
The Jodrell Bank Observatory houses the giant Lovell Telescope – its Discovery Centre is open to the public and hosts star parties.

### TRAIN TIME
Crewe is best known for its railways, hence Crewe Alexandra FC's nickname 'the Railwaymen'; the Crewe Heritage Centre tells the story of locomotives once built there.

### SEEING DOUBLE
Leek's double sunset at the summer solstice sees the sun set behind a hill called the Cloud, then reappear, and seem to set again.

### NUMEROUS NEWCASTLES
Newcastle-under-Lyme is one of over 100 Newcastles around the world.

**DERBYSHIRE**

### ROBBIE WILLIAMS
**B.1974**
The singer was born in Stoke-on-Trent. He was a member of *Take That* and is one of the best-selling British solo artist in the UK.

## NEWCASTLE-UNDER-LYME
## STOKE-ON-TRENT

### ANIMAL MAGIC

Trentham Monkey Forest is home to 140 Barbary macaques, while Chester Zoo is one of the UK's largest zoos, and has 500 animal species.

### FUN & GAMES
Theme parks include Alton Towers, Drayton Manor and Gulliver's World; Water World in Stoke-on-Trent; and the SnowDome in Tamworth.

### BURTON BREWING
Marmite was first produced in Burton upon Trent, using yeast from the Bass Brewery.

### GOING POTTY

Ceramics have been made in Stoke-on-Trent, known as the Potteries, since the 17th century.

### LEST WE FORGET
The National Memorial Arboretum, Alrewas, has memorials to fallen servicemen and women, set among 30,000 trees.

**STAFFORDSHIRE**

### STAFFORD KNOT
The three-looped Stafford knot is the symbol of Staffordshire and its county town, Stafford.

### HERITAGE CITY
Lichfield's sights include its unusual three-spired cathedral, Samuel Johnson's birthplace and Erasmus Darwin's house. The town also hosts a heritage weekend in September.

### BACK TO NATURE
Some of the best countryside to explore is Cannock Chase, Britain's smallest Area of Outstanding Natural Beauty and Delamere Forest, the biggest woodland in Cheshire.

### PINT-SIZED PARK
Prince's Park in Burntwood is the smallest park in the UK, and holds the shortest fun run: just 55 strides.

**LEICESTERSHIRE**

### PAULA RADCLIFFE

**B.1973**
The runner was born in Davenham and is the women's world record holder for the marathon, in a time of 2hrs 15mins and 25secs, set during the 2003 London Marathon.

**TAMWORTH**

### HOBBIT HOLES

The red sandstone Rock Houses at Kinver Edge may have inspired JRR Tolkien's hobbit holes. Occupied until the 1960s, these cave homes are open to visitors.

### HIDDEN TREASURE
In 2009, the Staffordshire Hoard, the biggest collection of Anglo-Saxon gold and silver ever found, was discovered near Hammerwich. You can see it at the Potteries Museum, Stoke.

### CAPITAL CITY
Tamworth was the capital of Mercia, the largest of the kingdoms in what is now England, from about AD584.

**WORCESTERSHIRE**

**WEST MIDLANDS**

**WARWICKSHIRE**

## GREATER MANCHESTER

## WEST YORKSHIRE

### WATER WORLD
There are dozens of reservoirs in the Peak District where you can sail, walk or cycle, including Carsington Water and Ladybower.

### CASTLE COUNT
Mighty castles include 17th-century Nottingham and Bolsover and ruined 11th- and 12th-century Peveril and Newark.

### RIGHT TO ROAM
In 1932, ramblers trespassed on Kinder Scout to fight for the right to walk on open land – their demands were finally met by a law passed in 2000.

### BESS OF HARDWICK
### 1527-1608
The 16th-century noblewoman outlived four husbands, became one of the wealthiest women in England, and built Chatsworth House and Hardwick Hall.

### PRECIOUS STONES
Blue John stone can only be found at Teak Cliff Cavern and Blue John Cavern in Castleton.

### CROOKED SPIRE
Chesterfield church tower's crooked spire twists 45 degrees and leans 2.9 metres – legend says the Devil knocked it out of shape.

### PLAGUE VILLAGE
During an outbreak of bubonic plague in 1665, the villagers of Eyam quarantined themselves to stop the disease spreading. 260 died.

### BUXTON
You can drink Buxton's famous spring water for free at St Ann's Well.

## CHESHIRE

### WILLIAM BOOTH
### 1829-1912
The preacher from Sneinton founded the Salvation Army, a Christian charitable organisation, in 1865; there is a statue of him outside his birthplace.

### HISTORIC HOUSES
Chatsworth House is known as the Palace of the Peak, while other impressive stately homes include Haddon Hall, Calke Abbey, Hardwick Hall, Ilam Hall and Kedleston Hall.

### CHESTERFIELD

### MANSFIELD

### TALKING TRAMS
The National Tramway Museum at Crich Tramway Village has more than 60 trams built between 1900 and 1930. Ride one into the countryside.

### TAKE A PEAK
The Peak District was the UK's first national park in 1951; one of the most beautiful areas is Dovedale, where you can climb Thorpe Cloud.

### WELL DRESSING
Villages Tissington and Aston-Upon-Trent dress their wells with flowers in summer to give thanks for clean water.

## DERBYSHIRE

### WHEELY GOOD
Raleigh, founded in Nottingham in 1885 is one of the oldest bicycle companies in the world, and is best known for its iconic children's bike, The Chopper.

## STAFFORDSHIRE

### BALL GAME
The medieval Royal Shrovetide Football Match is played on Shrove Tuesday and Ash Wednesday in Ashbourne between the Up'Ards and the Down'Ards.

### D.H. LAWRENCE
### 1885-1930
The writer from Eastwood wrote novels including *Sons and Lovers* and *Lady Chatterley's Lover*. There is now a museum and a festival devoted to him.

### CHILDHOOD MEMORIES
The Museum of Childhood at Sudbury Hall has a big toy collection, and shows what life was like for children working down a mine or up a chimney.

### DERWENT VALLEY MILLS
The first modern factories were built along the River Derwent in the 18th century.

### MARVELLOUS MUSEUMS
Wollaton Hall, a country house from the 1580s, now houses Nottingham's Natural History Museum and Industrial Museum.

### DERBY

### GOING POTTY
Royal Crown Derby has been making fine bone china since about 1750 – you can go on a factory tour and visit the museum.

### BEESTON

### EXPERT ENGINEERING
Rolls-Royce has been manufacturing in Derby since 1908, from top-of-the-range cars to jet engines.

### DERBYSHIRE DELICACIES
Derbyshire Foods include Bakewell pudding, pyclets (flattened crumpets) and sage derby cheese. Stilton is made here, too.

### LAND LOCKED
Church Flatts Farm at Coton in the Elms is the furthest place from the sea in Great Britain – a full 113km away.

### PARK LIFE
Derby Arboretum opened in 1840 and was the world's first planned public park – Central Park in New York is said to have been modelled on it.

### LEICESTERSHIRE

24

## SOUTH YORKSHIRE

## LINCOLNSHIRE

### EARLY SETTLERS
The Pilgrim Fathers left Bassetlaw in 1607 to start a new life, and reached Plymouth in the USA in 1620. Follow the historic sites on the Mayflower Trail.

### OLD MASTERS
Britain's only known Ice Age rock art is at Cresswell Crags – the 13,000-year-old engravings of animals and birds are the most northerly cave art in Europe.

### GOOD NEIGHBOURS
Four dukes once lived unusually close to each other in an area called the Dukeries: their huge homes are Clumber House, Thoresby Hall, Welbeck Abbey and Worksop Manor.

### PRINCE OF THIEVES
Robin Hood is said to have lived with his Merry Men in the Major Oak in Sherwood Forest; he married Maid Marion at St Mary's church, Edwinstowe.

### COOKING APPLES
Young Mary Ann Brailsford grew the first bramley apples from pips in 1809.

### HORSING AROUND
The Museum of the Horse in Tuxford has finds from equestrian history, including a 2,000-year-old bit, Roman stirrups, and a horse's gas mask.

### JOSEPH WRIGHT
**1734-1797**
The painter is famous for his dramatic use of light and his depictions of the scientific advances of the Industrial Revolution.

### ADA LOVELACE
**1815-1852**
The mathematician and writer is dubbed the world's first computer programmer; both she and her father, poet Lord Byron, are buried in Hucknall.

### FUN OF THE FAIR
The Nottingham Goose Fair, which started c.1284, is one of Europe's most famous travelling funfairs.

## NOTTINGHAMSHIRE

### CIVIL WAR
The National Civil War Centre in Newark tells the story of the deadly conflict between the Roundheads and the Cavaliers from 1642 to 1651.

### FLORENCE NIGHTINGALE
**1820-1910**
The nurse, brought up at Lea Hurst, cared for wounded soldiers during the Crimean War and became known as the Lady with the Lamp.

### HILARY MANTEL
**B.1952**
The writer was born in Glossop and grew up in Hadfield; she is the first woman to have won the Booker Prize twice, with *Wolf Hall* and *Bring Up the Bodies*.

### CITY OF CAVES
Take a tour of Nottingham's 500 manmade caves, which have been used as houses, pubs, cells and even bowling alleys.

### HARD WORK
The Workhouse in Southwell – now a museum – was built in 1824 to house the poor. It looks like a prison and the inmates were treated harshly.

NOTTINGHAM

### LACE UP
Nottingham made lace and exported it around the world in the 19th century from grand buildings in the Lace Market area.

### CRIME AND PUNISHMENT
The Sheriff of Nottingham worked at the city's old courthouse and jail, which is now the Galleries of Justice Museum.

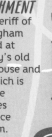

## Pack your bags for the Peak District!

The Peak District in Derbyshire was made England's first national park in 1951, and while the county is blessed with natural beauty, its architecture is just as impressive, with stately homes such as Chatsworth, and destinations such as Buxton (a spa town) and Bakewell (home of the Bakewell pudding) tempting just as many visitors to the region. Neighbouring Nottinghamshire is Robin Hood country! The Prince of Thieves and his Merry Men were said to live in Sherwood Forest, today, some of the most ancient woodland in the country, and home to Major Oak, thought to be up to 1,000 years old! Robin Hood's legacy of lawlessness has endured the ages; if you're intrigued by Nottingham's history of crime and punshiment, why not visit its National Justice Museum?

# NOTTINGHAMSHIRE & DERBYSHIRE

# CAMBRIDGESHIRE & LINCOLNSHIRE

## Find some high-flyers in Fenland!

Once an area of boggy marshland, the Fens were drained centuries ago and today, its numerous dykes and windmills remind visitors that much of the area has been reclaimed from the sea. Cambridgeshire has the UK's lowest land point: Holme Fen is 2.75m below sea level. But while its land might lie low, its IQ soars high! Cambridge is famous for its world-class university, and Grantchester is home to more Nobel prize-winners than anywhere else. And across the border in Lincolnshire, its county town, Lincoln, boasts an equally lofty claim to fame: its cathedral became the tallest building in the world after the Great Pyramid of Giza, in 1311, and retained the title for more than 200 years, setting the bar high for generations to come!

**NORTH SEA**

**NORFOLK**

### EDITH SMITH
### C.1880–1924
The former midwife became Britain's first official female police officer with full powers of arrest in Grantham in 1915 – she is commemorated in the Grantham Museum.

### DOUGLAS ADAMS
### 1952–2001
The writer was born in Cambridge and is best known for The Hitchhiker's Guide to the Galaxy, a comedy science fiction series.

### LINCOLNSHIRE FARE
Delicacies include stuffed chine (salt pork with herbs), pig's fry (pork and offal), sage-flavoured sausages, plum loaf, Lincolnshire Poacher cheese and Grantham gingerbread.

### BUCKETS & SPADES
Skegness had Butlin's first holiday camp, a big sandy beach, donkeys, rides and arcades; Mapleythorpe and Cleethorpes are further up the coast.

### ROCK ON
Britain's first proper rock festival was Barbecue 67 in Spalding, headlined by Jimi Hendrix, Pink Floyd and Cream – tickets cost just £1.

### STUMP UP
Boston's St Botolph's Church, known as the Stump, is one of the biggest parish churches in England and has a huge 83m tower that can be seen for miles.

### MUSEUM TIME
There is a branch of the Imperial War Museum near Duxford; On Your Marques is a model car museum in Mumby; and there is a Stained Glass Museum in Ely cathedral.

### CLOUDSPOTTING
The Cloud Bar, a wooden building on the beach at Anderby Creek, is the world's first official cloudspotting area, with viewing seats and swivelling mirrors.

### EGG-STRAVAGANZA
The World Egg Throwing Championships dates back to 1322 and is held each June in Swaton.

**LINCOLNSHIRE**

### POET'S CORNER
The poet Alfred, Lord Tennyson, was born and grew up in the Rectory in Somersby (now Somersby House), and baptised in St Margaret's church.

### HAXEY HOOD
The annual Haxey Hood dates back to the 14th century and is part rugby match, part pub crawl, as villagers compete to get a leather hood back to their favourite pub.

### UNUSUAL AUCTION
There has been an auction in Bourne for the right to graze animals on Whitebread Meadow since 1742 – people place their bids while two children run a race, and the money goes to charity.

WHITEBREAD MEADOW

### FISHY BUSINESS
Grimsby was the largest fishing port in the world in the 1950s; the Grimsby Fishing Heritage Centre tells the tale.

**GRIMSBY →**

**SCUNTHORPE**

### HENRY IV
### 1367–1413
Henry was born in Bolingbroke Castle and was King of England and Lord of Ireland from 1399 to 1413.

### CATHEDRAL CITY
Lincoln's cathedral was the tallest building in the world from 1311 to 1549 and is home to the Lincoln Imp; the city's Norman castle contains an original copy of the Magna Carta.

**LINCOLN**

### JETTING OFF
Frank Whittle invented the jet engine at RAF Cranwell and his first jet plane took off on 15 May 1941, while RAF Scampton is the base of the Red Arrows, the air force's acrobatic team.

### MIGHTY OAK
The Bowthorpe Oak in Manthorpe is thought to be Britain's oldest tree at more than 1,000 years old – it is hollow inside, and so big that 39 people once stood in it together.

**NOTTINGHAMSHIRE**

### FARMING FESTIVALS
Corby Glen has Britain's oldest sheep fair (from 1238), Lincoln has a big agricultural show, while Spalding has a pumpkin parade.

**LEICESTERSHIRE**

**ISAAC NEWTON**

**1643-1727**

The mathematician, astronomer and physicist discovered the laws of gravity and motion and invented calculus – he was born in Woolsthorpe and his house is open to the public.

**TREASURE TROVE**

More than 6,500 pieces of bronze from around 1,000BC were found in Isleham in 1959 – some of the Isleham Hoard is now on display in the archaeology museum in Cambridge.

**MARGARET THATCHER**

**1925-2013**

The controversial "Iron Lady" was Britain's first female prime minister, from 1979 to 1990 – she grew up above her parents' grocer's shop in Grantham.

**OLIVER CROMWELL**

**1599-1658**

The military and political leader was born in Huntingdon and became Lord Protector – historians argue about whether he was a hero or a villain (he banned Christmas!).

**ISLE OF EELS**

The cathedral city of Ely is built on an island and named after the eels in the waters around it – it has an eel festival in May where you can try jellied eels and eel pies.

**SUFFOLK**

**BACK TO NATURE**

Wicken Fen is the National Trust's oldest nature reserve, acquired in 1899, and one of Europe's most important wetlands, supporting over 9,000 species – you can sponsor a Konik pony!

**LISTED TOWN**

Stamford has more than 600 listed buildings, which means they are architecturally or historically important, including a theatre from 1768 and a Victorian steam-powered brewery.

**DANCING BEAR**

At the Whittlesea Straw Bear festival each January, a man covered in straw parades through the town with 250 performers; the bear costume is ceremonially burned the next day.

**CAMBRIDGESHIRE**

**FROZEN FUN**

The first record games of bandy, the precursor to ice hockey, took place on the fens during the great frost of 1813-14.

**ESSEX**

**FOOTBALL FACT**

The first games of Association football were played on Parker's Piece near Cambridge – the "Cambridge Rules" were adopted by the FA in 1863.

**CAMBRIDGE**

**PETERBOROUGH**

**FULL STEAM AHEAD**

The Heritage Nene Valley Railway runs from Peterborough Nene Valley to Yarwell Junction – you can ride on a full-scale replica of Thomas the Tank Engine.

**LOW POINT**

Holme Fen, a nature reserve and silver birch woodland, is the UK's lowest land point at 2.75m (9ft) below sea level.

**SMART CITY**

Cambridge university was founded in 1209 and has 31 colleges, more than 100 libraries, the world's oldest publishing house and a botanic garden.

**HAVE A PUNT**

You can go punting on the River Cam, on flat-bottomed boats propelled by a pole, from Cambridge to Grantchester – Scudamore's Punting Company is the oldest in the UK, founded in 1910.

**GREAT GRANCHESTER**

The village of Grantchester is said to have the highest population of Nobel prize winners in the world – some may take part in the annual barrel-rolling race on Boxing Day.

**GREAT GARDEN**

Tomatoes were first grown in Britain at Burghley House in 1562, but were believed to be poisonous – now you can visit the Garden of Surprises!

**HARD CHEESE**

Stitton cheese was first made in the Cambridgeshire village of Stilton, but now by law can only be made in Derbyshire, Leicestershire and Nottinghamshire.

**ROYAL CONNECTIONS**

Catherine of Aragon, Henry VIII's first wife, died in Kimbolton Castle in 1536 and is buried in Peterborough cathedral; King John is said to have lost the Crown Jewels in the Wash, near Sutton Bridge, in 1216.

**ANIMAL MAGIC**

Lincolnshire Wildlife Park in Friskney is home to the National Parrot Sanctuary; Shepreth Wildlife Park has a hedgehog hospital.

**HERTFORDSHIRE**

**BORDER LINE**

Lincolnshire and Northamptonshire have the shortest border in the country – just 19 metres long!

**NORTHAMPTONSHIRE**

**SHERIDAN SMITH**

**B.1981**

The actor was born in Epworth and has starred in TV comedies such as Gavin & Stacey, plays as well as dramas, plays and musicals.

**BEDFORDSHIRE**

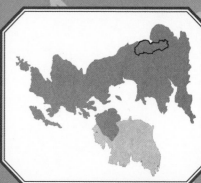

# SHROPSHIRE & HEREFORDSHIRE

SHROPSHIRE

## CHARLES BABBAGE
### 1791–1871
The polymath invented the first mechanical computer in the 1820s, which eventually led to the computers we use today – he lived at Dudmaston Hall near Quatt.

## MARY WEBB
### 1881–1927
The novelist and poet was born in Leighton and set her six novels in her beloved south Shropshire countryside – there are now four walking trails exploring the locations in her books.

### SPORTS CENTRE
Lilleshall Hall is one of three national sports centres for elite athletes – the England football team trained here before winning the World Cup in 1966.

### WOOLLY JUMPERS
In the sheep steeplechase at Hoo Farm Animal Kingdom, which takes place every day from April to September, sheep race over fences, ridden by teddy bear jockeys.

### HIGH FLYER
The RAF Museum Cosford has more than 70 historic aircraft, including the world's oldest Spitfire, plus a huge collection of missiles.

## BRIDGNORTH

### CASTLE COUNT
There are 32 castles in Shropshire, including Clun, Ludlow, Stokesay, Whittington and Bridgnorth, which leans at four times the angle of the leaning tower of Pisa.

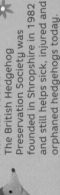

NEWPORT

TELFORD

### IRONBRIDGE GORGE
The world's first iron bridge opened in 1781 – it is now a world heritage site with 10 attractions including a working Victorian town.

### FULL STEAM AHEAD
Heritage railways include the Severn Valley Railway and the Telford Steam Railway; the Bridgnorth Cliff Railway is one of the oldest and steepest funiculars in the country.

### PRICKLY ISSUE
The British Hedgehog Preservation Society was founded in Shropshire in 1982 and still helps sick, injured and orphaned hedgehogs today.

SHROPSHIRE

### COLUMN INCHES
Shrewsbury, a Tudor market town, has the biggest freestanding Doric column in England: Lord Hill's Column.

### ROMAN REMAINS
Wroxeter Roman City (Viroconium) was once the fourth-largest city in Britain – explore the remains of a bathhouse and a reconstructed townhouse.

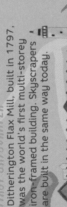

SHREWSBURY

### FLOWER POWER
Shropshire's county flower is the round-leaved sundew, a crimson-coloured, carnivorous plant that traps and eats insects.

## OSWESTRY

### ESCAPE TO NARNIA
Hawkestone Park, a magical 18th-century landscape of grottoes and ravines, was the setting for a TV adaptation of CS Lewis's Chronicles of Narnia.

### FIRST SKYSCRAPER
Ditherington Flax Mill, built in 1797, was the world's first multi-storey iron-framed building. Skyscrapers are built in the same way today.

### PROTO PARLIAMENT
England's first official parliament was held in a barn in Acton Burnell in 1283, when King Edward I met with barons and commoners.

### TASTY TOWN
Ludlow is the food capital of Shropshire with a festival featuring a famous sausage trail and a food centre where you can buy fidget pies filled with gammon, apples, potatoes and cheese.

Aston-on-Clun is the only British village still to celebrate Arbor Day, an ancient tree-dressing ceremony and public holiday held from 1660 to 1859.

## ELIZABETH BARRETT BROWNING
### 1806–1861
The poet grew up at Hope End near the Malvern Hills and is best known for her love sonnets. The Barrett Browning Institute in Ledbury is now a library.

## WILLIAM PENNY BROOKES
### 1809–1895
The social reformer founded the Olympian Games in Much Wenlock in 1850, which inspired the modern Olympics – the Wenlock Games still take place every July.

## MATTHEW WEBB 1848-1883

Born in Dawley, he became the first person to swim the English Channel, on 25 August 1875, in 21 hours 45 minutes (the record is now 6hr 55min).

## WILFRED OWEN 1893-1918

The soldier and poet was born near Oswestry and wrote brilliant poetry about the horrors of the first world war, such as Anthem for Doomed Youth.

## EGLANTYNE JEBB 1876-1928

The social reformer was born in Ellesmere and founded the Save the Children charity in 1919, which still helps children around the world.

### FOOTBALL FACT

Hereford FC's nickname is the Bulls, named after the Hereford Cattle breed. Their mascot, a bull called Hawkesbury Ronaldo, parades around the ground before matches.

**WORCESTERSHIRE**

### SCI-FI STOP

The Time Machine Museum of Science Fiction in Bromyard has amazing props and costumes from Doctor Who, Star Wars and Red Dwarf – you enter through a police box.

**BROMYARD**

### POETRY PLEASE

The 10-day Ledbury poetry festival in July is the biggest in the UK, and includes competitions for children and young people.

**LEDBURY**

### Behold the birthplace of a revolution!

While today Shropshire is one of England's most sparsely populated counties, it has been awarded UNESCO World Heritage status not for its bucolic charm (which is indeed plentiful!), but for its role in the industrial revolution: Ironbridge Gorge is home to the world's first cast iron bridge, marking for many the start of the Industrial Revolution in Britain. The county boasts all sorts of other Victorian attractions, including a steam train on the scenic Severn Valley Railway.

Over the border, the Wye Valley in rural Herefordshire is equally lovely to explore. The region is most famous for its apple and pear orchards... and its cider! The only city in this West Midlands county is Hereford, whose cathedral holds the Mappa Mundi, a medieval map of the world.

### FESTIVAL FEVER

Bromyard is known as the town of festivals, with all sorts of annual events including a scarecrow celebration and a noisy gathering of town criers.

### ANCIENT ARTEFACTS

Hereford Cathedral houses the c1300 Mappa Mundi, the biggest medieval map of the world, as well as the Chained Library, which has 8th-century manuscripts.

**LEOMINSTER**

**ROSS-ON-WYE**

### TOURIST TRAP

British tourism began in Ross-on-Wye in 1782 – people flocked there to take the Wye Tour after William Gilpin published a book about the area's "picturesque beauty".

### ACTIVITY BREAK

Symonds Yat is a top adventure spot, with climbing and caving at Yat Rock, kayaking and SUP boarding down the River Wye, and a cycleway to Monmouth.

**GLOUCESTERSHIRE**

### CASTLE COUNT

Castles in Herefordshire include Goodrich, one of the best preserved English medieval castles, plus Croft, Hampton Court and Eastnor.

### WARTIME HEROINE

Learn about WWII British secret agent Violette Szabo at a museum in Wormelow Tump. She was executed by the Nazis and posthumously awarded the George Cross.

**HEREFORD**

### BLACK AND WHITE

Herefordshire is known for its black and white villages with medieval timber-framed houses – you can cycle around them on a 64km circular trail from Leominster.

It is said that Hereford babies were baptised in cider in the 14th century because it was cleaner than water!

The Ryeland is one of the oldest English sheep breeds, first bred by Leominster monks 700 years ago – Queen Elizabeth I's stockings were made from their wool!

### BATTLE RE-ENACTMENTS

The Battle of Mortimer's Cross took place during the Wars of the Roses near Wigmore in February 1461, and is re-enacted at Hampton Court Castle each year.

See cute miniature donkeys and other pint-sized animals at the Small Breeds Farm Park & Owl Centre in Kington, or walk among butterflies at the Wye Valley Butterfly Zoo.

Aardvark Books in Brampton Bryan is an enormous bookshop with a special reading and playspace for children, called the BookBurrow.

**HEREFORDSHIRE**

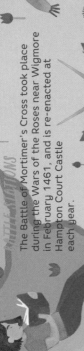

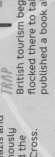

## DOROTHY CROWFOOT HODGKIN
### 1910-1994
The scientist lived in Ilmington and won the Nobel prize for chemistry in 1964 – she is still the only British woman to win a Nobel prize for science.

## WILLIAM SHAKESPEARE
### 1564-1616
The Bard lived in Stratford-upon-Avon and is considered the greatest writer in the English language; his plays include *Macbeth*, *Romeo and Juliet*, and *Hamlet*.

## GEORGE ELIOT
### 1819-1880
The writer was born Mary Anne Evans in Nuneaton and wrote under a male name so she would be taken seriously; her best-known novel is *Middlemarch*.

### FOOTBALL FACT
The West Midlands "big six" teams are West Bromwich Albion, Aston Villa, Birmingham City, Wolverhampton Wanderers, Walsall and Coventry City.

## WOLVERHAMPTON

### MACABRE MUSEUM
The Coffin Works museum is in the old Newman Brothers coffin furniture factory, where fittings were made for the Queen Mother's funeral.

## NEVILLE CHAMBERLAIN
### 1869-1940
The Conservative politician was born in Edgbaston and was Prime Minister at the outbreak of the Second World War, although he is best known for his policy of appeasement.

## LENNY HENRY
### B.1958
The comedian and actor was born in Dudley and has starred in TV shows, films and plays, including Shakespeare's *Othello*; he also co-founded the charity Comic Relief

## MALALA YOUSAFZAI
### B.1997
The activist was born in Pakistan and now lives in Birmingham, after the Taliban tried to kill her; she won the Nobel peace prize aged 17, the youngest ever laureate.

### CASTLE COUNT
Dudley Zoo is in the grounds of the ruined Dudley castle; other castles include Warwick, Kenilworth and a fragment of Caludon.

## WORCESTERSHIRE

### BLACK COUNTRY
The Black Country is an area named after the soot once produced by all the coal mines and factories – the Black Country Living Museum brings the period to life.

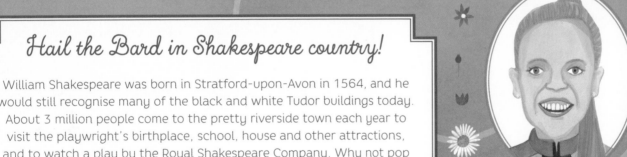

## *Hail the Bard in Shakespeare country!*

William Shakespeare was born in Stratford-upon-Avon in 1564, and he would still recognise many of the black and white Tudor buildings today. About 3 million people come to the pretty riverside town each year to visit the playwright's birthplace, school, house and other attractions, and to watch a play by the Royal Shakespeare Company. Why not pop by on his birthday weekend, 26 April, when there is a huge celebration? After you've visited the Bard, come to Brum! Birmingham is Britain's second-biggest city, known for its Bullring shopping centre, miles of canals and the Balti Triangle, the top spot for a curry. If you can smell chocolate, you must be near Cadbury World – it's a must-stop shop for chocoholics!

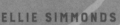

## ELLIE SIMMONDS
### B.1994
The swimmer was born in Walsall and won two gold medals at the Beijing Paralympics in 2008 aged 13, two golds at London 2012 and another at Rio 2016.

### ENCHANTED FOREST
The Heart of England Forest is a new native woodland stretching from the Forest of Arden (where Shakespeare's *As You Like It* was set) to the Vale of Evesham.

# WEST MIDLANDS & WARWICKSHIRE

**STAFFORDSHIRE**

**BACK TO NATURE**
Sutton Park is a huge, 9.7 sq km nature reserve with a donkey sanctuary, pools for sailing and kayaking, and a model aircraft flying field.

**NO MAN'S HEATH**
The four counties of Warwickshire, Staffordshire, Derbyshire and Leicestershire meet at a little village called No Man's Heath.

**LEICESTERSHIRE**

NO MAN'S HEATH

**BEST OF BRUM**
Birmingham, Britain's second-biggest city, has more kilometres of canals than Venice.

SUTTON COLDFIELD

**WEST MIDLANDS**

BIRMINGHAM

**LITERARY LEGEND**
Nuneaton is the biggest town in Warwickshire – its museum has an exhibition about local writer George Eliot, and there is a statue of her on Newdegate Square.

**BALL GAME**
Atherstone, a former hat-making town, has held a Shrove Tuesday Ball Game on Watling Street for more than 800 years – it is a free-for-all, with hundreds of players.

**CATHEDRAL CITY**
Coventry was heavily bombed in World War II and most of its 14th-century cathedral was destroyed – you can climb the spire that is still standing, beside the new cathedral.

**MUSEUM TIME**
Unusual museums include the MAD Museum of mechanical art in Stratford-upon-Avon, the Pen Museum in Birmingham and the National Motorcycle Museum in Solihull.

SOLIHULL

**LOCAL FOOD**
The Balti Triangle is an area of Birmingham with lots of Asian restaurants serving balti, a kind of curry.

**SENT TO COVENTRY**
The unkind practice of "sending someone to Coventry" means to ignore them and pretend they don't exist – it is thought to have originated during the English civil war.

COVENTRY

**SPORTS REPORT**
In 1994, batsman Brian Lara scored 501 not out for Warwickshire against Durham at Edgbaston, the highest ever individual score in first-class cricket.

**COUNTY TOWN**
Warwick's medieval buildings include St Mary's church, which has a 15th-century chapel and a tower that you can climb for views of the town.

**ANCIENT HISTORY**
The Lunt is a partially reconstructed turf and timber Roman fort with ramparts to climb on and the only known "gyrus": a ring that was used for training horses.

**BREAKING THE RULES**
Rugby is said to have been invented by William Webb Ellis when he picked up the ball and ran with it during a football match at Rugby School in 1823 – there is a rugby museum in Rugby town centre.

**CHOC'S AWAY**
At Cadbury World in Bourneville, you can learn about the history of chocolate (and eat lots of it too!).

**DOWN BY THE RIVER**
You can go boating on the River Avon in a canoe, gondola or motor boat, or join a river cruise. There is also a River Festival every July.

ROYAL LEAMINGTON SPA

**ROYAL TOWN**
Royal Leamington Spa is famous for its spring water – Queen Victoria gave it the 'Royal' prefix in 1838. You can sample the water outside the Royal Pump Rooms.

**SHAKESPEARE'S STRATFORD**
William Shakespeare was born in Stratford-upon-Avon. Visit his birthplace and school or watch a play at one of three Royal Shakespeare Company theatres.

**ON THE TRAIL**
Compton Verney, an 18th century mansion, has a woodland adventure play area, willow tunnels and nature trails.

**WARWICKSHIRE**

**ANIMAL MAGIC**
Stratford Butterfly Farm has 1,500 free-flying butterflies and one of the biggest insect collections in the UK.

**NORTHAMPTONSHIRE**

**HISTORY LESSON**
The Battle of Edgehill on 23 October 1642 was the first pitched battle of the English Civil War, between the Royalists (or Cavaliers) and the Parliamentarians (or Roundheads).

**GET THE HUMP**
At Joseph's Amazing Camels in Idlicote you can go camel trekking through the Warwickshire countryside on a Dromedary (one hump) or Bactrian (two humps).

**MEGALITHIC MONUMENTS**
The Rollright Stones on the border of Warwickshire and Oxfordshire are three ancient monuments: the King's Men, the King Stone and the Whispering Knights.

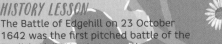

OXFORDSHIRE

# LEICESTERSHIRE, NORTHAMPTONSHIRE & RUTLAND

LINCOLNSHIRE

NOTTINGHAMSHIRE

DERBYSHIRE

STAFFORDSHIRE

**RICHARD III**
**1452-1485**
Richard was born at Fotheringay Castle and was King of England from 1483 until his death at the Battle of Bosworth – his remains were found under a car park in Leicester in 2012.

## MUSEUM TIME
Rutland's Rocks by Rail is an open-air railway museum in an ironstone quarry; Leicester's Abbey Pumping Station is a science and technology museum; the National Gas Museum tells the story of gas power.

## MUCH IN LITTLE
Rutland is the smallest historic county in England, just 29km long and 27 km wide; its county town is Oakham and its motto is Multum in parvo – "Much in little".

## SECRET BEACH
Rutland Water is the biggest reservoir in England by surface area – you can cycle 40km around it or sail on it, and there is even a beach.

## WORLD CHAMPIONS
The World Conker Championships are held in Southwick, and the Nurdling World Championships (tossing pennies into a hole) take place in Stretton.

## LUCKY HORSESHOES
The horseshoe is the emblem of Rutland and 240 of them are on display in the 12th-century Oakham Castle – the oldest was given by King Edward IV in 1470.

RUTLAND

## SPORTS DAY
Uppingham is the only other town in Rutland; Uppingham School has the biggest playing fields in the country – former pupil Stephen Fry had 26 hectares to play on (although he wasn't very sporty).

## SPACED OUT
The National Space Centre in Leicester is full of rockets, satellites, meteorites and space suits – plus you can find out how astronauts go to the toilet in space …

## BOOKWORMS
Ladybird books were first published in Loughborough in 1915; and the town's Loogabarooga Festival celebrates them.

## ROYAL CONNECTION
Follow in the footsteps of King Richard III in Leicester, from the city's castle to the cathedral where his body lies.

LEICESTER

LOUGHBOROUGH

## RINGS A BELL
Loughborough has been home to John Taylor & Co, the world's biggest bell foundry, since 1784 – it made the bell in St Paul's Cathedral, and has a bell museum to visit.

## CASTLE COUNT
Climb to the top of Ashby de la Zouch Castle's half-ruined tower and explore its underground passage and visit Kirby Muxloe, Belvoir and Rockingham castles.

## ENCHANTED FOREST
Since 1995, more than eight million trees have been planted to create the 520 sq km National Forest.

LEICESTERSHIRE

## FOOTBALL FACT
Leicester City FC won the 2015/16 Premier League in one of the greatest sporting upsets of all time: at the start of their season, the odds of victory were 5,000-1.

## CITY OF LIGHT
Cosmopolitan Leicester holds one of the biggest Diwali celebrations outside India, on and around the Golden Mile, and one of the UK's biggest Caribbean carnivals.

## TASTE OF LEICESTERSHIRE
Leicestershire is famous for Melton Mowbray pork pies, stilton and red Leicester cheese, and Walkers crisps.

## ANIMAL MAGIC
Twycross Zoo has all four types of great ape: gorilla, orangutan, chimpanzee and bonobo; Tropical Birdland has 250 birds; Bugtopia The Zoo in Rutland specialises in insects.

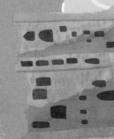

## CAMBRIDGESHIRE

### LOVE TOKENS
In the 1290s, King Edward I erected 12 monuments to his late wife between Lincoln (where she died) and London (where she was buried) – the Eleanor Cross in Geddington is the best-preserved.

### GARY LINEKER
#### B.1960
The footballer was born in Leicester – he scored 48 goals for England, won the Golden Boot in 1986 and never got a yellow or red card; he now presents Match of the Day.

## BEDFORDSHIRE

### FUN & GAMES
Wicksteed Park's Waterchute, which opened in 1926, is the oldest working ride in the UK; Twinlakes is a theme park aimed at young children.

### TASTE OF NORTHAMPTONSHIRE
'Ock 'n' dough, a sort of ham pie, is a traditional Northamptonshire dish – and gives Wellingborough Town FC their nickname, the Doughboys.

CORBY

KETTERING

NORTHAMPTON

### GONGOOZLERS GALORE
Gongoozlers (people who like canals) flock to the staircase locks and BoilerHouse museum at Foxton Locks, and the Canal Museum at Stoke Bruerne.

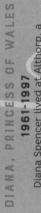

### LITTLE SCOTLAND
Corby is the most Scottish place in England, thanks to the Scottish migrants who worked in the steel industry – the town even hosts a Highland Gathering.

## NORTHAMPTONSHIRE

### LOAD OF COBBLERS
Northampton was once the centre of British shoemaking - the town made 50 million pairs of boots during the First World War, and Northampton Town FC are known as the Cobblers.

### NEED FOR SPEED
Silverstone Circuit hosts the British Grand Prix; Donington Park has a racing car museum; and Rockingham Motor Speedway is the fastest circuit in Europe.

## BUCKINGHAMSHIRE

### PARMINDER NAGRA
#### B.1975
The actress was born in Leicester and got her big break in the 2002 film Bend it Like Beckham; more recently she has appeared in Agents of S.H.I.E.L.D.

### UNDERWATER ADVENTURES
Stoney Cove, the National Diving Centre, is a flooded quarry up to 36m deep, with wrecks including a 16th century ship, a helicopter and a bus for divers to explore.

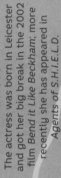

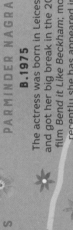

## WARWICKSHIRE

### PAST BATTLES
Historic battles include the Battle of Northampton in 1460 and the Battle of Bosworth in 1485, both in the Wars of the Roses, and the Battle of Naseby in 1645, in the English civil war.

## OXFORDSHIRE

### DIANA, PRINCESS OF WALES
#### 1961-1997
Diana Spencer lived at Althorp, a stately home, before marrying Prince Charles in 1981; she died in a car crash in 1997 and is buried in the grounds of Althorp.

### LADY JANE GREY
#### C.1537-1554
The noblewoman is thought to have been born in Bradgate Park – she was Queen of England for nine days in 1553 before being imprisoned in the Tower of London and beheaded.

### FRANCIS CRICK
#### 1916-2004
The scientist was born in Weston Favell – he co-discovered the structure of DNA in 1953 and won a Nobel Prize in 1962.

### DAVID ATTENBOROUGH
#### B.1926
The broadcaster and naturalist grew up in Leicester and is known for his wildlife documentaries, including the Life series, Planet Earth and Blue Planet.

## Get your binoculars out in Broadland!

Grab your binoculars – this is the birdwatching capital of Britain. Norfolk, part of East Anglia, is revered for its vast skies, nature reserves, and its unique landscape, which includes the Broads, the Fens, and the Brecks, and is a haven to a cornucopia of birds. No wonder the Queen likes to spend Christmas here, at Sandringham House! This royal association dates back centuries to Norman times, when Norfolk's county town, Norwich, became – and remained until the Industrial Revolution – England's second city. As a result, Norwich boasts a Norman castle and spectacular Cathedral at its heart, but it is perhaps better-known for its assocation with another kind of bird – the canary, the emblem of its football club, Norwich City, who wear a bright green and yellow strip.

### SUPER DUNES
Beautiful Holkham beach is often voted the best in Britain, and every summer, the Household Cavalry (the Queen's bodyguard) ride their horses here.

### SCOLT HEAD
Norfolk's only island is a nature reserve with beautiful beaches and sand dunes – there is a ferry in summer, or some people wade across at low tide (though this can be dangerous!)

### SEAHENGE
Seahenge, a prehistoric timber circle similar to the stone circle at Stonehenge, was discovered at Holme-next-the-Sea and is now on display at the Lynn Museum.

### TRAIN TIME
The miniature Wells and Walsingham light railway is the longest 10¼" narrow gauge steam railway in the world.

**THE WASH**

**LINCOLNSHIRE**

**WHOOPS**

### SUNNY HUNNY
Hunstanton has the only beach on the east coast where you can watch the sunset, as it faces west – and it is home to The World of Fun, one of Britain's biggest joke shops.

### ROYAL CONNECTIONS
The Queen spends Christmas at Sandringham House, Princess Diana was born nearby at Park House, and the Duke and Duchess of Cambridge (William and Kate) own Anmer Hall.

### PLACE OF PILGRIMAGE
Pilgrims have been visiting Walsingham since 1061, when a Saxon noblewoman had a vision of the Virgin Mary and built a Holy House.

### THOMAS PAINE
**1737-1809**
The philosopher was born in Thetford, became a supporter of the American Revolution and wrote *Common Sense*, *The Rights of Man* and *The Age of Reason*.

### ROBERT WALPOLE
**1676-1745**
Britain's first prime minister lived at Houghton Hall, which is now open to the public and has one of the biggest collections of model soldiers in the world.

**KINGS LYNN**

### WATER FESTIVALS
There are dragon boat races at Downham Market Water Festival, Wells has a Pirate Festival and Great Yarmouth hosts a Maritime Festival.

### WINDMILLS
Norfolk has lots of windmills, mainly for drainage: the tallest on the Broads is the Berney Arms High Mill, or you can climb a wind turbine at the Green Britain Centre in Swaffham.

### HORATIO NELSON
**1758-1805**
The naval hero was born in Burnham Thorpe and killed during his final victory at the Battle of Trafalgar; there is a monument to him in Great Yarmouth.

### EDITH CAVELL
**1865-1915**
The nurse from Swardeston saved the lives of soldiers on both sides in the first world war; she was shot by a German firing squad for helping 200 Allied soldiers escape.

### THE FENS
Several centuries ago, this was a marshy swamp, but since being drained it is flat, dry and a great place for a bike ride.

### THE BRECKS
This gorse-covered sandy heathland has an eight-mile 'pingo' trail – prehistoric hillocks that collapsed and became ponds – and unusual 'deal rows', which are lines of Scots pine trees.

**THETFORD**

### DAD'S ARMY
Thetford doubled as Warmington-on-Sea in the TV series *Dad's Army*, and has a statue of Captain Mainwaring and a museum, while Bressingham Steam and Gardens has vintage vehicles from the show.

# NORFOLK

**CAMBRIDGESHIRE**

## TWITCHERS
Norfolk is the bird-watching capital of Britain – with county nature reserves including Titchwell, Cley, Holkham, Blakeney, Snettisham and Welney. Listen out for the booming bittern in spring.

## BEESTON BUMP
You can fly kites on this hill, but watch out for Black Shuck, an evil dog with red eyes who inspired Arthur Conan Doyle's The Hound of the Baskervilles.

## CROMER CRABS
These crabs are so tasty and sweet because they grow slowly on the chalk reef just off the coast – you can go crabbing (AKA gillying) yourself in Cromer, Blakeney or Wells.

## SEAL SPOT
There is a colony of about 500 common and grey seals at Blakeney Point – you can take a boat trip to see them and they often swim around their visitors.

## DEEP HISTORY COAST
The oldest human footprints outside Africa were discovered on Happisburgh beach – more than 800,000 years old! A 700,000-year-old woolly mammoth skeleton was also found at West Runton.

## WOOL CHURCHES
Grand churches are all over Norfolk; many were built from the proceeds of the medieval wool trade.

## NORTH SEA

## SEA POWER
Coastal erosion is a problem along the soft North Norfolk cliffs – the village of Happisburgh, for example, is slowly slipping into the sea.

### BOUDICCA
### AD 30-61
The warrior queen of the Iceni tribe lived in what is now Norfolk and led an uprising against the Romans; today you can walk the Boudicca Way from Diss to Norwich.

## HISTORIC HOUSES
These include moated Oxburgh Hall, Felbrigg Hall, Holkham Hall and Blickling Hall, which is said to be haunted by Anne Boleyn's headless body.

## CHRISTMAS SPECTACULAR
The Thursford Collection, a museum of steam engines, organs and fairground attractions, puts on the biggest Christmas show in the country.

## NORFOLK CHILDREN'S BOOK CENTRE
For more than 30 years, this bookshop, in the tiny village of Alby, has stocked the biggest range of books!

## FUN AND GAMES
You can have a fun day out at BeWILDerwood, a treehouse adventure park; Banham Zoo, which has lots of monkeys; or the Dinosaur Adventure Park in Lenwade.

### JULIAN OF NORWICH
### 1342-1416
The mystic wrote Revelations of Divine Love, the first book in English known to have been written by a woman.

**NORFOLK**

**DEREHAM**

**NORWICH**

## KETT'S REBELLION
Robert Kett and his troops set up camp on Mousehold Heath before attacking Norwich in 1549, in protest at land enclosures – they were defeated and Kett was hanged.

## GREAT YARMOUTH

## TOP THEATRES
Catch a show at Norwich's Puppet Theatre or Maddermarket Theatre, a recreated Shakespearean playhouse, or go to the last end-of-the-pier show in the world in Cromer.

## THE BROADS
Explore Britain's magical waterland, a network of rivers and manmade lakes, by wherry (a wide, shallow boat), looking out for the unique swallowtail butterfly.

## CASTLE COUNT
Norfolk has seven castles open to the public, including Norwich Castle, built by William the Conqueror, and Castle Rising, which has one of the best-preserved keeps in England.

## FOOTBALL FACT
Fans of Norwich City sing the oldest known football song, On the Ball City, and in 1938 King George VI was the first British monarch to watch a football league match, at Carrow Road.

## GOLDEN MILE
Great Yarmouth's Golden Mile has all sorts of seaside fun, including a sandy beach, arcades, rides, a Sea Life Centre and crazy golf.

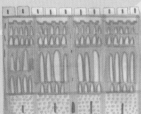
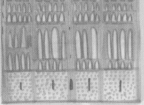

## RACING CARS
Lotus sports and racing cars have been built at RAF Hethel, a former second world war airfield, since 1966 – they test the new cars on the old runway.

## CUT THE MUSTARD
Colman's Mustard has been made in Norfolk since 1814, first in Stoke Holy Cross, now in Norwich.

## FRIENDLY INVASION
During the second world war, Norfolk housed 50,000 US troops in 17 bases – they brought the locals chewing gum, Coca Cola and peanut butter!

### PHILLIP PULLMAN
### B. 1946
The writer from Norwich is best known for the brilliant His Dark Materials trilogy, suitable for older children.

**SUFFOLK**

**BENJAMIN BRITTEN**

**1913-1976**

The classical music composer, conductor and pianist was born in Lowestoft and died in Aldeburgh. Visit his Red House or attend the festival he founded there.

**1924-2000**

The humanitarian, who helped displaced people in World War II and set up a charity to help people with life-threatening illnesses, is buried in Bury St Edmunds.

## ENCHANTED FOREST

Thetford Forest on the Suffolk/Norfolk border has Britain's first Go Ape course (there are now 30+), mountain bike trails and a Center Parcs holiday village.

NORFOLK

## PATRON SAINT

St Edmund was king of East Anglia from about AD855-869 – according to legend, he was beheaded by Norse warriors and a wolf helped his followers find the head in a forest.

**MAGGI HAMBLING**

**B.1945**

The painter and sculptor was born in Sudbury and lives near Saxmundham – her controversial sculpture Scallop is on Aldeburgh beach.

## PLACE YOUR BETS

Newmarket is the home of horse-racing, with two racecourses, the National Horse Racing museum, and a home for retired horses – visit at dawn to see the horses and jockeys on the gallops.

## TOP TOWN

Bury St Edmunds is a medieval market town that boasts Suffolk's only cathedral, and the Angel Hotel where Charles Dickens used to stay – you can sleep in his four-poster bed!

## VILLAGE PEOPLE

West Stow has a recreated Anglo-Saxon village, which holds an annual Lord of the Rings festival called RingQuest, and a Dragon Fest.

**BURY ST EDMUNDS**

## PIG TALES

Agriculture is important in Suffolk and it is said there are more pigs than people – feed them at Jimmy's Farm, see prime porkers at the Suffolk Show and learn more at the Museum of East Anglian Life.

CAMBRIDGESHIRE

## BEST BANGERS

Suffolk's famous Newmarket sausages can't be made anywhere else, Framlingham has an annual sausage festival and Jimmy's Festival has a sausage-eating competition.

**HAVERHILL**

## SILKY SKILLS

Sudbury is the UK's silk capital, with four firms making furnishings for palaces and stately homes, and clothes for royalty, including Princess Diana's wedding dress.

## WOOL TOWNS

Towns that grew rich from the 15th-century wool trade built elegant buildings – Lavenham is the best-preserved, and was used as Godric's Hollow in the Harry Potter films.

## NAME DROPPING

The writer George Orwell's real name was Eric Arthur Blair – he chose his 'pen name' because he loved Suffolk's River Orwell so much.

## CONSTABLE COUNTRY

Many of the places painted by John Constable are unchanged today – you can visit Flatford (seen in the Hay Wain) and Dedham Vale, or explore the River Stour by boat.

**RALPH FIENNES**

**B.1962**

The actor was born in Ipswich and played Lord Voldemort in the Harry Potter films.

ESSEX

## Come and see Constable country!

Visitors to this lovely East Anglian county certainly should bring their camera – or their sketchpad! – since Suffolk's coast and heathlands were declared an official Area of Outstanding Natural Beauty in 1970. But the charms of the county have been extolled for far longer, perhaps most notably by the painter John Constable, who was born Suffolk and immortalised its bucolic landscape in many of his famous oil paintings. And while the beauty of its landscape is well-known, Suffolk has its hidden treasures, too: several hauls have been discovered buried underground, including the Anglo-Saxon ship burial at Sutton Hoo, one of the most important discoveries in British archaeology. Dating back to the 7th century, Suffolk has been clearly been a destination of choice for centuries!

**JOHN CONSTABLE**

**1776-1837**

The Romantic painter was born in East Bergholt and painted Suffolk landscapes – you can visit the Constable exhibition at Flatford and see his artworks in the Christchurch Mansion.

**THOMAS GAINSBOROUGH**

**1727-1788**

The portrait and landscape painter was born in Sudbury – his house is now a museum and gallery, and some of his paintings are in the Christchurch Mansion, Ipswich.

**PLANESPOTTING**
See historic aircraft at the Norfolk and Suffolk Aviation Museum, ride a 1904 tram at the East Anglia Transport Museum and learn about the invention of the hovercraft at the Lowestoft Maritime Museum.

**EAST IS EAST**
Ness Point in Lowestoft is the most easterly settlement of the UK, so you can see the sunrise there before anywhere else.

  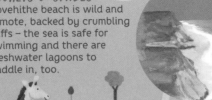 

LOWESTOFT

**ONE, TWO, THREE, FOUR ...**
I declare a thumb war! The Thumb Wrestling World Championships is held in Suffolk each August, often in Beccles.

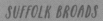

**SUFFOLK BROADS**
The Norfolk Broads are better-known but Suffolk has manmade waterways too – Oulton Broad is the largest lake and has a watersports centre with boats to hire.

**BUCKETS & SPADES**
Covehithe beach is wild and remote, backed by crumbling cliffs – the sea is safe for swimming and there are freshwater lagoons to paddle in, too.

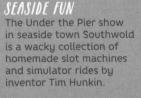

**EXOTIC ANIMALS**
You can see more than 80 species of animal from Africa at the 100-acre Africa Alive! wildlife park, and ride camels at the Oasis Camel Park.

**SEASIDE FUN**
The Under the Pier show in seaside town Southwold is a wacky collection of homemade slot machines and simulator rides by inventor Tim Hunkin.

**ALL SAINTS**
The Saints are a group of 12 villages that are all named after saints; St Michael is also a Thankful Village – one from which all men who fought in the first world war survived.

**DISAPPEARING DUNWICH**
Dunwich used to be the capital of the Kingdom of East Anglia and was a similar size to 14th-century London – now, thanks to storms and erosion, it is a tiny village.

**HEAVY HORSES**
The Suffolk Punch is a draught horse, bred during the 16th century in the county for use in farming. It is always chestnut brown and stockily built.

Stocklinch
A Thankful Village
All who served in World Wars I and II returned home safely

**MUSIC FESTIVALS**
Aldeburgh Festival in Snape Maltings is one of the best classical music festivals in the world, and Latitude in Henham Park is a great family-friendly pop festival.

**NATURE RESERVES**
Suffolk has more than 60 nature reserves, including RSPB Minsmere, one of the best places to see red deer rutting in autumn (fighting for mates), and Orford Ness, a remote shingle spit.

**BURIED TREASURE**
Sutton Hoo, the ship burial of an Anglo-Saxon king and his treasured possessions, is one of the greatest archaeological discoveries of all time.

**ALIEN INVASION**
Try to spot extraterrestrial life on the UFO trail in Rendlesham Forest, where unexplained lights were reported in 1980.

**SUFFOLK**

**ONLY ISLAND**
Havergate Island, a marshy nature reserve known for its avocets and terns, is the only island in Suffolk.

**COUNTY TOWN**
Ipswich, the county town, was an important trading port for centuries – it claims to be the oldest continuously inhabited English town.

**FINDING NEVERLAND**
The Thorpeness Meare is a shallow boating lake inspired by Peter Pan, with lots of channels to explore and tiny islands to land on.

IPSWICH

NORTH SEA

The physician was the first Englishwoman to qualify as a doctor and founded the first hospital staffed by women; she retired to Aldeburgh where she became the first female mayor.

**CASTLE COUNT**
Orford Castle was built in the 12th century by King Henry II – the Wild Man of Orford (a merman) is said to have been kept prisoner there; Framlingham Castle is another impressive 12th-century fortress.

FELIXSTOWE

SUFFOLK

**FEARSOME FORT**
Landguard Fort is the site of the last opposed seaborne invasion of England, by the Dutch in 1667, who were defeated by the Royal Marines in their first land battle.

**TASTE OF WORCESTERSHIRE**
Lea & Perrins Worcestershire Sauce was invented here in the 1830s.

**WORCESTERSHIRE**

REDDITCH

WARWICKSHIRE

**PD JAMES**
**1920-2014**
The crime fiction author was born, educated and died in Oxford. She was best-known for her books featuring poet and police commander Adam Dalgliesh.

**HARRY STYLES**
**B.1994**
The singer was born in Redditch – he was a member of the boy band One Direction and made his acting debut in the film *Dunkirk*.

**ANIMAL MAGIC**
Feed the giraffes at West Midland Safari Park; visit 260 species at Cotswold Wildlife Park; meet penguins at Birdland; and spot a croc at Crocodiles of the World.

**DOWN BY THE RIVER**
Stourport-on-Severn is great for boating, with the River Severn (the UK's longest), the River Stour, and the Staffordshire and Worcestershire Canal.

WORCESTER

**WARRING WORCESTER**
Worcester's cathedral dates from 1084 and houses the tomb of King John; the 1651 Battle of Worcester marked the end of the English Civil War.

**READ ALL ABOUT IT**
Berrow's Worcester Journal, which was founded in 1690 as *The Worcester Post-Man*, is the oldest newspaper in the world in continuous and current production.

**HEREFORDSHIRE**

**ROYAL FAVOUR**
Malvern is a spa town popular thanks to its pure spring water, favoured by Queens Victoria, Elizabeth I and Elizabeth II.

**HEAD FOR THE HILLS**
The Malvern Hills are great for paragliding – the highest point is the summit of Worcestershire Beacon (425m).

**HANNAH SNELL**
**1723-1792**
The soldier from Worcester fought in India in 1748 disguised as a man – more than 250 years before women were allowed to serve in combat roles!

**EDWARD ELGAR**
**1857-1934**
The famously English composer was born in Broadheath and wrote the *Enigma Variations* – his birthplace is now a museum.

**GREAT GLOUCESTER**
King Edward II is buried in Gloucester cathedral – climb the tower in summer for views of the city's Victorian docks.

**MEDIEVAL MANOR**
Tewkesbury holds Europe's biggest Medieval Festival each July, re-enacting the 1471 Battle of Tewkesbury, the final battle in the Wars of the Roses.

**CASTLE COUNT**
Catherine Parr, Henry VIII's sixth wife, is buried in Sudeley Castle; other castles include Berkeley, Beverston, Broughton, Hartlebury and Oxford.

CHELTENHAM

**TASTE OF GLOUCESTERSHIRE**
Single and Double Gloucester cheese is made from the milk of Gloucester cattle; Gloucestershire Old Spots are a rare breed of pig.

**ENCHANTED FOREST**
The Forest of Dean is an ancient woodland with wild boar and deer – you can visit Clearwell Caves and Puzzlewood.

GLOUCESTER

**CHEESE CHASE**
An annual cheese-rolling competition is held at Cooper's Hill, Brockworth.

**FESTIVAL FEVER**
Spa town Cheltenham has jazz, science, music and literature festivals, as well as the Cheltenham Gold Cup horse race.

**WALES**

**WATER WORLD**
The Cotswold Water Park offers lots of watersports; surfers ride the Severn Bore, a tidal river wave; kayaking is popular on the River Wye; and the National Diving Centre is in Tidenham.

**GLOUCESTERSHIRE**

**NEW BALLS, PLEASE**
A textile firm from arty Stroud makes the felt for Wimbledon tennis balls and the baize for World Championship snooker tables.

**TREE HOUSE**
Westonbirt, the National Arboretum, has 15,000 trees and 2,500 different species, including 170 'champion trees' – the biggest of their type growing in the British Isles.

**WHEN IN ROME**
Cirencester, the capital of the Cotswolds, was called Corinium Dobbunorum by the Romans, and the Corinium Museum has lots of Roman mosaics.

**BRISTOL**

**SPORTS REPORT**
Badminton is said to have got its name from the Duke of Beaufort's children who played it at Badminton House.

**WOOLLY WINNERS**
The Tetbury Woolsack Races sees competitors race up and down steep Gumstool Hill carrying heavy sackfuls of wool; a tradition from the 17th century.

SOMERSET

WILTSHIRE

# WORCESTERSHIRE, GLOUCESTERSHIRE & OXFORDSHIRE

**NORTHAMPTONSHIRE**

## TASTE OF OXFORDSHIRE
Banbury cakes have been made in the town since at least 1586; Oxford pork and veal sausages are sold in the city's Covered Market; and Cooper's Oxford Marmalade has spread from Oxford High Street all across the UK.

## MUSEUM TIME
Snowshill Manor displays thousands of objects, including 26 suits of Japanese samurai armour; another unusual museum is the Forge Mill Needle Museum in Redditch.

## INGENIOUS INVENTION
The lawnmower was invented in Thrupp in 1830, by Edwin Budding, to cut the grass on sports grounds=.

### J.K. ROWLING
### B.1965
The author was born in Yate and wrote the *Harry Potter* books, which have sold more than 400 million copies and are the bestselling book series in history.

**OXFORDSHIRE**

## COTSWOLDS CALLING
Climb Broadway Tower for the best views of the Cotswolds' hilly countryside and pretty yellow-stone villages.

## PECULIAR PALACE
Blenheim is the only English palace that isn't home to a royal or a bishop. Winston Churchill was born there in 1874.

**OXFORD**

**BUCKINGHAMSHIRE**

## DREAMING SPIRES
Oxford University dates from c.1096 – the oldest in the English-speaking world. It includes 38 colleges, the Sheldonian Theatre and the Ashmolean Museum.

## HORSING AROUND
The Uffington White Horse is a 110m-long Bronze Age hill carving. Climb White Horse Hill to view the chalk trenches.

## STORY TIME
Alice's Day in July at Oxford's Story Museum celebrates the first telling of *Alice's Adventures in Wonderland* by Charles Lutwidge Dodgeson (a.k.a. Lewis Carroll) in 1862.

## ROW YOUR BOAT
Henley-on-Thames is the UK's rowing capital: it hosts the five-day Royal Henley Regatta in July, and has a River and Rowing Museum.

**BERKSHIRE**

## Call in on the Cotswolds!
Oxford is known as the city of dreaming spires, and has the oldest university in the English-speaking world. Winston Churchill was born Blenheim Palace, one of the biggest houses in England. Henley-on-Thames is the centre of rowing and has a famous regatta. Gloucestershire has lots of pretty countryside and villages, especially in an area called the Cotswolds, studded with medieval architecture and yellow, limestone buildings. Westonbirt arboretum has one of the best collections of trees in the world, and the Forest of Dean is an ancient woodland. Witness the centuries-old tradition of cheese-rolling at the annual contest on Cooper's Hill every year!
Worcester has a lot of history – not least of which is that it hosted the last battle of the English civil war in 1651, when Cromwell's 'New Model Army' defeated King Charles II's army. Outdoor activities in Worcestershire include boating at Stourport-on-Severn and paragliding in the Malvern Hills. Worcestershire Sauce is its most famous export!

### STEPHEN HAWKING
### 1942-2018
The theoretical physicist was born in Oxford and studied the basic laws that govern the universe – his books included the bestselling *A Brief History of Time*.

### DICK WHITTINGTON
### C.1354-1423
Richard Whittington was born in Pauntley and became four-times Lord Mayor of London, inspiring the pantomime *Dick Whittington and His Cat*.

## ANTHONY JOSHUA
### B.1989
The boxer was born in Watford and won a gold medal at the 2012 Olympics – he turned professional in 2013 and became the unified world heavyweight champion in 2017.

**LITTLE ITALY**
Bedford has one of the UK's biggest Italian communities, as a result of immigration in the 1950s, and has lots of Italian restaurants.

**PILGRIM'S PROGRESS**
The John Bunyan Museum in Bedford celebrates the 17th-century writer and preacher who wrote *The Pilgrim's Progress*.

**BACK TO NATURE**
The Lodge is an RSPB nature reserve with Iron Age hill forts, and lots of woodland birds.

## NANCY ASTOR
### NEE LANGHORNE, 1879-1964
The American-born politician was the first female MP to take her seat, in 1919 – she lived at Cliveden House, which is now owned by the National Trust.

**NEW TOWN**
Milton Keynes is a "new town", designed in the 1960s on a grid system – it is known for artist Liz Leyh's Concrete Cows.

## BEDFORDSHIRE

BEDFORD

**CRACK THE CODE**
Bletchley Park was the top-secret home of Britain's codebreakers in the Second World War – see the cipher machines and learn about cryptanalyst Alan Turing.

**LOCAL FOOD**
The Bedfordshire Clanger is a suet pudding with a savoury filling at one end and a sweet one at the other; the Buckingham Bacon Badger is similar but all savoury.

**ANIMAL MAGIC**
Woburn Safari Park has more than 1,000 animals; Whipsnade Zoo is the biggest zoo in Britain; Paradise Wildlife Park has big cats and meerkats.

MILTON KEYNES

**ENCHANTED FOREST**
The Forest of Marston Vale is a community forest – more than a million trees have been planted so far.

**MUSEUM TIME**
The Shuttleworth Collection has Edwardian aeroplanes; the de Havilland Aircraft Museum has fighter planes; and the Mossman Collection has horse-drawn carriages.

## OXFORDSHIRE

## BUCKINGHAMSHIRE

**FULL STEAM AHEAD**
The Buckinghamshire Railway Centre is a museum and has steam train rides; Leighton Buzzard Light Railway is a heritage line.

**LOOKOUT POINT**
You can climb the 172 steps to the top of the Bridgewater Monument on the Ashridge Estate – on a clear day, you can see Canary Wharf in London!

**TREE CATHEDRAL**
See the trees, hedges and shrubs planted by Edmund K. Blyth in the shape of a medieval cathedral in tribute to his fallen WWI comrades.

LUTON

## BEN WHISHAW
### B.1980
The actor was born in Clifton and his film roles include the voice of Paddington Bear in the Paddington films, and Michael Banks in *Mary Poppins Returns*.

**TOP TAXIDERMY**
The Natural History Museum at Tring is a branch of the more famous one in London, and has a big collection of stuffed animals.

**CASTLE COUNT**
Berkhamsted Castle is the remains of an 11th century motte and bailey castle.

**PARTY TIME**
Luton holds the biggest one-day carnival in Europe each May, and is the home of the UK Centre for Carnival Arts.

**ESCAPE TO THE COUNTRY**
Chequers has been the official country house of every British prime minister since David Lloyd George in 1921.

**GOLDEN TICKET**

**STORY TIME**
Roald Dahl lived in Great Missenden from 1954 until his death in 1990 – there is a museum and story centre there, and the Roald Dahl Children's Gallery is in Aylesbury.

**BEHIND THE SCENES**
On The Making of Harry Potter tour, you can walk down Diagon Alley, board the Hogwarts Express on Platform 9¾, explore Hogwarts' Great Hall and visit Hagrid's hut.

WATFORD

**TOY TOWN**
Bekonscot is the oldest model village in the world, dating from the 1920s, and is said to have inspired Enid Blyton's Noddy books.

HIGH WYCOMBE

**LIGHTS, CAMERA, ACTION**
James Bond films are made at Pinewood Studios, Star Wars is made at Elstree Studios and the Harry Potter films were made at Leavesden Studios.

**HEAD FOR THE HILLS**
The Chiltern Hills are an Area of Outstanding Natural Beauty – landmarks include Ivinghoe Beacon, Coombe Hill and Whiteleaf Cross.

**A RIVER RUNS THROUGH IT**
Marlow, a town on the River Thames, holds an annual regatta and is home to five-times Olympic gold medal-winning rower Steve Redgrave – there is a statue of him in Higginson Park.

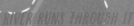

# BEDFORDSHIRE, BUCKINGHAMSHIRE & HERTFORDSHIRE

**CAMBRIDGESHIRE**

### GOING UNDERGROUND
Royston Cave is covered in medieval carvings; Scott's Grotto is decorated with shells, stone and glass; and Hellfire Caves extend 500m underground.

### GARDEN CITY
Letchworth was the world's first garden city in 1903, followed by Welwyn, and inspired the planned city of Canberra, capital of Australia.

### PARLIAMENT SQUARE
Hertford has a Parliament Square, like London, because the Parliament of England moved there during a plague outbreak in the capital in 1563.

**HERTFORDSHIRE**

**MARY NORTON**

**1903-1992**
The author was raised in Leighton Buzzard and wrote *The Borrowers* and *The Magic Bedknob*, which was turned into the Disney film *Bedknobs and Broomsticks*.

**ESSEX**

### ART ATTACK
The Henry Moore Foundation at Perry Green includes the artist's house and studios, plus gardens and fields containing many of his enormous sculptures.

### WRITERS' RETREATS
You can visit George Bernard Shaw's house in Ayot St Lawrence and John Milton's cottage in Chalfont St Giles.

### WHITE WATER
The Lee Valley White Water Centre hosted the canoe slalom events at the 2012 Olympics, and is now a venue for white-water rafting and canoeing.

### HISTORIC CITY
St Albans was once the Roman city of Verulamium, and some Roman walls survive; its cathedral has a shrine to St Alban, Britain's first Christian saint.

## Check out the charming Chilterns!

The Chiltern Hills are an Area of Outstanding Beauty stretching for 833 sq km across all three of these south-eastern counties (as well as Oxfordshire). There are several long-distance walks here, including the Ridgeway national trail, which has been used by travellers for more than 5,000 years and is thought to be England's oldest road. The scenic route passes through woodland and valleys, finishing at Ivinghoe Beacon (233m) for panoramic views.

The beautiful countryside surely inspired local resident Roald Dahl, who lived in Great Missenden, while Bekonscot model village was an inspiration for Enid Blyton. Today you can celebrate another legendary children's author, JK Rowling, on the Making of Harry Potter tour at the Warner Bros Studios in Leavesden. Magical stuff!

**POPE ADRIAN IV**

**C.1100-1159**
Nicholas Breakspear was born in Bedmond and went to school in St Albans – he is the only Englishman ever to become Pope.

**LEWIS HAMILTON**

**B.1985**
The Formula One racing driver was born in Stevenage – he started karting aged eight, became Formula One world champion aged 23, and has won the title three more times so far.

**TERRY PRATCHETT**

**1948-2015**
The author was born in Beaconsfield and is best known for his Discworld novels – *The Amazing Maurice and his Educated Rodents* won the Carnegie Medal for best children's book.

41

## MAGGIE SMITH
### B.1934

The actor was born in Ilford, then part of Essex – she has appeared in more than 50 films, including the Harry Potter series, in which she played Professor McGonagall.

## HISTORIC HOUSES

Audley End House is a Jacobean mansion with horses in the Victorian stableyard, Ingatestone Hall is a 16th-century manor house and Hylands House is a neoclassical villa.

## AMAZING MAZES

Saffron Walden has two historic mazes: an ancient turf maze on the common and a Victorian hedge maze in Bridge End Gardens – there is a Maze Festival in August.

## CAMBRIDGESHIRE

## CASTLE COUNT

Colchester and Hedingham castles have impressive Norman keeps, Stansted Mountfitchet has a reconstructed castle and Hadleigh Castle is a romantic ruin.

## HERTFORDSHIRE

## ESSEX

## COUNTRY PARKS

Essex has lots of country parks, such as Great Notley, which has a 1.2km play trail, and Thorndon, which has a Gruffalo trail.

## DICK TURPIN
### 1705-1739

The highway robber was born in Hempstead; he became a folk hero after his execution for horse theft.

## TRUE LOVE

At the Dunmow Flitch Trials, held since the 13th century, married couples try to prove that they love each other, haven't argued for a year and don't regret their marriage – the prize is a 'flitch' of bacon.

## HORSE SANCTUARY

Redwings Ada Cole, a branch of Britain's largest horse sanctuary, has 70 rescued horses, ponies, donkeys and mules to visit – or even adopt.

## PLACE YOUR BETS

Chelmsford City Racecourse was built in 2008, making it the first new course to to open since Taunton Racecourse in 1928.

## OLD WOOD

The 11th-century Greensted church is the oldest wooden church in the world, while the 13th-century Cressing Temple is the oldest timber-framed barn.

## HARLOW

## RADIO STAR

Chelmsford is known as the birthplace of radio: Marconi opened the first wireless factory here in 1899, and the first official broadcast was made in 1920.

## OPENING NIGHT

Shakespeare's A Midsummer Night's Dream is thought to have been first performed in the long gallery at Copped Hall, a stately home, around 1595.

## BIG BANG

The Royal Gunpowder Mills started making gunpowder in the 18th-century; the site is now a museum devoted to explosives and rocket propellants.

## SECRET NUCLEAR BUNKER

There is a cold war-era underground bunker at Kelvedon Hatch where the government would have gone in the event of a nuclear attack; it is now a museum.

## CHELMSFORD

## GO WILD

There are lots of places to visit wildlife, including Colchester Zoo and Tropical Wings Zoo, Lee Valley Parks Farm and Barleylands.

## SAMUEL PEPYS
### 1633-1703

The diarist, who wrote about the Great Fire of London and the Great Plague, was elected MP for Harwich in 1679 and 1685.

## LONDON

## ROYAL FORESTS

Epping, Hainault, Hatfield and Writtle have ancient royal forests (only royalty could hunt there) – you can visit Queen Elizabeth I's hunting lodge in Epping Forest.

## PEASANTS' REVOLT

The Peasants' Revolt started in Brentwood in 1381, when John Bampton's attempt to collect unpaid poll taxes led to a violent confrontation with the villagers.

## BASILDON

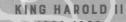

## KING HAROLD II
### 1022-1066

Harold Godwinson was the last Anglo-Saxon king of England – he was killed at the Battle of Hastings and legend has it that he is buried at Waltham Abbey.

## KENT

## FORT TO FORT

You can walk three miles from Tilbury Fort to Coalhouse Fort along a Thames path; Queen Elizabeth I came to Tilbury to rally the troops to face the Spanish Armada in 1588.

## TRAIN TIME
Take a trip on the heritage Colne Valley and Epping Ongar railways, and visit the East Anglian Railway Museum, which has a collection of steam locomotives.

## ART ATTACK
Essex has plenty of galleries: the Alfred Munning museum in Dedham; the Fry art gallery in Saffron Walden, which is devoted to the Great Bardfield artists; and Firstsite – a contemporary gallery in Colchester.

## FIRST CINEMA
The Electric Palace in Harwich was one of Britain's first cinemas when it was built in 1911 – you can still watch films there today.

### JAMIE OLIVER
#### B.1975
The celebrity chef was born in Clavering; he has campaigned for better school dinners.

### CHARLOTTE SCHREIBER
#### 1834-1922
The artist was born in Colchester and emigrated to Toronto, where she became one of Canada's best female painters.

## COLCHESTER

## OLDEST TOWN
Colchester is Britain's oldest recorded town – called Carmulodunum by the Romans – and has ancient town walls, the remains of a theatre and the site of a circus (a chariot-racing arena).

## NATURE RESERVES
Spot owls at Fingringhoe Wick and brown hares at Thurrock Thameside.

## SHIP BUILDING
The Mayflower, which the Pilgrim Fathers sailed to America in 1620, was built in Harwich and its captain was born there; a maritime heritage trail takes in all the historic sites.

## MUD RACE
The Maldon Mud Race is an annual charity fun run across the bed of the River Blackwater at low tide – the runners get covered in thick, squelchy mud!

## A PINCH OF SALT
Maldon Sea Salt has been produced since 1882 and is used by top chefs around the world; you can also take a boat trip on a traditional Thames Sailing Barge at Maldon.

## MERSEA ISLAND
This island is famous for its delicious oysters and has a Town Regatta in August – the final event is Walk the Greasy Pole!

## NEW BEACHES
A recent coastal protection scheme to prevent erosion along a 5km stretch from Holland Haven to Clacton has created 23 brand-new beaches.

### GRAYSON PERRY
#### B.1960
The ceramic artist was born in Chelmsford; he won the Turner prize in 2003 and often dresses as his female alter-ego Claire.

## FLYING HIGH
The Stow Maries Great War Aerodrome was a base for the Royal Flying Corps from 1916-19; it is now a museum and memorial.

## RAYLEIGH

## CRACKING COCKLES
The Thames Estuary is known for its tasty cockles; Osborne Bros in Leigh-on-Sea has been selling them since 1881.

## ESSEX ARCHIPELAGO
There are 35 islands in Essex, many of them important habitat for birds, including Foulness, Wallasea and Northey.

# ESSEX

## LONGEST PIER
Seaside resort Southend-on-Sea has Britain's longest pleasure pier (2.14km), an Adventure Island theme park and 11km of beaches.

### Take a tour of Roman Britain!
Colchester – or Carmulodunum, as the Romans called it – was mentioned by Pliny the Elder in AD77, making it the first British town on record. The biggest town today is Southend-on-Sea, which has Britain's longest pier, and the county town is Chelmsford, which is also the only city in this county. Who would have thought that Essex has 35 islands, including Mersea, a tidal island that you can walk to at low tide. One of Britain's most famous living artists, Grayson Perry, is from Essex – you can sometimes see his work at Firstsite, an art gallery in Colchester. Marvellous museums include a former secret nuclear bunker and a gunpowder museum, and one of the more unusual traditions is the really messy Maldon mud race.

## KARL MARX
### 1818-1883
The philosopher was born in Trier and moved to London in 1849; he wrote *Das Kapital* and co-wrote the Communist Manifesto, and is buried in Highgate Cemetery.

## SADIQ KHAN
### B.1970
The politician was born in Tooting and became a Labour MP in 2005 and mayor of London in 2016.

## ZADIE SMITH
### B.1975
The writer was born in Brent – her books include the bestselling debut *White Teeth*, and *On Beauty*, which won the Orange Prize for fiction.

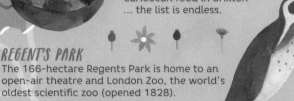

**WORLD MENUS**
Try Chinese food in Chinatown; curry on Brick Lane; kebabs on Green Lanes; Middle Eastern food on Edgware Road; Caribbean food in Brixton ... the list is endless.

**BARNET**

**REGENT'S PARK**
The 166-hectare Regents Park is home to an open-air theatre and London Zoo, the world's oldest scientific zoo (opened 1828).

**BLOOMSBURY GROUP**
This cultural quarter is home to the British Library, the British Museum and Platform 9 ¾ at Kings Cross Station.

### THE TUBE
The London Underground is the oldest underground railway in the world: the first line opened in 1863.

**ANNUAL EVENTS**
Notting Hill Carnival in August is one of the world's biggest street festivals; other annual events include the Lord Mayor's Show and Trooping the Colour.

**WEST END**
This entertainment hub hosts 40 theatres, Leicester Square's glitzy film premieres, and Piccadilly Circus.

## BUCKINGHAMSHIRE

**LONDON**

**EALING**

### FLOWER POWER
Kew Gardens has the biggest collection of plants in the world, plus an 18m-high treetop canopy and King George III's Kew Palace.

**ALBERTOPOLIS**
"Albertopolis" in South Kensington includes the Natural History Museum, Science Museum and Victoria and Albert Museum, plus the Royal Albert Hall.

**CITY OF WESTMINSTER**

**CITY OF LONDON**

### DEER STALKER
Richmond Park is Greater London's biggest royal park (1,000 hectares) and is home to 650 deer.

**DAILY POLITICS**
The Palace of Westminster includes the Houses of Parliament and Big Ben; coronations are held next door, at Westminster Abbey.

**BERKSHIRE**

**SOUTH BANK**
The South Bank's attractions include the 135m-tall London Eye, Tate Modern, Southbank Centre, Royal Festival Hall and National Theatre.

## CITY OF WESTMINSTER

### HIT THE SHOPS
Hamleys is the oldest and biggest toy shop in the world, while famous department stores include Harrods, Fortnum & Mason, Liberty and Selfridges.

### TRAFALGAR SQUARE
Trafalgar Square is named after the 1805 Battle of Trafalgar, and Nelson's Column is a memorial to Admiral Horatio Nelson, who died in the battle.

### PARK LIFE
There are eight royal parks – Hyde Park is the biggest in central London, and is known for Speakers' Corner and the Serpentine lake.

**MARKET DAY**
London's many markets include New Covent Garden (fruit and veg), Billingsgate (fish), Smithfields (meat), Borough and Leadenhall (food) and Spitalfields (fashion).

### FAMOUS NEIGHBOURS
The prime minister lives at 10 Downing Street and the chancellor lives next door at number 11.

### VISIT THE QUEEN
Buckingham Palace is the Queen's London home – the state rooms are open to the public in the summer, and you can see the Changing of the Guard most days.

**ROYAL PALACES**
Henry VIII owned Hampton Court Palace, which is now open to the public; William and Kate live in Kensington Palace; Princess Anne lives in St James's Palace.

**CROYDON**

**SPORTS DAY**
Annual sporting events include the Boat Race in March or April, the London Marathon (also April) and Wimbledon tennis championships in July.

**SURREY**

# ENFIELD

## LITERARY LONDON
You can see a Shakespeare play at the Globe, a reconstructed Elizabethan theatre, and have a Dickensian Christmas at the Charles Dickens Museum.

## OLYMPIC PARK
The London 2012 Olympics were held at the Queen Elizabeth Olympic Park; swim in the Olympic pool, cycle at the velodrome, or slide down the Orbit!

**NEWHAM**

## SHIP MATES
Climb aboard warship HMS Belfast, tea clipper Cutty Sark, and replica of Sir Francis Drake's galleon, the Golden Hind.

## SKY HIGH
The Shard is the tallest skyscraper in the UK at 310m – three others are nicknamed the Gherkin, the Walkie Talkie and the Cheesegrater.

## MARITIME MATTERS
Greenwich is home to the O2 (or Millennium Dome), the National Maritime Museum and the Royal Observatory, where Greenwich Mean Time was calculated.

**KENT**

## MUSEUM TIME
Don't miss the Imperial War Museum and London Transport Museum, plus the lesser-known Horniman Museum.

## LOCAL FOOD
Traditional cockney dishes include pie and mash with parsley liquor, winkles, cockles and jellied eels.

### DAVID BOWIE
### 1947-2016
The groundbreaking musician was born in Brixton – his career spanned five decades, from the 1969 single "Space Oddity" to the 2016 album *Blackstar*.

### DANIEL RADCLIFFE
### B.1989
The actor was born in Hammersmith and is best known for playing Harry Potter in eight films.

### ROSALIND FRANKLIN
### 1920-1958
The chemist was born in Notting Hill and helped to discover the double-helix structure of DNA.

**ESSEX**

## EAST END
People from the East End of London are known as cockneys – learn about rhyming slang at the Ragged School Museum.

**CITY OF LONDON**

## DOME DAY
St Paul's Cathedral was designed by Christopher Wren in the 17th century and its mighty dome survived the bombs during the Blitz.

## BUILDING BRIDGES
There are 33 bridges over the River Thames in Greater London: the most famous is Tower Bridge, which opens to let tall ships through.

## GREAT FIRE
The Great Fire of London in 1666 destroyed most of the City of London; climb the 62m-high Monument built to commemorate the disaster.

## CASTLE COUNT
The 11th-century Tower of London has been a fortress, prison and palace – you can see the Crown Jewels there, guarded by the "Beefeaters".

### ELEANOR RATHBONE
### 1872-1946
The politician was born in London and campaigned for child benefits to be paid to mothers – her campaign began in 1918 and the law was finally passed in 1945.

## Have a capital time in the Big Smoke!

London is one of the most-visited cities in the entire world – and no wonder! It has been the capital of England since the 11th century (and the UK's capital from 1707). Parliament meets at the Palace of Westminster, the Prime Minister lives at No. 10 Downing Street and the Queen's home is Buckingham Palace. But it's not all about politics and power – London is also a cultural capital, with world-class museums and galleries, amazing architecture, fun attractions and plenty of parks. And as befits a global city, it is truly cosmopolitan – more than 300 languages are spoken here, and you can tuck into food from all over the planet. London's nickname is the Big Smoke, after the smog that used to choke the city – but don't worry, it has long since cleaned up its act!

## CHARLES DICKENS
### 1812–1870
The writer loved Broadstairs and spent his holidays here; a Dickens House Museum and a June festival commemorate him.

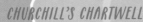

### DOWN HOUSE
The great scientist Charles Darwin lived here for 40 years, and his desk, chair, instruments and notebooks are all on display.

### LULLINGSTONE ROMAN VILLA
Amazing artefacts at this site from AD80 include a mosaic of the fire-breathing Chimera: a monster with a lion's head, goat's body and snake's tale.

### SWEEPS' FESTIVAL
A May Day festival in Rochester celebrates 19th-century chimney sweeps, with Morris dancing and folk music.

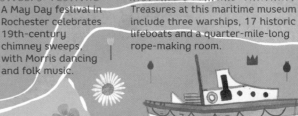

### HISTORIC DOCKYARD CHATHAM
Treasures at this maritime museum include three warships, 17 historic lifeboats and a quarter-mile-long rope-making room.

### ROCHESTER
Roman Rochester is one of the five 'Medway towns' with Chatham, Strood, Gillingham and Rainham.

### CHURCHILL'S CHARTWELL
Winston Churchill lived in this Tudor house from 1924 until his death in 1965, and his books, maps and paintings are all on display.

### BACK TO NATURE
Kent has 61 nature reserves, included Tyland Barn, a microcosm of the county's habitats (pond, meadow, chalk bank, hedge, scrub and shingle beach).

### MAIDSTONE

### LEEDS CASTLE
A fairytale castle surrounded by water, with an exotic aviary, maze, grotto and dog-collar museum.

### KNOLE
Henry VIII hunted in the parkland of this palace, where 600 fallow and sika deer still roam.

## DANTE GABRIEL ROSSETTI
### 1828–1882
The poet, painter and co-founder of the Pre-Raphaelite Brotherhood is buried in Birchington.

### HEVER CASTLE
King Henry VIII's second wife, Anne Boleyn, was born in this tiny moated castle. Anne of Cleves lived here too.

### TUNBRIDGE WELLS
Royals started coming here to drink the spring water in 1630, and you can still sample it there today.

### SCOTNEY CASTLE
A half-ruined castle by a lake with a 16th-century priest-hole, where Father Richard Blount hid from Elizabeth I's priest-hunters.

### SISSINGHURST
Kent has 180 gardens open to the public; those planted by poet Vita Sackville-West at Sissinghurst are the most beautiful.

# KENT

### ENCHANTED FOREST
Bedgebury National Pinetum has more than 10,000 trees, many of them conifers, plus a Go Ape! course and mountain bike tracks.

## Go green in the Garden of England!

King Henry VIII gave Kent its nickname after sampling some Kentish cherries, and no wonder: the county is bursting with fruit, flowers, hops and vines. Kent is in south-east England and borders Greater London, Surrey, East Sussex and Essex; the county town is Maidstone. It is full of important sites from history: Roman remains, ancient castles and Canterbury Cathedral, the home of the Church of England. World-famous former residents include Charles Dickens, Charles Darwin and Winston Churchill; their houses are now open to the public. Another claim to fame is Pluckley, said to be the most haunted village in England. Kent boasts lots of traditional seaside resorts and all kinds of weird and wonderful attractions – even a museum devoted to dog collars.

### HIGH WEALD
This 1,450-square-kilometre area of Outstanding Natural Beauty on the Kent/East Sussex border has ancient woods and rolling fields. Hops for ale and beer have been grown here since the sixteenth century.

### RAISE A GLASS
Kent has more than 50 vineyards, including Chapel Down in Tenterden, which has tours and wine tastings.

## ISLE OF SHEPPEY
Separated from the mainland by the Swale channel, this is known as Kent's Treasure Island.

## WHITSTABLE
An old fishing town renowned for its excellent oysters, which once fed the poor and are now an expensive delicacy.

## RAMSGATE
The proud location of the UK's only Royal Harbour, where boat trips set off to see seals on Goodwin Sands.

## BUCKETS AND SPADES
The Isle of Thanet (which hasn't been an island since the Wantsun Channel silted up in the 17th century) has lots of lovely sandy beaches.

## CANTERBURY
Canterbury cathedral was founded by Augustine in AD597, although the oldest part still standing is the 11th-century crypt.

## CHEERS!
Shepherd Neame has been making beer in Faversham since 1698, making it Britain's oldest brewer.

## MARGATE
A seaside town with the UK's first ever amusement park, 1920s Dreamland, and a modern art gallery, the Turner Contemporary.

MARGATE

## PICK YOUR OWN
Sample the fruit at Brogdale, the National Fruit Collection, which grows 2,000 kinds of apples and 500 types of pear.

## LUNCHTIME
In 1762, John Montagu, the fourth Earl of Sandwich, is said to have invented sandwiches by eating his meat between two pieces of bread while playing cards.

## WILD WOOD
At 28 square kilometres, the Blean is the largest area of ancient woodland in England.

CANTERBURY

## DEAL CASTLE
This unusual fort built for Henry VIII looks like a Tudor rose when viewed from above.

## WALMER CASTLE
The Duke of Wellington and stationer WH Smith both died in this Tudor castle.

## KENT DOWNS
This Area of Outstanding Natural Beauty covers 878 square kilometres from the White Cliffs of Dover to the Surrey border.

## HAUNTED HOUSES
The village of Pluckley claims to be the most haunted in England with 12 ghosts, including a pub poltergeist and a Red Lady.

## DOVER CASTLE
An impressive hilltop castle with a Roman lighthouse and secret wartime tunnels.

KENT

ENGLISH CHANNEL

## ROMNEY AND DENGE MARSHES
The southernmost part of Kent was reclaimed from the sea, and is now marshland where prized sheep graze.

## TOY TRAINS
The miniature R, H & DR railway from Hythe to Dungeness is one of the smallest in the world, with 15in track and one-third-sized trains.

DOVER

## DOVER
One of the Cinque Ports (with Hythe, Sandwich, New Romney and Hastings), famous for its bright White Cliffs.

FOLKESTONE

## SIR QUENTIN BLAKE
B.1932
This much-loved children's illustrator was born in Sidcup. He won the Hans Christian Anderson Award in 2002.

## MARY TOURTEL
1874-1948
This Canterbury resident created comic strip character Rupert Bear. The city's Heritage Museum has a wing dedicated to his adventures.

## ORLANDO BLOOM
B.1977
This actor rose to fame with his roles in The Lord of the Rings and Pirates of the Caribbean.

## GEOFFREY CHAUCER
C.1343-1400
The author wrote the Canterbury Tales, bawdy stories about pilgrims, at the end of the 14th century.

## ELIZABETH FRY
1780-1845
This social reformer was a well-known Quaker, and was know as the 'angel of prisons' for her humanitarian work there.

# BERKSHIRE & SURREY

## HEAVENLY VILLAGE
The artist Stanley Spencer is best known for painting biblical scenes as though they occurred in his village, Cookham – view them at the gallery there.

OXFORDSHIRE

## THE LIVING RAINFOREST
Three glasshouses are home to more than 700 species of plants and animals, including a bird-eating spider.

BERKSHIRE

## FARMING FACTS
The Museum of English Rural Life in Reading tells the story of farming, food and the countryside from 1750 to the present day.

### DAVID CAMERON

B.1966
The former prime minister grew up in Peasemore and was educated at Eton College.

## TOAD HALL
Mapledurham House, an Elizabethan stately home, is said to have inspired Toad Hall in The Wind in the Willows by Kenneth Graham.

READING

## CLEVER COOKING
Chef Heston Blumenthal's Fat Duck at Bray has served bacon and egg ice-cream, snail porridge and an Alice in Wonderland-inspired mock turtle soup.

## HORSE BOATS
From Roman times to the mid-20th century, horse-drawn boats carried cargo on the Kennet and Avon Canal.

## WOLF WALKS
Take a walk with wolves at the UK Wolf Conservation Trust in Beenham. Learn how to howl – and see if the wolves howl back!

BRACKNELL

## PAST BATTLES
Berkshire has seen many battles: Englefield and Ashdown, against the Danes; two Battles of Newbury in the English Civil War; and the Battle of Reading in the Glorious Revolution.

## PEACE CAMP
Greenham Common Women's Peace Camp was set up in 1981 to protest against nuclear weapons, and was active for 19 years.

HAMPSHIRE

WILTSHIRE

### MICHAEL BOND
1926-2017
The author was born in Newbury and grew up in Reading, and was best known for his Paddington Bear books.

## Roam the Royal County!

The Queen granted Berkshire royal status in 1957 in honour of Windsor Castle, built there by William the Conqueror in the 11th century. The county's other famous institution is Eton College, a boarding school founded by Henry VI in 1440. The county town is Reading, and attractions include Legoland and the Living Rainforest, where you can see a bird-eating spider.

Surrey is a millionaires' playground! There are more millionaires here than anywhere else in the UK. The county town is Guildford, and historic sites include Runnymede, where the Magna Carta was sealed by King John in 1215. Surrey has more woodland than any other English county, including at Box Hill in the North Downs. But don't try to visit Harry Potter's Muggle relatives, the Dursleys, in Little Whinging – it is a fictional town.

### HILDA HEWLETT
1864-1943
The first British female to earn a pilot's licence, she set up Braitain's first flying school at Brooklands near Weybridge.

### EDITH MORLEY
1875-1964
The literary scholar became England's first female university professor in 1908 at University College, Reading (now Reading University).

## BAD REP
Ricky Gervais' sitcom *The Office* is set in Slough, while poet John Betjeman wrote: "Come, friendly bombs and fall on Slough! It isn't fit for humans now".

## JUICY APPLES
Cox's Orange Pippins were first grown in the county and are now grown worldwide.

### KING EDWARD III
#### 1312-1377
The king of England was born in Windsor Castle. Crowned at age 14, his 50-year rule oversaw military success, and the Black Death.

## SCHOOL DAYS
Eton College is the most famous public school in the world – it has educated 19 British prime ministers.

## MAGNA CARTA
The Magna Carta was sealed at Runnymede in 1215 by King John. It was a series of written promises to the people that the king would rule within the law of the land.

## SLOUGH

## RADICAL POLITICS
Surrey was the birthplace of two radical political movements during the 1640s: the Levellers and the Diggers.

**GREATER LONDON**

## ROYAL RESIDENCE
Windsor Castle was built in the 11th century by William the Conqueror. It is the biggest inhabited castle in the world and is the Queen's favourite weekend home.

## PLACE YOUR BETS
Horse racing is huge here: courses include Ascot, Newbury and Windsor in Berkshire, and Epsom Downs, Lingfield Park, Kempton Park and Sandown in Surrey.

## SWAN UPPING
Each July, Swan Uppers row up the River Thames in skiffs from Sunbury to count the swans and check their health on behalf of the Queen, who owns them.

### WILLIAM COBBETT
#### 1763-1835
The radical farmer, journalist and reformer was born in Farnham and is best known for his book *Rural Rides*, an account of his journeys on horseback through the countryside.

## THRILLS AND SPILLS
Thorpe Park, between Chertsey and Staines, has more than 30 roller coasters and rides, and a shark-themed hotel.

## MINIATURE HEROES
Legoland Windsor Resort has more than 50 rides, including Miniland, with London landmarks made from 40 million bricks.

## WOKING

## FIRST MOSQUE
The Shah Jahan Mosque in Woking was the first purpose-built mosque in the UK, built in 1889 by Gottlieb Wilhelm Leitner.

**SURREY**

## WACKY RACES
Surrey has some unusual annual contests, such as the pram races in Windlesham and Oxted, and the yellow plastic duck races in Leatherhead, Chilworth and other villages.

**KENT**

## CASTLE COUNT
Historic sites in Surrey include Guildford and Farnham castles, and the ruins of Waverley Abbey and Woking Palace.

## REST IN PEACE
Brookwood Cemetery is the largest burial ground in the UK, while Woking Crematorium is the first custom-built crematorium (1878).

## MOTOR MUSEUM
Brooklands was the world's first purpose-built motor racing circuit; it is now a motoring and aviation museum.

## GUILDFORD

## RICH LIST
Surrey is thought to have the highest proportion of millionaires in the UK, and East Horsley is dubbed Britain's richest village.

### GERTRUDE JEKYLL
#### 1843-1932
The horticulturist grew up in Bramley House and later lived in Munstead Wood – she designed more than 400 gardens and worked closely with the architect Edwin Lutyens.

## BEST VIEWS
Scenic viewpoints include Box Hill, Leith Hill and the Devil's Punch Bowl.

## LEADING LIGHT
Godalming was the first town in the world to install a public electricity supply and electric street lighting.

## CRICKETING COUNTY
The first written mention of cricket was in 1598, when John Derrick wrote that children played the sport at Guildford's Royal Grammar School.

## HARRY'S HOUSE
The Dursleys, Harry Potter's Muggle relatives, live at Number 4 Privet Drive, Little Whinging – a fictional town in Surrey.

**WEST SUSSEX**

**EAST SUSSEX**

# WEST & EAST SUSSEX

SURREY

HAMPSHIRE

**CLEAR AS MUD**
The Sussex dialect has more than 30 different words to describe mud, from "gawm" (sticky, smelly mud) to "stug" (watery mud).

**LOOKOUT POINTS**
Blackdown is the highest point in West Sussex and was once the home of the poet Alfred, Lord Tennyson, while Ditchling Beacon is the highest point in East Sussex.

**HAIL IN HORSHAM**
Britain's heaviest hailstones fell in Horsham in September 1958, the size of tennis balls, each weighing up to 140g.

**FIRST TWENTY20**
Stoolball, a game similar to Twenty20 cricket, started in Sussex in the 15th century, where milkmaids used their stools as wickets; it is still played today.

CRAWLEY

**HERE BE DRAGONS**
In Sussex folklore, it was said that fearsome water dragons called knuckers lived in bottomless ponds, or knuckerholes.

**BUDDHIST RETREAT**
Cittaviveka, AKA the Chithurst Buddhist Monastery, has been a peaceful residence for monks and nuns since 1979.

**EARLY HUMANS**
The oldest human remains in Britain were found at Eartham Pit in Boxgrove in the 1990s – they were 500,000 years old.

**ANCIENT HISTORY**
Chanctonbury Ring is an Iron Age hillfort, the Devil's Jumps is a Bronze Age site, while the Long Man of Wilmington is an ancient hill figure.

**ARTY PARTY**
The Brighton Festival in May is the second-largest arts festival in the UK, after Edinburgh, and opens with a Children's Parade starring 5,000 local children.

**HISTORIC HOUSE**
Goodwood House is the site of the Festival of Speed, Goodwood Circuit and Goodwood Revival (for cars), and the Goodwood Racecourse (for horses).

**MUSEUM TIME**
See a collection of costumes at the Worthing Museum, and 10,000 toys at the Brighton Toy and Model Museum.

**SPORTS REPORT**
Sussex CCC were founded in 1839, making them the oldest first-class county cricket club in England and Wales.

WEST SUSSEX

**ART ATTACK**
Pallant House Gallery in Chichester has a great collection of 20th-century British art, while the Cass Sculpture Foundation in Goodwood displays British sculpture.

**ROMAN REMAINS**
Fishbourne Roman Palace was built in the first century AD and has amazing mosaic floors.

**BIRDMEN OF BOGNOR**
Bognor Regis, the sunniest place in mainland England, has an annual Birdman competition, where people try to 'fly' off the pier.

WORTHING

BRIGHTON AND HOVE

**CATHEDRAL CITY**
Chichester is the county town of West Sussex and has a 12th-century cathedral, Roman walls, a Tudor market cross and an excellent modern theatre.

**TOP TRAIN**
Volk's Electric Railway runs along Brighton's seafront – it opened in 1883, making it the world's oldest operating electric railway.

**CITY SIGHTS**
Brighton landmarks include the Royal Pavilion, built by King George IV; the Palace Pier and West Pier; the i360 observation tower; and narrow shopping streets called the Lanes.

**PROUD CITY**
The city of Brighton and Hove has one of the biggest LGBT communities in the UK and holds the biggest Pride event – which includes a Pride Dog Show.

**ANOHNI**
**B.1971**
The singer formerly known as Antony Hegarty was born in Chichester and is the second transgender person to be nominated for an Oscar, for her song *Manta Ray*.

**TOM CRUISE**
**B.1962**
The Mission Impossible star is reported to live at Saint Hill Manor in East Grinstead, the UK headquarters of the controversial Church of Scientology.

## DALEY THOMPSON
### B.1958
The decathlete grew up in Bolney and became the first athlete in any event to hold the Olympic, World, European and Commonwealth gold medals simultaneously.

## RUDYARD KIPLING
### 1865-1936
The writer lived at Bateman's in Burwash from 1902 and his house is now a museum; his children's books include the *Jungle Book* and the *Just So Stories*.

The chalk hills of Sussex form a national park and include the Seven Sisters and Beachy Head. Brighton in East Sussex is the gay capital of Britain, and Lewes has the UK's biggest Bonfire Night celebrations. Hastings is the site of William the Conqueror's first castle, and nearby Battle is where he won the Battle of Hastings in 1066. Why not play a game of poohsticks in Ashdown Forest, home of A.A. Milne's mischievous bear, Winnie-the-Pooh? Chichester is the county town of West Sussex, and Crawley is its biggest town. The oldest human remains were found at Boxgrove, and you can see flying humans at the Birdman contest in Bognor Regis. Pack your wellies – squelchy Sussex has more than 30 words to describe mud!

## CASTLE COUNT
Sussex's many castles include Arundel, Bodiam, Amberley, Lewes, Hastings and Herstmonceux, plus the Eastbourne Redoubt, a coastal defence fort from 1805.

**KENT**

## POOH'S FOREST
Ashdown Forest is the setting for the *Winnie-the-Pooh* stories written by AA Milne: you can play poohsticks at Poohsticks Bridge and visit Eeyore's Gloomy Place.

## LOCAL FOOD
Sussex was once known for "seven good things": Pulborough eels, Selsey cockles, Chichester lobster, Rye herring, Arundel mullet, Amberley trout and Bourne wheat.

## SUSSEX CITADEL
The hilltop centre of Rye is called the Citadel: climb St Mary's church tower for a view of the medieval Ypres Tower (the castle) and Landgate Arch.

**EAST SUSSEX**

## FULL STEAM AHEAD
Steam railways include the Bluebell Railway from Sheffield Park to East Grinstead; the Kent and East Sussex Railway from Tenterden to Bodiam; and the Lavender Line near Uckfield.

## A NIGHT AT THE OPERA
Glyndebourne opera house has held a festival every year since 1934, showing six operas from May to August.

## PAST BATTLES
The Battle of Hastings was fought in 1066 in Battle, seven miles from Hastings, between William the Conqueror and King Harold – Battle Abbey stands on the spot.

## GET BUSY AT THE BEACH
Camber Sands has a wide bay and dunes, while Brighton beach has courts for beach volleyball and other sandy sports.

## BIGGEST BONFIRES
The Lewes Bonfire Night celebrations on 5 November are the biggest in the UK, featuring flaming crosses, burning barrel races, bonfires and fireworks.

**HASTINGS**

**ENGLISH CHANNEL**

## ANIMAL MAGIC
Drusillas Park near Alfriston has a Hello Kitty-themed secret garden, a Safari express train, lots of rides and small animals such as meerkats.

## HISTORIC HASTINGS
Hasting's sights include William the Conqueror's first English castle, an underground Smugglers' Adventure at St Clement's Caves and the Blue Reef aquarium.

**EASTBOURNE**

## PERCY BYSSHE SHELLEY
### 1792-1822
The Romantic poet (and husband of *Frankenstein* author Mary Shelley) was born near Horsham – his poems include *Prometheus Unbound*, and he drowned aged 29.

## DOWNS AND OUT
The South Downs national park includes the Seven Sisters, and Beachy Head, has the highest chalk sea cliff in England at 162 metres.

## ELIZABETH BLACKWELL
### 1821-1910
The British-born doctor was the first woman to graduate from medical school in the United States, and the first woman on the UK Medical Register; she died in Hastings.

## ANITA RODDICK
### 1942-2007
The entrepreneur was born in Littlehampton and founded the Body Shop, one of the first beauty companies to ban animal testing and promote fair trade.

# HAMPSHIRE & THE ISLE OF WIGHT

## Set Sail for the Solent!

Hampshire's long maritime history dates back to the Middle Ages. At the SeaCity Museum in Southampton, learn about famous ships to have set sail here, including the Mayflower and the Titanic. The Historic Dockyard in Portsmouth exhibits historic ships the 16th-century Mary Rose and Lord Nelson's flagship HMS Victory. Many of the other warships that fought at the Battle of Trafalgar were built in Bucker's Hard, an 18th-century village in the New Forest that is now an open-air museum. After boning up on boats, embark on your own voyage across the Solent by hovercraft, ferry or catamaran to the Isle of Wight, England's biggest island. Cowes is the island's yachting capital – its annual regatta began in 1826 and now attracts 1,000 boats!

### NEIL GAIMAN
**B.1960**
The author was born in Portchester – *The Graveyard Book* is one of his award-winning children's novels.

### ISAMBARD KINGDOM BRUNEL
**1806-1859**
The engineer was born in Portsmouth and designed groundbreaking bridges, tunnels, railways and ships.

### ALFRED THE GREAT
**849-899**
The King of Wessex fought off the Vikings and ruled most of England by the time of his death – he died in Winchester and there is a huge bronze statue of him there.

### LAURA MARLING
**B.1990**
The folk singer-songwriter is from Eversley – she won a Brit Award in 2011 for her album *I Speak Because I Can*.

### JANE AUSTEN
**1775-1817**
The author was born in Steventon and died in Winchester – she wrote six major novels, including *Pride and Prejudice*. Her former home in Chawton is now a museum.

### FUN & GAMES
The New Forest Water Park in Fordingbridge has wakeboarding and an inflatable aqua park, while Paultons Park near Romsey is a family theme park.

### ROYAL FOREST
The New Forest was proclaimed a royal forest in 1079 by William the Conqueror. It is now a national park where you can go walking, cycling and horse riding.

**DORSET**

### QUEEN VICTORIA
**1819-1901**
The Queen spent holidays at Osborne House on the Isle of Wight, which was designed by her husband Prince Albert. She also died there – the house is now open to the public.

### JIM CALLAGHAN
**1912-2005**
Born in Portsmouth, he is the only person to have held the four Great Offices of State: Prime Minister (1976-79), Chancellor, Home Secretary and Foreign Secretary.

### ROCK STAR
The Needles is an Isle of Wight landmark: three pointed chalk sea stacks extend out into the sea near Alum Bay. There is a lighthouse at the end.

## ANIMAL MAGIC
Animal attractions include the Hawk Conservancy Trust in Andover; Liberty's Owl, Raptor and Reptile Centre in Ringwood; and the Isle of Wight Zoo in Sandown.

## SEEN ON SCREEN
TV period drama *Downton Abbey* was filmed at Highclere Castle; it is open to the public for part of the year.

## UP, UP AND AWAY
Farnborough has an International Airshow every other July, and a museum of Air Sciences; there is also a Museum of Army Flying in Middle Wallop.

**HAMPSHIRE**

BASINGSTOKE

## WATERCRESS CAPITAL
Alresford has a watercress festival every May, while its heritage Watercress Line railway runs to Alton.

## MILITARY MATTERS
Aldershot is the home of the British Army: the first training camp was set up there in 1854, and it now has a military museum; there are six regimental museums in Winchester.

## SHIPSHAPE
See the *Mary Rose* at the Portsmouth Historic Dockyard; learn about the *Titanic* at the SeaCity Museum, Southampton; or visit Buckler's Hard on the Beaulieu River, where Nelson's fleet was built.

## COUNTY TOWN
Winchester was once the capital of England and is now the county town of Hampshire; it has one of the longest cathedrals in Europe and a medieval Great Hall.

## CURIOUS COLLECTIONS
Gilbert White was a pioneering naturalist and his family home in Selborne is now a museum – part of it is devoted to the Antarctic explorer Lawrence Oates.

## PONY TALES
About 3,000 ponies roam free around the New Forest – they are owned by local people, who round them up in autumn.

## CASTLE COUNT
Castles include the ruins of Medieval Wolvesey; the shore fort of Portchester; and Carisbrooke on the Isle of Wight, where King Charles I was imprisoned before his execution in 1649.

## LOCAL LANDMARK
Portsmouth's Spinnaker Tower is 170m high and looks like sails blowing in the wind.

## GREAT GRAPES
Parts of Hampshire have a similar soil and climate to the Champagne region of France, and produce similar sparkling wines.

## DEER LIFE
There are five species of deer in the New Forest – red, fallow, sika, roe and muntjac – spot them at the Bolderwood Deer Sanctuary.

EASTLEIGH

## CRADLE OF CRICKET
Hambledon Club, formed c.1750, is one of the oldest known cricket clubs.

SOUTHAMPTON

**WEST SUSSEX**

## WHEELY GOOD
The National Motor Museum at Beaulieu has a collection of more than 280 vintage vehicles.

## LIVING HISTORY
Little Woodham is a "living history" museum that recreates life in a 17th-century village.

## FLYING HIGH
Kite fliers from all over the world travel to the Portsmouth International Kite Festival in August.

PORTSMOUTH

GOSPORT

## PIG OUT
The New Forest still carries out the ancient practice of 'pannage' – up to 600 pigs are released each autumn to eat all the acorns, which are poisonous to other animals.

## YACHT SPOT
Cowes Week in August is one of the biggest and longest-running regattas in the world.

## WATER SPORTS
It is claimed that windsurfing was invented on Hayling Island by Peter Chilvers in 1958.

THE SOLENT

**ISLE OF WIGHT**

## FESTIVAL FEVER
The 1970 Isle of Wight music festival, starring Jimi Hendrix, was even bigger than Woodstock – it was revived in 2002 and is held every June.

## DINOSAUR ISLAND
The 17km coastline between Compton and Sandown is one of the best places in Europe to find dinosaur fossils and footprints, and there is a Dinosaur Isle museum in Sandown.

## ADVENTURE TIME
Blackgang Chine near Ventnor is one of the UK's oldest theme parks – it opened in 1843 and has a whale skeleton that washed up near the Needles in 1842.

## VAMPIRE-PROOF
Garlic has been grown here for more than 50 years – try garlic fudge at the festival every August!

## TOP TRAINS
The Island Line from Shanklin to Ryde uses London Underground trains from the 1930s.

**ENGLISH CHANNEL**

# BRISTOL, SOMERSET & WILTSHIRE

## Go back in time to Bronze-age Britain!

Stonehenge in Wiltshire is a famous ancient monument and, along with the stone circles at Avebury, a world heritage site. The county town is historic Salisbury, and one of Wiltshire's top attractions is Longleat safari park. Bath in Somerset is also a world heritage site, while the county's other city, Wells, is one of the smallest in the UK. Somerset has a national park, Exmoor, and seaside resorts such as Weston-super-Mare. Glastonbury festival is the biggest event, and Cheddar Gorge is is a fantastic day out. Bristol is unusual in being a city AND a county. One of its landmarks is the Clifton Suspension Bridge, the site of the first modern bungee jump, and the city hosts Europe's biggest hot-air balloon festival.

### BUCKETS & SPADES
Weston-super-Mare is Somerset's biggest seaside resort, with a long sandy beach and an annual sand sculpture festival from April to September.

### A LOT OF HOT AIR
The Bristol International Balloon Fiesta is Europe's biggest hot-air balloon event, with hundreds of balloons floating over the city every August.

**WESTON-SUPER-MARE**

### SAY CHEESE!
Somerset is known for its cider and cheddar cheese, which was first made in the village of Cheddar.

**BRISTOL CHANNEL**

### TURNING TIDES
The Bristol Channel has a tidal range of 13 metres – second only to the Bay of Fundy, Canada – so its a great place to see wading birds and go rockpooling.

### FLOWER POWER
The island of Steep Holm is a nature reserve and bird sanctuary. It's also the only place in the UK where wild peonies grow. Take a boat trip there from Weston-super-Mare.

**SEVERN ESTUARY**

### EIGHT TO ONE
The stretch of sand between Brean Down and Burnham-on-Sea is one of the longest in Europe, and includes eight different beaches.

### GOING UNDERGROUND
Cheddar Gorge is Britain's biggest gorge with 137-metre cliffs, stalactite caverns and caving tours. Wookey Hole also has spectacular caves.

### NATIONAL PARK
Exmoor national park is made up of hilly moorland with 54 kilometres of cliffs and beaches – you can ride a rare-breed native pony at the Exmoor Pony Centre.

### BEST BASE
The seaside resort of Minehead is the start of the South West Coast Path and the northern gateway to Exmoor.

**SOMERSET**

### CARNIVAL SEASON
Illuminated carnivals take place across Somerset each autumn – the best is at Bridgwater, with 40 carts, 22,000 lights and 150 "squibbers" letting off fireworks.

### LOOKOUT POINTS
Somerset has six "360" hills that you can climb for great views: Glastonbury Tor, Brean Down, Brent Knoll, Burrow Mump, Crook Peak and Lollover Hill.

**TAUNTON**

### WIND IN THE WILLOWS
Willow has been grown on the Somerset Levels for centuries: you can visit the Willow and Wetlands centre, Musgrove Willows craft centre and Willow Man sculpture.

### JACQUELINE WILSON
**B.1945**
The writer was born in Bath and her children's novels include the *Tracy Beaker* books, which were made into TV series on CBBC.

### COUNTY TOWN
Taunton has been Somerset's county town since 1366 - its 12th-century castle now houses the county museum.

### HIGHS AND LOWS
Somerset has lots of hilly areas such as the Blackdown, Mendip and Quantock Hills; and a low, flat area called the Somerset Levels.

### FLYING SAILORS
The Fleet Air Arm museum is devoted to the Royal Navy's flying division – it has Europe's largest collection of naval aircraft on display.

**DEVON**

**DORSET**

## GLOUCESTERSHIRE

## OXFORDSHIRE

## BERKSHIRE

**CITY AND COUNTY**
Bristol is a city AND a county: it was first made a county in 1373, and today includes the city centre and suburbs such as Clifton.

**BUILDING BRIDGES**
The Clifton Suspension Bridge over the Avon Gorge is based on a design by Isambard Kingdom Brunel – in 1979, the first modern bungee jump was made here.

**CAPITAL IDEA**
Malmesbury claims to be the first capital of England, under King Athelstan in 925: he is buried in the abbey, as is Hannah Trynnoy, who was killed by a tiger in 1703.

**TWIN TOWNS**
In 2009, Swindon beat 24 other British towns to be twinned with Walt Disney World in Florida.

SWINDON

### ATHELSTAN
### C.894-939
King Athelstan reigned from 925 to 939, first as king of the Anglo-Saxons and then as king of the English. He was Alfred the Great's great grandson.

**PANCAKE RACE**
On Shrove Tuesday, there is a Pancake Race across Bradford on Avon's Norman bridge.

**MOON RAKING**
People from Wiltshire are nicknamed the Moonrakers after a trick that was played on customs officials at Crammer pond in Devizes in the 18th century.

BRISTOL

WILTSHIRE

**BACK IN TIME**
The Herschel Museum of Astronomy and the Jane Austen Centre are both in Bath, while Swindon has the Museum of Computing.

**SCHOOL STORIES**
The mysterious Marlborough Mound in Marlborough College is said to be the burial place of the wizard Merlin. Catherine, Duchess of Cambridge is an Old Marlburian.

BATH

**SMALL CITY**
Medieval Wells is England's smallest city (after the City of London) and has an impressive cathedral and moated Bishop's Palace.

**BUILT TO LAST**
Bath is a world heritage site thanks to its architecture, including the Roman baths and Georgian Royal Crescent – Jane Austen lived there in the early 19th century.

**SPINNING JENNY**
Trowbridge, the county town of Wiltshire, was once famous for its woollen cloth – the town's textile museum displays a rare spinning jenny from the 1790s.

**STONE CIRCLES**
Stonehenge, a ring of standing stones, is one of the most famous prehistoric monuments in the world, while Avebury is the biggest stone circle in Europe.

**CLIMBING THE RAMPARTS**
Somerset castles include Dunster and Nunney, while Wiltshire boasts Old Sarum and Old Wardour. Farleigh Hungerford castle is on the border between the two counties.

**CATHEDRAL CITY**
Salisbury Cathedral has the tallest spire in the UK (123 metres), the oldest working mechanical clock (from 1386) and one of four surviving copies of the Magna Carta.

**FESTIVAL FEVER**
The Glastonbury Festival is one of the world's biggest and best-known pop festivals, taking place every June at Pilton, near Glastonbury.

**ANIMAL MAGIC**
Longleat was the first drive-through safari park outside Africa when it opened in 1966 – today it has more than 500 animals in 36.42 km² of Wiltshire countryside.

HAMPSHIRE

### JACOB ANDERSON
### B.1990
The actor was born in Bristol and plays Grey Worm in *Game of Thrones* – he is also a singer under the stage name Raleigh Ritchie.

### BANKSY
### C.1974
The anonymous graffiti artist is thought to have been born in Bristol. There is a walking trail of his artworks around the city.

### MARGARET BONDFIELD
### 1873-1953
The politician was born in Chard and became the first female cabinet member when she was appointed minister of labour in 1929.

### BLACKBEARD
### C.1680-1718
Edward Teach was born in Bristol and became the fearsome pirate, Blackbeard – there is a character based on him in *Pirates of the Caribbean: On Stranger Tides*.

### CHRISTOPHER WREN
### 1632-1723
The architect was born in East Knoyle, Wiltshire, and his most celebrated building is St Paul's Cathedral in London.

# DORSET

## Take a jaunt along the Jurassic Coast!

Three-quarters of Dorset's incredible Jurassic Coast is a world heritage site, and it is the best place in the UK to find fossils. Dinosaur skeletons have been discovered here, and there is a Dinosaur Museum in Dorchester, the county town. There are lots of sandy beaches and amazing rock formations, and seaside fun at towns such as Swanage, Poole, Bournemouth and Weymouth, which has a sand sculpture park. The most famous person from Dorset is the writer Thomas Hardy, whose house you can visit. See the red squirrels on Brownsea Island, take a donkey for a walk in Beaminster or visit the baby orang-utans at Monkey World. There is even a music festival especially for children, Camp Bestival at Lulworth Castle.

**TASTE OF DORSET**
Local delicacies include blue vinny cheese, Dorset apple cake and Blandford pudding, made with gooseberries.

**SOMERSET**

**FUNNY NAMES**
Dorset is full of giggle-inducing place names: Happy Bottom, Scratchy Bottom, River Piddle, Piddlehinton...

River Piddle

**DORSET**

**BADGER WATCH**
At hides in Buckland Newton, you can spend the night watching elusive badgers emerge from their setts and forage for food.

**WALK WITH THE ANIMALS**
Take a donkey for a walk in Beaminster or trek with a llama in Mosterton.

**TAKE THE BISCUIT**
A Dorset Knob biscuit throwing competition takes place in Cattistock every May.

**GIANT MYSTERY**
The Cerne Abbas Giant is a 55-metre naked man wielding a club, carved into the chalk hillside – nobody knows when or why.

**ON THE ROPES**
Bridport used to make ropes and nets, including ones for the gallows; the main street is very wide because hemp and flax cords were stretched between the buildings.

**T. REX AND PALS**
There's a wealth of dino museums, such as the Dinosaur Museum in Dorchester, the Etches Collection in Kimmeridge and Swanage Museum.

**ON THE DEFENSIVE**
Maiden Castle is one of the biggest Iron Age hillforts in Europe – it's the size of 50 football pitches.

**DORCHESTER**

**MARY ANNING**
**1799-1847**
The fossil collector and palaeontologist made amazing dinosaur discoveries in Lyme Regis, such as an the first full ichthyosaur skeleton.

**FOSSIL FINDS**
The Jurassic Coast World Heritage Site is full of fossils from the age of the dinosaurs – the best place to hunt for them is on Charmouth beach.

**SWANNING ABOUT**
Abbotsbury Swannery has been there for 600 years; take a walk among the swans and cygnets.

**PLAGUE PORT**
The Black Death entered Britain at Melcombe Regis in 1348.

**DEVON**

**THOMAS HARDY**
**1840-1928**
The great novelist and poet was born in Stinsford and died in Dorchester. Many of his books are set in Dorset, which he called Wessex – you can visit his cottage and his house.

**ENID BLYTON**
**1897-1968**
The children's author went on holiday to Purbeck three times a year for 20 years and it inspired many of her books, including the *Famous Five* series.

**ON CHESIL BEACH**
Chesil Beach is an enormous, 28-kilometre bar of pebbles of different sizes; it joins Portland to the mainland.

**SEASIDE FUN**
Enjoy Weymouth's five-kilometre beach, the Sea Life adventure park and giant sand sculptures at Sandworld.

**WEYMOUTH**

**THE ENGLISH CHANNEL**

**ISLE OF PORTLAND**
This 'tied island' is home to many of Britain's 57 butterfly species, the rare scaly cricket and the even rarer Portland sea lavender – but don't mention rabbits: they are bad luck!

**STONE AGE**
Portland Stone was used to build St Paul's Cathedral and Purbeck Marble was used in Westminster Abbey; some old quarries are now sculpture parks and nature reserves.

## HOVIS HILL

Gold Hill, a steep, cobbled street in Shaftesbury, was used for the 'Boy on a Bike' advert for Hovis bread in 1973, voted the nation's favourite advert.

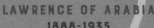
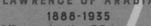

## FILLY LOO

This midsummer celebration takes place in Ashmore, Dorset's highest village, with live music, country dancing and a torchlit procession.

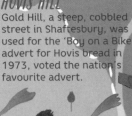

## HAUNTED HOUSE

Thought to be the most haunted house in Dorset, Athelhampton House has seven ghosts – including a spectral pet ape.

## STEAM POWER

At the Great Dorset Steam Fair in Tarrant Hinton each August, there is an old-fashioned, steam-powered funfair.

## FUN AND GAMES

There are lots of fun places to visit in Hurn, including the Adventure Wonderland theme park and skiing and snowboarding centre Snowtrax.

## ALAN CARR
### B.1976

The Chatty Man comedian was born in Weymouth – his footballer dad Graham played for Weymouth FC.

## LAWRENCE OF ARABIA
### 1888-1935

Officer and author T.E. Lawrence lived at Cloud's Hill cottage, near Wareham, which is now a museum.

## CHAINED LIBRARY

Wimborne Minster has one of the first public libraries in the country, built in 1686 – the books were chained up so they could be read but not stolen.

## MONKEY WORLD

This sanctuary near Wool has 250 rescued and endangered primates, including gibbons, chimpanzees, lemurs, all kinds of monkeys and even an orang-utan creche.

## FOOTBALL FACT

AFC Bournemouth, a.k.a. The Cherries, are Dorset's only Football League team.

## MARY SHELLEY
### 1797-1851

The author of Frankenstein is buried in St Peter's church, Bournemouth, beside her parents (Mary Wollstonecraft and William Godwin), and her husband Percy Shelley's heart.

## TOLPUDDLE MARTYRS

Six farm labourers formed a trade union in 1831, and were arrested and shipped to Australia in chains. Today they are heroes, with a museum and a festival every July.

## TOP TANKS

Bovington's Tank Museum tells the story of 100 years of armoured warfare, with more than 200 vehicles, including Little Willie, the world's first tank.

## HUGE HARBOUR

Poole is thought to have the biggest natural harbour in the Europe and the second biggest in the world, after Sydney, Australia.

**BOURNEMOUTH**

## SUPERSIZE CHURCH

Christchurch Priory is said to be the longest church in England, bigger than 21 cathedrals.

## BEAR NECESSITIES

Visit the Wareham Bears, 200 dressed-up teddies, at The Blue Pool; there is also a Teddy Bear Museum in Dorchester.

**POOLE**

## BROWNSEA ISLAND

Robert Baden-Powell held the first ever Scout camp here in 1907.

## BEACH HUTS

Bournemouth has 11km of sandy beach – no wonder beach huts were invented here in 1908.

**CHRISTCHURCH**

## BEST FESTIVAL

Camp Bestival at Lulworth Castle every July is a music festival where kids are king.

## KING OF THE CASTLES

The 1,000-year-old ruins of Corfe Castle have murder holes, where boiling water was poured on to invaders.

## REMARKABLE REPTILES

The heathland behind the Studland Bay is home to all six species of British reptile: adders, grass snakes, smooth snakes, sand lizards, common lizards and slow worms.

## CURIOUS COAST

The coastline has been carved by the sea into spectacular shapes, such as circular Lulworth Cove, arched Durdle Door and Old Harry Rocks – see it all from the Jurassic Skyline viewing capsule, Weymouth.

## SNORKEL TRAIL

There is a snorkel trail in Kimmeridge Bay, leading swimmers from sandy seabed to rocky reef and Japanese seaweed garden.

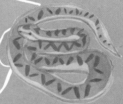

## FULL STEAM AHEAD

The 19-km Swanage Steam Railway puffs passengers into the Victorian seaside resort.

## WILLIAM BARNES
### 1801-1886

The poet and priest wrote more than 800 poems, many in Dorset dialect – learn about him at the Dorset County Museum in Dorchester.

# DEVON

## Relax on the English Riviera!

The Devon seaside towns of Torquay, Paignton and Brixham have lovely sandy beaches, and have been compared to the more famous French Riviera (on a sunny day). The city of Exeter is Devon's county town, and the port of Plymouth holds an annual Fireworks Championship.
If the great outdoors takes your fancy, then you're in luck, as Devon is home to Dartmoor national park, a huge area of moorland that is home to ponies and other wildlife – big wild cats are even rumoured to roam the moors, but nobody has ever proved it. You can see dolphins off the coast of Devon; sometimes they even swim up the River Dart. The island of Lundy is the place to spot puffins, and you can visit rescued donkeys at a sanctuary near Sidmouth. Dartmouth Castle is such a pretty setting.

### CASTAWAY
The island of Lundy is a great place to spot puffins, seals and other wildlife. You can camp there or stay in a lighthouse, a signal station or a castle.

### IT'S TRUE!
Verity, a 20-metre steel and bronze statue of a pregnant woman holding a sword, by Damien Hirst, overlooks the harbour at Ilfracombe.

CORBOROUGH    WESTWARD HO!

### WHERE?!
Westward Ho!, named after a novel by Charles Kingsley, is the only place name in the British Isles to have an exclamation mark – Saint-Louis-du-Ha! Ha! in Canada is the only place to have two.

### PAST MASTER
Barnstaple is thought to be the oldest borough in England, dating back to the 900s – the heritage centre and the museum celebrate its long history.

### WITCH HUNT
Temperance Lloyd, Mary Trembles and Susannah Edwards from Bideford were three of the last women to be hanged as witches in England (1682).

Tarka Trail
Public Footpath

### THE TARKA TRAIL
Cycle or walk along the River Taw and River Torridge, following the route of *Tarka the Otter* in Henry Williamson's famous 1927 book.

**FRANCIS DRAKE**
**1540-1596**
Born in Tavistock, Drake was the first English sea captain to circumnavigate the globe. A hero at home, he was thought of as a pirate by the Spanish.

**SAMUEL TAYLOR COLERIDGE**
**1772-1834**
The poet was born in Ottery St Mary and wrote poems including *The Rime of the Ancient Mariner* and *Kubla Khan*.

### LOCAL FOOD
A Devon cream tea is a scone with clotted cream topped with strawberry jam (in that order!).

### GO OUTDOORS
Go kayaking on the River Dart, where dolphins sometimes swim; mountain-biking at Gawton Gravity Hub; or Tree Surfing at the Tamar Trails Centre.

### MUSEUM TIME
Unusual museums include the Museum of British Surfing in Braunton, Dingles Fairground Heritage Centre in Lifton and the House of Marbles in Bovey Tracey.

**AGATHA CHRISTIE**
**1890-1976**
The bestselling novelist of all time was born in Torquay and wrote the Hercule Poirot and Miss Marple detective stories.

**BERYL COOK**
**1926-2008**
The artist lived in Plymouth from 1968 until her death. Her first exhibition was at the Plymouth Arts Centre in 1975.

CORNWALL

### HOUSES OF PRAYER
Two of Britain's oldest synagogues are in Plymouth and Exeter, built in 1762 and 1763, respectively.

### GRAND DESIGNS
Plymouth cathedral opened in 1858 and was designed by architect Joseph Hansom, who also invented the Hansom cab, a horse-drawn taxi.

PLYMOUTH

### BIG BANGERS
The British Firework Championships are held in Plymouth every August – professional firework companies compete to put on the best show.

## CLIFFHANGER

Great Hangman is the highest sea cliff in England at 318 metres and the highest point on the 1,000km South West Coast Path.

## SHAGGY DOG STORY

Vicar of Swimbridge, Jack Russell (1795–1883), first bred the dogs named after him. The village pub is called the Jack Russell Inn in his honour.

## FUN & GAMES

Theme parks include Crealy Great Adventure Park near Exeter; Woodlands Family Theme Park near Dartmouth; and Diggerland in Cullompton.

## WHIMPLE WASSAIL

On 17 January, villagers in Whimple go wassailing: they visit the cider orchards to wake up the trees and scare away evil spirits, for a good harvest.

MIRANDA HART
**B.1972**
The actor and comedian was born in Torquay and is best known for her sitcom *Miranda*.

SOMERSET

## SECRET PASSAGES

Take a guided tour of the network of underground passages beneath Exeter, built in medieval times to bring drinking water into the city.

## HISTORIC HALL

Exeter Guildhall is thought to be the oldest town hall in England (800 years) still in use today.

## TAR BARRELS

On 5 November, people carry flaming tar barrels through the streets of Ottery St Mary in a risky tradition dating back to the 17th century.

DEVON

## CASTLE COUNT

Castles include Dartmouth, a 14th-century fort that guards the entrance to the harbour, plus Powderham, Compton, Totnes and the ruins of Okehampton.

## MIGHTY MOOR

Dartmoor is famous for its exposed granite hilltops called tors. The film *War Horse* was shot there, too

DORSET

## HEXADECAGON HOUSE

Visit 'A la Ronde' near Lympstone and count the house's 16 sides. Built in 1796 for cousins Jane and Mary Parminter, the public gallery houses nearly 25,000 shells.

EXETER

## ZOOTOPIA

Animal attractions include the Butterflies and Otter Sanctuary in Buckfastleigh, the Donkey Sanctuary near Sidmouth and Paignton Zoo.

WALTER RALEIGH
**C.1552–1618**
The adventurer and politician was born in Hayes Barton and is credited with bringing potatoes and tobacco back to Britain from the Americas.

EXMOUTH

## QUEEN'S DAY

Berry Pomeroy still celebrates Queene's Day on 17 November, marking the accession of Elizabeth I to the throne in 1558.

TORBAY

## ENGLISH RIVIERA

Torbay – the seaside towns of Torquay, Paignton and Brixham – is known as the English Riviera; the Gleneagles Hotel in Torquay inspired John Cleese to write the series *Fawlty Towers*.

ENGLISH CHANNEL

## FULL STEAM AHEAD

The Dartmouth Steam Railway runs between Paignton and Kingswear, where you can take a ferry across the river to Dartmouth.

TORQUAY

## SHIPSHAPE

The fishing village of Brixham has a replica of Francis Drake's ship the *Golden Hind* moored in its harbour, and it holds an annual pirate festival.

PAIGNTON

## TOTNES POUND

Arty Totnes was the first 'transition town' (trying to reduce their carbon footprint); it has had its own currency, the Totnes Pound, since 2007.

## ROYAL CONNECTION

Lots of royal cadets have trained at the Britannia Royal Naval College in Dartmouth, including Princes Phillip, Charles and William.

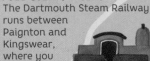

## SEA TRACTOR

South Sands beach in swanky Salcombe is reached by ferry, then sea tractor, an amphibious vehicle that travels on water and sand.

## BUCKETS AND SPADES

Devon has lots of lovely beaches – Saunton Sands is a big sandy beach backing on to dunes, and Blackpool Sands is sheltered and great for swimming.

JOSHUA REYNOLDS
**1723–1792**
Born in Plympton, he became the leading portrait painter of the 18th century and the first president of the Royal Academy of Arts.

# CORNWALL

**SHIVER ME TIMBERS**
Pirates were a real problem around the Cornish coast 300 years ago, but these days, the Pirate's Quest attraction in Newquay is a lot of swashbuckling fun.

**RICHARD TREVITHICK**
**1771-1833**
The inventor and engineer was born in Tregajorran; he built the first steam-powered vehicle, the *Puffing Devil*.

**WILLIAM GOLDING**
**1911-1993**
The author was born in Newquay and died in Perranarworthal; he is best known for his novel *Lord of the Flies*.

**MORWENNA BANKS**
**B.1961**
The actor was born in Redruth and is the voice of Mummy Pig, Madame Gazelle and Dr Hamster in *Peppa Pig*.

**DOLLY PENTREATH**
**C.1692-1777**
The fishseller from Paul, near Mousehole, is believed to have been the last fluent speaker of the original Cornish language.

**BARBARA HEPWORTH**
**1903-1975**
The artist and sculptor lived in St Ives from 1949 until her death; her work is on display at the Barbara Hepworth Museum there.

**DAPHNE DU MAURIER**
**1907-1989**
The novelist spent much of her life in Cornwall and many of her books are set there, including *Rebecca* and *Jamaica Inn*.

**HAROLD WILSON**
**1916-1995**
The Labour prime minister spent his summer holidays in the Isles of Scilly and is buried on St Mary's.

CELTIC SEA

**ART ATTACK**
Tate St Ives exhibits work by modern British artists, and Penlee House in Penzance has a collection by the Newlyn School of painters.

**SOUTHERN POINT**
Land's End is the most south-westerly point of mainland Britain; attractions there include the Shaun the Sheep Experience.

CAMBORNE

**FLOWER POWER**
Flowers grow earlier on the Scilly Isles than in the rest of Britain, thanks to the milder climate – flower farms grow scented narcissi (fancy daffodils) for export.

**INSPIRING ISLANDS**
Several books by Michael Morpurgo, the former Children's Laureate, are set on Scilly, including *Why the Whales Came*.

LANDS END 2018
NEW YORK 3147    JOHN O'GROATS 874
ISLES OF SCILLY 28

**TIN TRADE**
In the 1900s, half the world's tin came from Cornwall – you can take an underground tour and the visit mining museums.

**SCILLY SHREW**
The isles are the only place in the UK where the lesser white-toothed shrew lives.

**OPEN-AIR THEATRE**
The Minack Theatre, an outdoor theatre carved into the cliff overlooking Porthcurno Bay, was built in 1930 in the style of an ancient Greek amphitheatre.

**TWINKLE, TWINKLE**
Mousehole is famous for its amazing Christmas lights, using 7,000 bulbs each year.

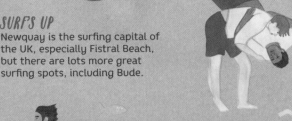

## SURF'S UP
Newquay is the surfing capital of the UK, especially Fistral Beach, but there are lots more great surfing spots, including Bude.

## MARVELLOUS MUSEUMS
Bodmin Jail is now an attraction showing what life was like for prisoners; Boscastle has a Museum of Witchcraft and Magic.

## CORNISH CONCERNS
Cornwall is one of six Celtic nations and has its own language (dydh da means hello), flag, patron saint and unofficial anthem – some people would even like it to be an independent country.

DEVON

## WRESTLE MANIA
Cornish wrestling is the county's oldest sport and can be seen at the Royal Cornwall Show in Wadebridge each June; referees are known as sticklers.

## KING ARTHUR
The legend of King Arthur lives on at his birthplace, Tintagel Castle; and Dozmary Pool, where he is said to have pulled out Excalibur.

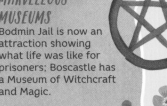

## BEAST OF BODMIN
A huge wild cat is rumoured to roam Bodmin Moor, 200 square kilometres of rugged moorland that contains Cornwall's highest peak, Brown Willy.

## SMUGGLED GOODS
Silk, tea, tobacco and brandy were smuggled into Cornwall in the 18th century to avoid paying high taxes – you can see some of them at the Smugglers Museum, Jamaica Inn.

## COOL COASTLINE
Cornwall has up to 400 beaches, which are wilder on the north coast and more sheltered in the south: the three-kilometre beach at Perranporth is one of the best for family fun.

## SEEN ON SCREEN
*Doc Martin* is filmed in Port Isaac and *Poldark* locations include Charlestown, Kynance Cove and Porthcurno.

## ON YOUR BIKE
You can cycle along the Camel trail, a disused railway line through beautiful countryside, from Padstow to Wenford Bridge.

## GARDENERS WORLD
You can visit a rainforest at the Eden Project, a global garden in a crater the size of 30 football pitches, and explore a jungle at the Lost Gardens of Heligan.

NEWQUAY

CORNWALL

## SOLE CITY
Truro is the only city in Cornwall and the most southerly city in mainland Britain.

## CHINA CLAY
The Cornish Alps are man-made peaks from china clay mining – Charlestown is the centre of the industry and Wheal Martyn is a museum devoted to clay mining.

## LOCAL FOOD
The Cornish pasty is the county dish and was eaten by miners; pilchard heads poke through the pastry in a stargazy pie; and a Cornish cream tea is a scone with jam and cream (in that order!).

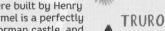

## CASTLE COUNT
Pendennis and St Mawes castles were built by Henry VII, Restormel is a perfectly circular Norman castle, and St Michael's Mount can only be reached on foot at low tide.

ST AUSTELL

TRURO

## ANIMAL RESCUE
The Wild Futures Monkey Sanctuary is near Looe; the Cornish Seal Sanctuary is in Gweek and the Screech Owl Sanctuary is near Saint Columb Major.

THE ENGLISH CHANNEL

## SHIP SHAPE
Falmouth's National Maritime Museum Cornwall tells the story of seafaring, and the Charlestown Shipwreck Centre shows what happens when it goes wrong.

FALMOUTH

## FOLK FESTIVALS
Enjoy ancient Cornish customs, including the Furry Dance in Helston, the 'Obby 'Oss festival in Padstow and the Montol festival in Penzance.

## CORNISH REBELS
The 1497 Cornish Rebellion against war taxes began in St Keverne on the Lizard Peninsula; today Cornwall's rugby league team are the Cornish Rebels.

## *Pack your bags for pirate paradise!*

Pack your bucket and spade – Cornwall has 400 beaches, as well as Britain's best surfing at Newquay and Bude. Truro is the only city (although more people live in Falmouth), and there are lots of seaside resorts and pretty villages. Inland you'll find wild Bodmin Moor – watch out for the Beast of Bodmin! Land's End is the furthest you can go on mainland Britain, but the flower-filled Isles of Scilly are part of Cornwall, too, despite being located 45 kilometres off the coast. Tin mining was once a major industry in Cornwall, and you can explore the old mines on underground tours. The county's most famous attraction, the Eden Project, is in a huge reclaimed mining pit. Don't leave the county before you've sampled a delicious Cornish pasty and a cream tea.

# SCOTLAND

## Discover this northern star!

Scotland is divided into three areas: the Highlands, Islands and Lowlands – there are nearly 800 islands across Shetland, Orkney, the Inner Hebrides and the Outer Hebrides, and the nation has some of the most stunning scenery in the world. Its mountains, lochs, glens and firths shelter golden eagles, wildcats, red deer and bottlenose dolphins. Its cities don't disappoint either, including the capital, Edinburgh, and the biggest city, Glasgow. If you're keen to find out about its fascinating traditions, you'll find them best showcased at the Highland Games, from tossing the caber to playing the bagpipes (and wearing a kilt). It's possible you'll hear all three of the nation's official languages – English, Scots and Scottish Gaelic – spoken, and its floral emblem the thistle proudly on display. And if you spot a unicorn, don't be surprised – this is the country's national animal! You'll find the true spirit of Scotland on Burns Night, when the national poet is celebrated with a supper of neeps, tatties and, of course, haggis.

STIRLING

FALKIRK

## EAST DUNBARTONSHIRE

## NORTH LANARKSHIRE

CUMBERNAULD

### BUILDING BRIDGES
The Forth Bridge across the Firth of Forth was built between 1883 and 1890 and is now a world heritage site; the Queensferry Museum tells the story of its construction.

### HISTORIC HOUSES
Mary Queen of Scots was born in Linlithgow Palace in 1542; nearby Hopetoun House is one of Scotland's grandest stately homes.

LIVINGST

### KEIR HARDIE
**1856-1915**
The politician worked in the mines from the age of ten, but taught himself to read and write and became the first leader of the Labour party.

### DOWN ON THE FARM
Meet Aberdeen Angus cows, Tamworth pigs, Ayrshire cattle, and Clydesdale horses on the farm at the National Museum of Rural Life.

### GO EXPLORE
The David Livingstone Centre in Blantyre documents Scotland's most famous explorer's adventures in Africa.

### WEST LOTHIAN

### FUN AND GAMES
M&D's, Scotland's theme park in Motherwell, has white-knuckle rides, fairground attractions and glow-in-the-dark bowling.

### FUN RUN
The Red Hose Race in Carnwath dates back to 1508 and is believed to be the oldest footrace in the world – join in in July to win a pair of red socks!

## GLASGOW CITY

HAMILTON

EAST KILBRIDE

### ELSIE INGLIS
**1864-1917**
The doctor was born in India and studied in Edinburgh – she set up the Scottish Women's Hospitals who helped on the frontlines of the First World War.

### FIRE & FIREWORKS
Edinburgh's Hogmanay is one of the world's biggest New Year's Eve parties; the Beltane Fire Festival in April celebrates the start of summer.

### WORLD HERITAGE
The medieval Old Town and Georgian New Town have together been a world heritage site since 1995.

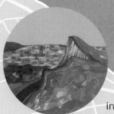

### LOOKOUT POINT
For the best views over the city, climb Arthur's Seat, a 251-metre extinct volcano in Holyrood Park.

### MILLING ABOUT
New Lanark was an 18th-century cotton mill village and is now a world heritage site – meet mill girl Annie, and then visit the Falls of Clyde.

### RAINY DAYS
Visit the Museum of Childhood, Our Dynamic Earth, The Writers' Museum, the Surgeons' Hall Museum, Museum on the Mound, The People's Story or the Museum of Edinburgh.

### DAVID TENNANT
**B.1971**
The actor was born in Bathgate – he played the Tenth Doctor in *Doctor Who* and Barty Crouch in *Harry Potter and the Goblet of Fire*.

### SHAGGY DOG STORY
Pat the statue of Greyfriars Bobby, a loyal Skye Terrier who is said to have spent 14 years guarding the grave of his owner.

### EDINBURGH CITY CENTRE

## SOUTH LANARKSHIRE

### TOP TRAIN
The Leadhills and Wanlockhead Railway runs between Scotland's two highest villages – visit the Leadhills Miners' Library and Wanlockhead's mining museum.

### EAST RENFREWSHIRE

### ROBERT LOUIS STEVENSON
**1850-1894**
The writer was born in Edinburgh, travelled widely and settled in Samoa – his most famous book is the adventure novel *Treasure Island*.

### EAST AYRSHIRE

### DUMFRIES & GALLOWAY

## ROYAL YACHT
Step aboard the Royal Yacht *Britannia*, the Queen's official yacht from 1954-1997, in the historic port of Leith.

EDINBURGH

## TREASURE COVE
Beautiful beaches include Gullane Bents and Yellowcraig – the latter has views of Fidra Island, which inspired Robert Louis Stephenson's Treasure Island.

## NATIONAL COLLECTIONS
Visit Dolly the sheep, the first cloned mammal, at the National Museum of Scotland; you can also go to the National Library, the National Gallery and the National War Museum.

## BIRD WATCHING
The Scottish Seabird Centre has interactive live cameras showing gannets on Bass Rock and puffins on the Isle of May, and runs boat trips to the islands.

## CASTLE COUNT
Tantallon Castle is a 14th-century clifftop fortress; other castles include Craignethan, Dirleton, Borthwick, Crichton and Dalhousie.

NORTH SEA

## BRIDGE TO NOWHERE
At Belhaven Bay, a surfing beach, there is a footbridge over a stream – at high tide the bridge gets submerged and looks like it is stranded in the middle of the sea!

## CAPITAL CITY
Edinburgh is the capital of Scotland – its landmarks include Edinburgh Castle and Holyrood Palace, which bookend the Royal Mile, and the Scottish Parliament Building.

## FESTIVAL FEVER
The festival capital of the world hosts the Edinburgh Festival and Fringe (the world's biggest arts festival), plus a host of others from book festivals to military tattoos.

MIDLOTHIAN

## HIGH FLIERS
At the National Museum of Flight, you can see a Spitfire, a Harrier jump jet and a Tornado F3 – and board Scotland's only Concorde.

EAST LOTHIAN

## UNICORN SPOTTING
Did you know that Scotland's national animal is a unicorn? Keep your eyes peeled for symbols on 9 April – national unicorn day.

## HIT THE SLOPES
The Midlothian Snowsports Centre is Britain's longest dry ski slope, with two main slopes, three nursery slopes and a jump slope, plus tubing runs.

## MEET THE BEASTIES
At Edinburgh Butterfly & Insect World, you can hold a giant millipede, a snake and a tarantula, and see butterflies flying around an indoor rainforest.

## GOING UNDERGROUND
At the National Mining Museum Scotland in Lady Victoria Colliery, Newtongrange, you can tour the pithead and drive the country's biggest steam engine.

## ALEXANDER GRAHAM BELL
**1847-1922**
The scientist was born in Edinburgh and emigrated to Canada and then the US – he invented the telephone in 1876, which led to the mobile phones we use today.

## BHAGVAT SINGH
**1865-1944**
The Maharaja of Gondal graduated from the University of Edinburgh, the only princely ruler to have a degree, and introduced education for girls as well as boys.

## MARIE STOPES
**1880-1958**
The campaigner for women's rights was born in Edinburgh – she became a pioneer in the field of family planning, which was very controversial at the time.

## Have a laugh in the Capital of Comedy
Edinburgh became the capital of Scotland in the 15th century. The city is divided into two main areas: the Old Town with its medieval castle, and the neoclassical New Town; together they are a world heritage site. Today the city is the festival capital of the world! The Edinburgh International Festival and Fringe began in 1947.
Lots of comedians including Harry Hill got their big break at the Fringe, the world's biggest annual arts festival.
The nearby Forth Bridge set another world record when it opened in 1890: the longest single cantilever bridge in the world (521m). It is still the second longest, after Quebec Bridge in Canada, and has become a symbol of Scotland.

SCOTTISH BORDERS

# EDINBURGH AND AROUND

# GLASGOW AND AROUND

## BONNIE BANKS
Loch Lomond is huge, with 22 named islands including Inchconnachan, where wallabies live!

## LOCHSIDE LARKS
Balloch is on the banks of Loch Lomond and its attractions include, an aerial adventure course, a bird of prey centre and the Maid of the Loch paddle steamer.

## ART & SCIENCE
Greenock's McLean Museum has an exhibition about inventor James Watt, born in the town in 1736; its Beacon Arts Centre is a top theatre.

## CASTLE COUNT
Two of the best-preserved castles are Dumbarton, which is built on a volcanic rock, and 15th-century Newark in Port Glasgow.

### WEST DUNBARTONSHIRE

## MODEL SHIPS
Dumbarton was once the capital of the ancient kingdom of Strathclyde; today, its Denny Tank museum has a huge water tank for testing ships.

### ARGYLL AND BUTE

### INVERCLYDE

### GREENOCK

## SHIP SHAPE
Port Glasgow was once a centre of shipbuilding – a replica of the 1812 PS *Comet*, the first commercial steamboat in Europe, stands in the town centre today.

## STATELY STATION
Wemyss Bay's wrought iron-and-glass railway station is one of the finest in Scotland – the station also houses the ferry terminal to Rothesay on the Isle of Bute.

## PAISLEY PATTERN
Paisley is Scotland's biggest town, best known for the patterned shawls its weavers once made – see them at the Paisley Museum.

## CHILDREN'S HOMES
Quarrier's Village was founded in 1876 by William Quarrier where orphaned children could be cared for in cottages instead of orphanages.

## GET OUTDOORS
Clyde Muirshiel is Scotland's biggest regional park: build rafts on Castle Semple Loch, make sandcastle at Lunderston Bay and climb Windy Hill.

## BRAVEHEART'S BIRTHPLACE
Elderslie is thought to be the birthplace of William Wallace (c.1270-1305), who led the Wars of Scottish Independence; he is celebrated every August.

### GORDON BROWN
**1951**
The Labour politician was born in Giffnock – he was Prime Minister of the UK from 2007 to 2010 and Chancellor from 1997-2007.

### DAME CAROL ANN DUFFY
**B.1955**
This Scottish poet and playwright was born in Glasgow, and appointed Poet Laureate in 2009.

### RENFREWSHIRE

### NORTH AYRSHIRE

## BACK IN TIME
Medieval buildings include Glasgow Cathedral (1136), Crookston Castle, Provand's Lordship, and the Trongate and Tolbooth steeple.

### IRISH SEA

### ALEX FERGUSON
**B.1941**
The football manager was born in Govan – he managed Manchester United from 1986-2013, winning 38 trophies, including 13 Premier League titles, five FA Cups and two Champions Leagues titles.

### CHARLES RENNIE MACKINTOSH
**1868-1928**
Scotland's most celebrated architect and designer was born in the Townhead area of Glasgow – he was a pioneer of the Glasgow Style, a variant of art nouveau.

## GOING GREEN
Dams to Darnley is a new country park between Barrhead, Darnley and Newton Mearns, where you can go walking, cycling and horse riding.

## STIRLING

### CLACHAN OF CAMPSIE
Spot the ruined "kirk" (church) and 300-million-year-old lava flows, that turned to rock resembling a set of steps in the Campsies.

### GRUFFALO HUNT
Kilmardinny Loch is a nature reserve – spot the Gruffalo sculptures carved in honour of author Julia Donaldson, who used to live in the town.

### CANAL CAPITAL
Kirkintilloch, on the Forth and Clyde Canal, is known as the canal capital of Scotland and holds a canal festival in August.

**KATHERINE GRAINGER**
**B.1975**
The rower has won one Olympic gold medal and four silvers, and is a six-time world champion.

**PETER CAPALDI**
**B.1958**
The actor played the 12th incarnation of the Doctor in Doctor Who, and was Mr Curry in the Paddington films.

### CLYDEBANK CRANE
Clydebank was another major shipbuilding town: learn about ships such as the QE2 at the Clydebank Museum, then watch bungee-jumpers drop from the 45m Titan Crane!

**CLYDEBANK**

### STARCHITECT
Charles Rennie Mackintosh designs include the Glasgow School of Art, Mackintosh House, The Lighthouse, House for an Art Lover and Scotland Street School.

### EAST DUNBARTONSHIRE

### CITY OF THE DEAD
The Necropolis is a Victorian cemetery modelled on Père Lachaise in Paris – you can go on a guided tour of the 15-hectare site.

### FESTIVAL FEVER
Aye Wright! is Glasgow's annual book festival; other festivals include Celtic Connections, The West End, Merchant City, Jazz Festival and Glasgay.

### NORTH LANARKSHIRE

**RENFREW**

### CULTURE VULTURE
Glasgow is home to the Royal Scottish National Orchestra, the BBC Scottish Ballet, the National Theatre of Scotland, the Scottish Symphony Orchestra and Scottish Opera.

**GLASGOW**

### WOMEN'S LIB
The Glasgow Women's Library is also a unique museum that celebrates women's lives, histories and achievements.

### GLASGOW PATTER
In Glasgow patter, "how" means "why" and your "geggy" is your mouth, with which you might eat a "piece" (a sandwich).

**PAISLEY**

### GLASGOW CITY

### GOING UNDERGROUND
Glasgow Subway, opened in 1896, is the third-oldest underground metro line in the world after London and Budapest – it has just 15 stops.

**GORDON RAMSAY**
**B.1966**
The Michelin-starred celebrity chef was born in Johnstone – he has starred in cooking shows such as *Hell's Kitchen* and *Ramsay's Kitchen Nightmares*.

### SCIENCE LESSON
At the Glasgow Science Centre, you can run on a giant hamster wheel and try other interactive exhibits, watch science shows and visit the planetarium.

### SPORTS REPORT
Hampden Park is Scotland's national football stadium and home to the Scottish Football Museum, which houses the 1873 Scottish Cup.

### SOUTH LANARKSHIRE

### BACK TO NATURE
Highland cattle roam Pollok Country Park, which also contains the Burrell Collection of art and historic Pollok House.

### WAR STORY
Rudolf Hess was the deputy leader of the Nazis – in 1941 he flew solo to Scotland and parachuted into a field in Eaglesham, where he was arrested.

### EAST AYRSHIRE

### EAST RENFREWSHIRE

## Practise your patter in Scotland's biggest city!

Glasgow has been the biggest city in Scotland for a century. A small settlement on the River Clyde grew into Britain's biggest trading seaport in the 18th century, and then became a major shipbuilding centre during the Industrial Revolution. The city is characterised by the grand Victorian buildings built at the height of its wealth, and the architecture of the Glasgow School, especially the designs by Charles Rennie Mackintosh. Listen in as you walk the streets, and see if you can pick up some of the local dialect, Glaswegian, also known as the Glasgow patter! Or, if it's a match day, you could hear football chants, especially if the city's two rival football teams, Celtic F.C. and Rangers F.C., – who are often vying for the Scottish Premiership Table top spot – are playing one another!

# Go trekking through the Trossachs!

Venture north out of Edinburgh or Glasgow, and you'll soon reach central Scotland. This region is dominated by Loch Lomond and the Trossachs National Park, which is often called the Highlands in miniature. You can climb mountains, explore forests and swim in icy lochs. Legend tells of the daring deeds of the outlaw Rob Roy in these parts, and the area inspired Walter Scott's historical novels.

For more Scottish history, head to Stirling, a city that straddles the Highlands and the Lowlands. Its strategic importance means that lots of fighting took place here, including the Battle of Stirling Bridge in 1297, and the mighty castle built here still stands today. The world's oldest football was found in the castle – it is almost 500 years old!

## RIP ROB ROY
The kirkton (village) of Balquhidder at the head of Loch Voil is the final resting place of the outlaw Rob Roy – visitors come from all over the world to see his grave.

## ROB ROY
### 1671-1734
Red-haired Rob Roy MacGregor was an outlaw and hero, said to be the Scottish Robin Hood – you can now walk the 148-km Rob Roy Way.

## LADY OF THE LAKE
Sir Walter Scott wrote his 1810 poem "The Lady of the Lake" after visiting Loch Katrine, and the Sir Walter Scott steamboat has sailed on the loch since 1900.

## FAULT LINE
Callander is a town on the Highland Boundary Fault, which divides the Highlands from the Lowlands.

## ON SAFARI
At Blair Drummond Safari Park, you can drive through the reserves to see rhinos, lions and zebras, and take a boat around Chimp Island.

## NATIONAL PARK
Loch Lomond and the Trossachs National Park has 21 Munros (peaks over 3,000ft/914.4m), 20 Corbetts (2,500-3,000ft/762-914.4m), 22 large lochs and two forest parks.

## POPULAR PEAK
Ben Lomond – the most southerly Munro in Scotland – has namesakes in the US, Australia, New Zealand, Canada, Jamaica, and Trinidad and Tobago!

## BIRD WATCHING
Cycle the Trossachs Bird of Prey Trail from Aberfoyle to see owls, eagles and buzzards, or watch footage of the birds at the Lodge visitor centre.

**STIRLING**

## READ ALL ABOUT IT
Dunblane has Scotland's oldest purpose-built library, Leighton Library, with 4,500 books in 89 languages – the oldest was printed in 1504.

## ENCHANTED FOREST
The Queen Elizabeth Forest Park is 200 sq km of woods, mountains, moor, rivers and lochs – you can go cycling and pony trekking here.

## ISLAND ESCAPE
Sail across the Lake of Menteith to Inchmahome Priory, an island monastery founded in 1238, and picnic under the ancient chestnut trees.

## OLDEST FOOTBALL
The world's oldest football is in the Stirling Smith Art Gallery and Museum: it was made from a pig's bladder in the 1540s and found in Stirling Castle in 1981.

**ARGYLL & BUTE**

## ALAN HANSEN
### B.1955
The footballer was born in Sauchie and played for Partick Thistle, Liverpool and Scotland – he then worked as a pundit on Match of the Day for 22 years.

## BATTLE OF BANNOCKBURN
Scotland's Robert the Bruce defeated England's Edward II at the Battle of Bannockburn in 1314 – the visitor centre uses 3D technology to bring the battle to life.

**WEST DUNBARTONSHIRE**

**EAST DUNBARTONSHIRE**

## WALK THE WALL
The Antonine Wall was the northern frontier of the Roman Empire: see some remains at Watling Lodge, Rough Castle fort or Seabegs Wood.

**NORTH LANARKSHIRE**

# CENTRAL SCOTLAND

### JAMES IV
#### 1473-1513
The king was born in Stirling Castle – he was the most successful of the Stewart kings of Scotland until his defeat and death at the Battle of Flodden.

## LITERARY LINK
Bridge of Allan is a Victorian spa town – authors Robert Louis Stevenson and Charles Dickens used to visit the town in the 19th century.

## MIGHTY MONUMENT
See William Wallace's sword at the National Wallace Monument, and learn about his victory in 1297 over Edward I at the Battle of Stirling Bridge.

### PERTH & KINROSS

## CASTLE COUNT
Castle Campbell was known as Castle Gloom and has a 15th-century tower; 14th-century Doune has a 30m gatehouse; Blackness looks like a great stone ship.

## OVER THE HILLS
Ben Cleuch (721m) is the highest peak in the Ochil Hills, which stretch from the Firth of Tay to Stirling.

### CLACKMANNANSHIRE

## THIEVES POT
Stirling was once the capital of Scotland – visit its 16th-century jail, the Thieves' Pot, in the Thistles shopping centre!

## STIRLING'S CITADEL
Mary, Queen of Scots was crowned at Stirling Castle in 1543 – today you can tour her castle.

STIRLING

ALLOA

## FRUITY FOLLY
The Dunmore Pineapple was built by the Earl of Dunmore as a summer house in 1761 and looks exactly like a pineapple!

### ANDY MURRAY
#### B.1987
The tennis player grew up in Dunblane – he has won Wimbledon twice and the US Open once, and is the only tennis player to have won two Olympic singles titles.

### JOHN GRIERSON
#### 1898-1972
The pioneering film-maker was born in Deanston – he is regarded as the father of the documentary and his films include *Drifters* and *Night Mail*.

### FIFE

## NATIONAL DISH
Haggis is made from sheep's offal, oatmeal, onion and spices, cooked in a sheep's stomach and served with neeps and tatties (swede and potatoes).

### ELIZABETH BLACKADDER
#### B.1931
The painter and printmaker was born in Falkirk – she is the first woman to be elected to both the Royal Scottish Academy and the Royal Academy.

NORTH SEA

## FULL STEAM AHEAD
Take a steam train on the Bo'ness and Kinneil Railway, and visit Scotland's biggest railway museum at Bo'ness station.

BO'NESS

### FALKIRK

FALKIRK

## WHEELY GOOD
Ride on the Falkirk Wheel, the world's only rotating boatlift, which lifts boats between the different levels of the Union and Forth & Clyde canals.

## LOCAL LANDMARK
The present Falkirk Steeple has stood in the centre of the town since 1814, but there has been a steeple on the site for centuries – it appears on the crest of Falkirk FC.

## HISTORIC HOUSE
Callendar House looks like a French chateau – its grounds include a big play park and a section of the Antonine Wall, with an accompanying exhibition.

### WEST LOTHIAN

### MARGARET KIDD
#### 1900-1989
The advocate (lawyer) was born in Bo'ness – she was the first woman to be called to the Faculty of Advocates and the first female King's Counsel in Britain.

# AYRSHIRE AND ARRAN

## ROBERT BURNS
### 1759-1796
The poet was born in Alloway and has been voted the greatest Scot of all time – he wrote "Auld Lang Syne", which is sung at Hogmanay (New Year's Eve).

**SOUTH LANARKSHIRE**

**EAST RENFREWSHIRE**

**RENFREWSHIRE**

**INVERCLYDE**

**NORTH AYRSHIRE**

### OLYMPIC CHAMPIONS
Kays Curling in Mauchline has been making curling stones from Ailsa Crag granite since 1851 – their stones are used in the Winter Olympics!

### HISTORIC HOUSE
Dumfries House is an 18th-century stately home – in the grounds is a rare-breeds farm, a woodland adventure playground and a maze.

### LOOKOUT POINT
Kilwinning Abbey Tower was built in 1816 in the ruins of a 12th-century abbey – you can climb the 143 steps for the best view in North Ayrshire.

### CASTLE COUNT
Castle ruins include 14th-century Dundonald, which holds a Highland Games, plus Dunure, Lochranza and Loch Doon.

**KILMARNOCK**

**KILWINNING**

### VISIT FROM THE KING
Glasgow Prestwick airport is the only place in the UK that Elvis Presley is known to have visited, when his plane refuelled here in 1960.

**PRESTWICK**

**AYR**

**IRVINE**

### MUSEUM TIME
Victorian grain mill Dalgarven Mill now houses the Museum of Ayrshire Country Life and Costume.

### ART ATTACK
13th-century Kelburn Castle had a 21st-century makeover in 2007, when it was covered in graffiti by Brazilian artists!

### TEE OFF IN TROON
Troon has seven golf courses including Royal Troon, which often hosts the Open Championship.

### SPORTS REPORT
The seaside resort of Ayr has a racecourse that dates back to the 16th century – it hosts the Scottish Grand National in April.

### ROYAL PARADE
See who is crowed Marymass Queen at the Marymass Festival in Irvine every August.

### ISLE OF ARRAN
Arran is known as "Scotland in miniature" because it has both highlands and lowlands, mountains, forests, lochs and beaches.

### VIKING INVASION
The seaside resort of Largs was the site of a Viking battle in 1263 – visit the Vikingar! museum and watch a longship burn at the annual Viking Festival.

### COME TO CUMBRAE
Cycle 18km around Great Cumbrae, go jetskiing at the national watersports centre, and visit the aquarium at Millport, the island's only town.

## ANDREW FISHER
### 1862-1928
The politician was born in Crosshouse and emigrated to Australia in 1885 – he became the country's fifth prime minister, serving three separate terms.

### TOP TOWN
Brodick is Arran's main tourist town with a heritage museum and Brodick Castle – from here you can climb Goatfell (874m), the highest peak.

### WILDLIFE WATCH
Look for red squirrels, red deer, eagles, seals and dolphins, plus three endemic species of tree, the Arran whitebeams.

### GET OUTDOORS
Hike up Glenashdale Falls and visit the Giants' Graves, or the six prehistoric stone circles on Machrie Moor.

### BUCKETS & SPADES
Arran's beaches include Whiting Bay, Kildonan, Sannox, and Cleats Shore, Scotland's first

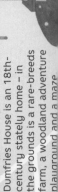
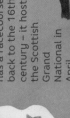
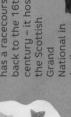
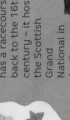
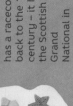
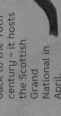
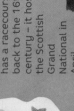

## FULL STEAM AHEAD
At the Scottish Industrial Railway Centre, you can ride a steam train, play with the steam-powered model railway and look at the historic locomotives.

## STAR GAZING
The Scottish Dark Sky Observatory near Dalmellington has two powerful telescopes – book a visit to observe the wonders of the night sky.

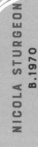

### NICOLA STURGEON
### B.1970
The politician was born in Irvine – she has been leader of the Scottish National Party and First Minister of Scotland since November 2014.

### ALEXANDER FLEMING
### 1881-1955
The scientist was born in Darvel – he discovered penicillin in 1928, which has saved millions of lives, and won the Nobel Prize in Medicine in 1945.

## Sail away to Scotland in miniature!

If you can visit only one place in Scotland, the Isle of Arran is a good choice – it is like a pint-sized version of the whole country. That's because the Highland Boundary Fault runs across the island, dividing it into highland and lowland areas, so you get the best of both worlds! There are mountains, forests, lochs and beaches; bustling towns and villages; prehistoric monuments and medieval castles; and iconic Scottish wildlife such as red deer, eagles and dolphins.

Ayrshire, on the mainland is an agricultural region of south-west Scotland that was the birthplace of the national bard, Robert Burns. You can visit attractions devoted to his life, poetry and song, and find out why he is the most-loved Scot of all time.

## BARD OF AYRSHIRE
Visit the Robert Burns Birthplace Museum in Alloway and the Bachelors' Club that the poet co-founded in Tarbolton, and celebrate Burns Night anywhere in Scotland on 25 January.

## ANCIENT ABBEY
Crossraguel Abbey near Maybole was founded in 1244 – you can wander around the monks' church, cloister, chapter house and dovecote.

## ON THE ROAD
Ayrshire native John McAdam invented "macadamisation", a new, more economic way of building roads with layers of broken stone and asphalt.

### LILLY ASPELL
### B.2007
The actor was born in Kilmarnock and played the young Wonder Woman in the 2017 film – her next role is in the sci-fi movie Extinction.

## DEFYING GRAVITY
The Electric Brae near Dunure is a gravity hill – it creates an optical illusion where it looks as if your car is going uphill, when actually it is rolling downhill.

## PRESIDENT'S PAD
Culzean is a clifftop castle surrounded by beaches and woods – you can stay overnight in an apartment that once belonged to US President Eisenhower.

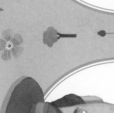

## FUN & GAMES
At the Heads of Ayr Farm Park, you can meet Ralph the camel, Troy the tapir and almost 50 other kinds of animal, plus play on the bumper boats and tackle the assault course.

## BIRD WATCHING
Boat trips run from Girvan to Ailsa Craig, an island formed from a volcanic plug – today it is a bird sanctuary with thousands of gannets and puffins.

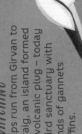

IRISH
SEA

### FLORA DRUMMOND
### 1878-1949
The suffragette grew up in Pirnmill on the Isle of Arran – she campaigned for women to get the vote and was sent to prison nine times.

## ROBERT THE BRUCE
## 1274-1329
The King of Scots is thought to have been born in Turnberry Castle – he fought against the English, made Scotland independent again and is a national hero.

# Go Gaelic or Norse in Britain's far north!

The Western Isles, or Outer Hebrides, is an enchanting archipelago off the coast of west Scotland. The 15 inhabited islands are a stronghold of Scottish Gaelic – today, almost 99% of Scots speak English, except in the Western Isles, where the majority can still talk in the old tongue. Learn a few phrases yourself at a Gaelic festival on Barra!

The Northern Isles comprise Orkney, off the north coast, and Shetland, in the far north-east. These remote island groups have their roots in a different culture entirely: Norwegian. The isles were invaded by Vikings and annexed by Norway in the ninth century, and didn't become Scottish for another 600 years. Remnants of Norse culture survive in Orcadian tales of trolls and Shetland's exciting Viking fire festivals!

### RECORD BREAKER
Out Stack is the northernmost point of the British Isles; Skaw is the most northerly settlement; Muness the most northerly castle.

### FIRE FESTIVAL
Up Helly Aa is a Viking fire festival in Lerwick in January; a parade of 1,000 torchbearers set light to a replica Viking ship.

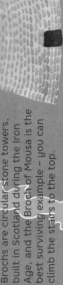

### PINT-SIZED PONY
Shetland ponies are small and stocky, while the Shetland Sheepdog, or Sheltie, is a small, friendly herding dog.

### UP NORTH
Shetland is as far north as St Petersburg, Russia, and Anchorage, Alaska, and as close to the North Pole as parts of Greenland and Alaska.

### SHETLAND FOOD
Traditional dishes make use of the Shetland black potato's purplish flesh; liver muggies (fish stomachs stuffed with fish livers), and reestit (air-dried) mutton.

### NORTHERN LIGHTS
Shetland is the best place in the UK to see the Aurora Borealis, or Northern Lights. The "merrie dancers" shimmer green in the winter night sky.

## SHETLAND ISLANDS

### FIDDLESTICKS!
The fiddle is the traditional instrument of Shetland – you can hear it played at the annual folk festival in spring.

### JUMP TO IT
Fair Isle is famous for its colourful knitwear, which became popular when the Prince of Wales (later King Edward VIII) wore a Fair Isle jumper in 1921.

SCALLOWAY

LERWICK

### BROCH STOP
Brochs are circular stone towers, built in Scotland during the Iron Age, and the Broch of Mousa is the best surviving example – you can climb the stairs to the top.

---

### ARTHUR ANDERSON
### 1792–1868
The businessman and Liberal MP was born in Lerwick. Shetland – he co-founded the P&O shipping company which went on to offer its famous cruise holidays.

### CHECKMATE
A hoard of 12th-century chess pieces was found on Lewis in 1831 – some are now on display in the museum at Lews Castle.

### PROPER PUDDING
Stornoway black pudding is made on Lewis from beef suet, oatmeal, onion and blood.

STORNOWAY

### STONE CIRCLE
The Callanish Stones on Lewis date from about 2900 BC, and form one of the most complete stone circles in Europe.

### TOP TWEED
Harris Tweed is cloth that, by law, must be handwoven and finished in the Outer Hebrides using wool dyed and spun there.

### SILVER SANDS
Luskentyre on Harris is one of the most beautiful beaches in the Outer Hebrides, with its wide expanse of white sand.

### ISLAND EMIGRATION
During the Highland Clearances of the 19th century, many islanders emigrated; hundreds left North Uist for Cape Breton, Canada.

## WESTERN ISLES

### MOON STONES
Roineabhal, a hill on Harris, has a plateau made from anorthosite – the same kind of granite that is found in on the moon.

### HIGH-PROTEIN DIET
According to the 1764 census, the 90 inhabitants of St Kilda ate 36 eggs and 18 seabirds every day – each!

### WILDLIFE WATCH
The Outer Hebrides is home to sealife such as basking sharks, orca, minke whales, porpoises and dolphins.

### MINIMAL MAMMALS
Red deer and otters are the only two native land mammals in the Outer Hebrides.

### BRITISH MUMMIES
Cladh Hallan on South Uist is the only place in the UK where prehistoric mummies have been found – they were discovered in 2001.

### MERMAID MYTH
In 1830, crofters cutting seaweed on Benbecula reported seeing a mermaid – her body is said to have washed up two days later and was buried near the sea.

CANADA

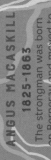

## DONALD TRUMP
### B.1946
The controversial US president has Scottish heritage: his mother was born in Tong, Lewis, in 1912, and emigrated to New York at the age of 18.

## FLORENCE MARIAN MCNEILL
### 1885-1973
The folklorist was born in Holm, Orkney, and helped revive Scottish literature and culture, writing *The Silver Bough* and *The Scots Kitchen*.

## ANGUS MACASKILL
### 1825-1863
The strongman was born on Berneray and moved to Canada – he is the tallest recorded "giant" at 2.36m. There is a museum devoted to him on Skye.

## JOHN RAE
### 1813-1893
The surgeon and explorer was born in Orphir, Shetland, and explored northern Canada – he discovered part of the Northwest Passage and there is a statue of him in Stromness.

## RACHEL JOHNSON
### 1922-2016
The last of the native St Kildans was born on Hirta and was evacuated with the 35 other inhabitants in 1930, when life on the remote archipelago became too difficult.

## FLORA MACDONALD
### 1722-1790
The Jacobite heroine was born on South Uist and helped Bonnie Prince Charlie hide on Benbecula and escape to Skye after the Battle of Culloden in 1746.

*WHISKY GALORE*
In 1941, the SS Politician was wrecked near Eriskay and Calvay – the locals helped themselves to its cargo of 28,000 cases of whisky, inspiring Compton Mackenzie's novel *Whisky Galore*.

*FISH OUT OF WATER*
During winter storms, small fish can be blown onto the top of 190m cliffs at Barra Head, the southernmost island in the Outer Hebrides.

*SCOTTISH GAELIC*
More than half the population of the Outer Hebrides speak Scottish Gaelic; Fèis Bharraigh, on Barra, is an annual Gaelic culture festival.

*ALL DAY LONG*
On the longest days of the year, it never gets completely dark in Orkney and Shetland, a phenomenon known as "simmer dim".

*SEAWEED SHEEP*
North Ronaldsay, Orkney's most isolated island, is home to sheep that have evolved to feed on seaweed.

*SPEED OF FLIGHT*
The flight from Westray to Papa Westray is the shortest scheduled flight in the world – just two minutes!

*TALL TALES*
Orkney's rich folklore is full of mischievous creatures such as trows – you can hear the tales around a peat fire at the Orkney Folklore and Storytelling Centre.

*ANCIENT TOMB*
Rousay is known as the "Egypt of the North" because it has more than 160 archaeological sites, including Midhowe Broch, a 5,000-year-old chambered tomb.

*ORKNEY FOOD*
Bere bannocks are thick scones made from an ancient kind of barley grown and milled in Orkney, baked on a girdle (iron) and served warm with cheese.

*SEA STACK*
The Old Man of Hoy is one of the tallest sea stacks in Britain at 137m; you can spot puffins, known as "Tammie Norries" on Orkney, from the viewpoint overlooking it.

ORKNEY

KIRKWALL

STROMNESS

ATLANTIC OCEAN

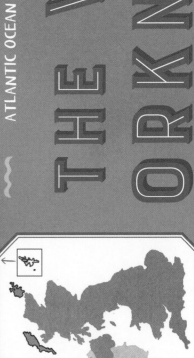

73

# NORTH-EAST SCOTLAND

### LOOKOUT POINT
Nelson's Tower in Forres was built in 1806 to commemorate the Battle of Trafalgar – climb the tower for views over the Moray Firth.

## Get royal treatment at the Highland Games!

Visit Braemar, a village in Aberdeenshire, to witness one of the most famous Highland Games in Scotland. The Braemar Gathering is said to have originated with King Malcolm III in the 11th century; events include tossing the caber, piping and tug o' war. It still has the royal seal of approval: the Queen has a front-row seat each year! The area around Braemar is known as Royal Deeside because the royal family have spent their summers here ever since the reign of Queen Victoria. Speaking of royalty, Aberdeen was once of the first places to be granted a royal charter, by King David I in the mid-12th century. The Granite City, so-called because of its sparkling stone buildings, is Scotland's third-biggest city, and the centre of the UK's oil industry.

### WHISKY GALORE
Speyside is one of Scotland's five whisky regions and contains more than half the country's distilleries – grown-ups can follow the Malt Whisky Trail.

HIGHLANDS

### SPOOKY SUMMIT
Ben Macdui (1,309m) is the second-highest mountain in the UK after Ben Nevis, and the highest in the Cairngorms – the summit is said to be haunted by a Big Grey Man.

**DENIS LAW**
**B.1940**
The footballer was born in Aberdeen and is the only Scottish player to have won the Ballon d'Or, in 1964.

**ETHEL GORDON FENWICK**
**1857–1947**
The nurse was born in Elgin and campaigned to make nursing a profession with training, exams and a register of qualified people.

**EMELI SANDÉ**
**B.1987**
The singer grew up in Alford – so far she has won three Mobo awards and four Brits, including best British female solo artist (twice).

PERTH AND KINROSS

### GREAT GATHERING
The Braemar Gathering is one of the most famous Highland Games, featuring traditional tests of strength and speed, dancing and piping – the Queen attends every year.

**PETER MULLAN**
**B.1959**
The actor and director was born in Peterhead – he is the only person to have won awards for best actor and best film at the Cannes and Venice film festivals.

**EVELYN GLENNIE**
**B.1965**
The musician was born in Aberdeen and is a virtuoso percussionist – she has been profoundly deaf since the age of 12 but can feel music in different parts of her body.

**ANNIE LENNOX**
**B.1954**
The singer was born in Aberdeen and became famous as the lead singer of the Eurythmics – she is now a solo artist and has won eight Brit awards.

## ROCK ON
Bow Fiddle Rock near Portknockie is a sea arch shaped like the tip of a fiddle bow – you can kayak past it and see the nesting seabirds.

## SEA LIFE
The Macduff Marine Aquarium has creatures from the Moray Firth, Scotland's biggest bay, including sharp-toothed wolf fish and jellyfish.

## FAR EAST
Busy fishing port Peterhead is known as the Blue Toun, and is the easternmost point of mainland Scotland.

### ELGIN

## PICTISH PERFECT
Elgin has the oldest independent museum in Scotland, whose collection includes Pictish stones from the sixth century.

## SAIL AWAY
Portsoy's 17th-century harbour hosts the Scottish Traditional Boat festival, where you can row coracles, watch races and whiz down waterslides.

### FRASERBURGH

## LOCAL FOOD
Cullen skink is a thick soup made from smoked haddock, potatoes and onions; the Aberdeen buttery (or rowie) is a sort of flaky, salty bread roll.

## HISTORIC HOUSE
Art gallery Duff House in Banff was designed by the Scottish architect William Adam in the 1730s and was a prisoner of war camp during the second world war.

## FISHY BUSINESS
Fraserburgh is the biggest shellfish port in Europe, holds the low level British wind speed record (228kph!) and had the first lighthouse in Scotland.

### PETERHEAD

## BUILDING BRIDGES
Craigellachie Bridge spans the River Spey – it was built by Thomas Telford in 1812-14, making it the oldest cast-iron bridge in Scotland.

## FULL STEAM AHEAD
The Keith and Dufftown Railway is known as the Whisky Line, chugging 18km to Dufftown, the malt whisky capital of the world.

## STRANGE STONES
There are up to 100 recumbent stone circles in Aberdeenshire – Easter Aquhorthies is one of the best-preserved examples.

## ANIMAL MAGIC
The Forvie National Nature Reserve is a huge area of shifting sand dunes with the UK's biggest populations of eider ducks (up to 5,000!), and seals in the estuary.

### MORAY

### ABERDEENSHIRE

## BACK TO NATURE
Muir of Dinnet National Nature Reserve includes Burn O'Vat, a giant pothole; other reserves include RSPB Fowlsheugh; RSPB Loch of Strathbeg; St Cyrus; and Glen Tanar.

### INVERURIE

## YOUNG STARS
The Aberdeen International Youth Festival is one of the world's biggest arts festivals for young performers of dance, drama and music.

## COAST WITH THE MOST
There are sandy beaches all along the coastline, including 23-km Balmedie beach and dunes.

### NORTH SEA

## ROYAL CONNECTION
Royal Deeside is so-called because it is home to Balmoral Castle, a royal residence since Queen Victoria's reign, and Birkhall, now owned by Prince Charles.

### ABERDEEN

## GRANITE CITY
Aberdeen is Scotland's third-biggest city – it is known as the Granite City because lots of its buildings are made from this local rock, which sparkles in the sunshine.

## PARK LIFE
Aberdeen has 45 parks and gardens, and a long sandy beach between the rivers Dee and Don, next to an amusement park called Codona's.

## ART & CULTURE
The Aberdeen Art Gallery has reopened after a £30m refurbishment, and the Aberdeen Maritime Museum has displays on North Sea oil and gas.

## SPORTS REPORT
Golf courses in north-east Scotland include Braemar, the highest 18-hole course in the country (366m above sea level), and one owned by US president Donald Trump.

## VICTORIAN VILLAGE
Ballater is a Victorian village that holds an annual Victoria Week with duck races, a scarecrow trail, a pet show and all kinds of children's activities.

## DIVE IN
The Olympic-sized Stonehaven swimming pool is the northernmost lido (outdoor pool) in the UK – luckily it is heated!

### RAMSAY MACDONALD
### 1866-1937
The politician was born in Lossiemouth and became the first Labour prime minister in 1924 – he was later expelled from the party and led a coalition government.

"Da Ken fit yer saying"

"I don't know what you're saying"

## TALKING POINT
People from north-eastern Scotland speak a dialect called Doric: words include "quines" (girls) and "louns" (boys), and there is an annual Doric festival.

### ANGUS

## CASTLE COUNT
North-east Scotland has more castles than anywhere else in the UK, such as Dunnottar, a ruined clifftop fortress – the Castle Trail takes in 19 of the best.

# PERTH & KINROSS
# ANGUS, DUNDEE AND FIFE

**PERTH & KINROSS**

### MARGARET FAIRLIE
**1891-1963**
The gynaecologist was born in Balmirmer – she worked at a hospital and taught at a university in Dundee, and became Scotland's first female professor in 1940.

**TOP TREES**
The Fortingall Yew, Britain's oldest tree, is up to 9,000 years old; the Birnam Oak appears in Shakespeare's Macbeth; the Meikleour Beech Hedge is the world's highest hedge.

**SCOUTING AROUND**
Blair Castle is the garrison of the only legal private army in Europe, the Atholl Highlanders, and hosts the Jamborette, Scotland's biggest Scout Camp.

**ROYAL PALACE**
Scone Palace is the ancient crowning place of Scottish kings – Macbeth, Robert the Bruce and Charles II were all crowned here on the Stone of Scone.

**ISLAND LIFE**
In the Iron Age, people lived in thatched roundhouses on crannogs (artificial islands) – go inside a reconstructed dwelling at the Scottish Crannog Centre on Loch Tay.

**TARTAN ARMY**
Balhousie Castle houses the Black Watch museum, which tells the story of Scotland's oldest Highland regiment.

### SHIRLEY HENDERSON
**B.1965**
The actor grew up in Kincardine – she played Moaning Myrtle in the Harry Potter films and voiced the Gruffalo's Child in the animated version of Julia Donaldson's book.

**STIRLING**

### J.M. BARRIE
**1860-1937**
The author was born in Kirriemuir, where you can visit the weaver's cottage in which he grew up – he is best known for writing *Peter Pan*.

**SHAKY TOUN**
Comrie is known as the Shaky Toun because it has more earth tremors than anywhere else in the UK; it holds a Flambeaux (flaming torch) parade at Hogmanay.

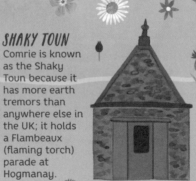

**PERTH**

**THE FAIR CITY**
Perth, a city on the River Tay, was once the capital of Scotland and is known as the Fair City, after a novel called *The Fair Maid of Perth* by Walter Scott.

**CLACKMANNANSHIRE**

**AULD GREY TOUN**
Dunfermline Abbey is the burial place of Robert the Bruce and 11 other kings, queens and princes; Dunfermline also has a world-class waterskiing and wakeboarding.

## Dabble in design in Dundee!

Dundee is said to be built on the "three Js", referring to its big industries: jute, jam and journalism. The latter is still going strong – the Dundee company D.C. Thomson publishes *The Beano*, Britain's longest-running children's comic, and Dundee was named the UK's first City of Design in 2014. Now this design heritage is celebrated at the V&A Dundee, where exhibits include Dundee-made video games such as *Lemmings* and *Grand Theft Auto*. The museum is on the River Tay waterfront, where you will also find the historic ships RSS *Discovery* and HMS *Unicorn*.
If Dundee is Scotland's design capital, then St Andrews is the home of golf! There are seven golf courses, and the British Golf Museum tells the history of the sport.

**DUNFERMLINE**

**WALK WITH SHARKS**
Deep Sea World is an aquarium with the longest underwater tunnel in the UK – you can walk through it to see the sharks, stringrays, seahorses and seals.

### EWAN MCGREGOR
**B.1971**
The actor was born in Perth and grew up in Crieff – his films include *Trainspotting*, the Star Wars prequel trilogy, *Beauty and the Beast* and *Christopher Robin*.

### SHAKESPEARE'S CASTLE
Glamis Castle is the setting for Macbeth, the real-life childhood home of Queen Elizabeth the Queen Mother and the birthplace of Princess Margaret.

### PICTISH STONES
Lots of Pictish Stones were found in Angus and Fife – you can see some at the Meigle Sculptured Stone Museum, and the Montrose Museum.

### LOCAL FOOD
The Forfar bridie is a meat pasty while the Arbroath smokie is a smoked haddock.

**ABERDEENSHIRE**

### ARTY TOWN
The sculptor William Lamb (1893-1951) was born in Montrose – you can see his sculptures around town and visit his studio.

### GAGGLE OF GEESE
The Montrose Basin is a nature reserve that attracts up to 80,000 pink-footed geese in winter – the visitor centre has telescopes and binoculars to see them up close.

**ANGUS**

### CLIMB A VOLCANO
Dundee Law is a 400-million-year-old extinct volcano – you can walk to the top for views of the city.

### SHIP SHAPE
Step aboard the RSS *Discovery*, the ship that took Scott and Shackleton on their first expedition to Antarctica, or HMS *Unicorn*, Scotland's only surviving wooden warship.

### ANCIENT ABBEY
Arbroath Abbey, founded by King William the Lion in 1178, is known for the 1320 Declaration of Arbroath, which asserted Scotland's independence from England.

### FOOTBALL FACT
Arbroath FC hold the world record for the biggest win in a professional football match – they beat Bon Accord 36-0 on 12 September 1885.

**MOIRA SHEARER**
**1926-2006**
The ballet dancer and actress was born in Dunfermline – her most successful film was Powell & Pressburger's *The Red Shoes*.

**DUNDEE**

**DUNDEE CITY**

### ROUND TOWERS
There are only two 11th-century round towers still standing in Scotland, in Brechin and Abernethy – you can climb to the top of the Abernethy tower.

### SEASIDE SPOT
Broughty Ferry is a seaside suburb just outside Dundee, where you can play on the beach and visit the 15th-century coastal fort.

### LEADING LIGHT
Bell Rock Lighthouse is the world's oldest surviving sea-washed lighthouse – it was first switched on in 1811 on a reef 18km off the coast of Angus.

### HOME OF GOLF
St Andrews has Scotland's oldest university (Prince William studied there), a golf club founded in 1754, and the British Golf Museum.

**DULEEP SINGH**
**1838-1893**
The last Maharaja of the Sikh Empire was born in Lahore – he came to power aged five, was exiled to Britain at 15 and later lived in Castle Menzies.

### ANYONE FOR TENNIS?
Falkland Palace has the world's oldest real tennis court still in use – it was built for King James V in 1539.

### ANIMAL MAGIC
The Scottish Deer Centre in Cupar has 14 species of deer including reindeer, plus wolves, lynx and Scottish wildcats.

**GLENROTHES**

**FIFE**

### EASTER FAIR
Kirkcaldy's Links Market, held around Easter, is Europe's longest street fair, with more than 200 fairground rides and attractions.

### PUFFIN PATROL
The Isle of May is a nature reserve – boats call there between April and September; June and July is the best time to see the breeding puffins and other seabirds.

**NORTH SEA**

**KIRKCALDY**

### CASTLE COUNT
Aberdour Castle was built in the 1100s and is one of the oldest standing stone castles in Scotland; other castles include Menzies, Drummond and Claypotts.

**ADAM SMITH**
**1723-1790**
The philosopher and political economist was born in Kirkcaldy – his most famous book is *The Wealth of Nations*.

## A WEE DRAM
Whisky is Scotland's national drink and has been made here since at least 1494. The Highlands has lots of whisky distilleries, tours and festivals.

## HIGHLAND GAMES
Every weekend in summer, somewhere in the Highlands, men in tartan kilts compete in feats of strength such as tossing the caber and tug o' war, while bagpipers play and people dance.

## GOLD RUSH
Gold was found in the Strath of Kildonan, leading to the Great Sutherland gold rush of 1869 – you can still pan for small amounts of gold today.

## CASTLE COUNT
Spectacular castles and ruins include the Castle of Mey, Urquhart, Invergarry, Dunrobin, Cawdor and the Old Man of Wick.

## SMOO CAVE
This cave has a 15-metre-high entrance and was formed by the sea on one side and a waterfall on the other – see the inner chamber by boat.

## SNOW SPORTS
The Highlands is the UK's top destination for outdoor skiing, with several ski centres including: Cairngorm Mountain, Glencoe Mountain, and Nevis Range.

## SHINTY
This ancient sport is similar to hockey, played with a stick called a caman. The Camanachd Cup is the top prize.

## SUNBATHING
Balnakeil is a beautiful Highland beach, Nairn is one of the driest and sunniest places in Scotland, and Ullapool is best for a seaside holiday.

## HIGHLAND CLEARANCES
In the 18th and 19th centuries, many Highland families were evicted; the Exiles statue in Helmsdale is a tribute to them.

## SKYE HIGH
Skye is the biggest island in the Inner Hebrides and is famed for its natural wonders such as the Old Man of Storr, the Cuillin, the Quiraing and the Fairy Pools.

## PORT OF CALL
Portree is the main town on Skye; other places to visit include the Skye Museum of Island Life and Dunvegan Castle.

**HIGHLAND**

## LAST BATTLE
At the Battle of Culloden in 1746, the final battle of the Jacobite Rising, up to 2,000 Highlanders were killed in an hour; the visitor centre tells the tale.

## GREAT GLEN
This 100-km glen (valley) is dotted with lochs (lakes) linked by rivers and the Caledonian Canal; you can walk, cycle or canoe the Great Glen Way from Fort William to Inverness.

## CASTLE COUNT
Eilean Donan is one of the most-photographed castles in Scotland; other Instagram-worthy castles include Dunrobin Castle.

## HUNT FOR NESSIE
Search for the elusive Loch Ness Monster on a boat trip, and learn about the mythical beast at the exhibition centre in Drumnadrochit.

**INVERNESS**

## REALLY WILD
Amazing wildlife includes rare wildcats, pine martens, golden eagles, sea eagles and red deer – you can see lots of them at the Highland Wildlife Park in Kincraig.

## SMALL ISLES
The Small Isles archipelago includes Rùm, Eigg, Muck and Canna – Rùm, the biggest, is a national nature reserve and the site of Kinloch Castle.

## HOGWARTS EXPRESS
The Jacobite Steam Train from Fort William to Mallaig on the West Highland Line was the Hogwarts Express in the Harry Potter films.

## MIGHTY MOUNTAIN
Ben Nevis in the Grampians is the highest mountain in Britain; the first recorded ascent was in 1771 and now 100,000 people climb it every year.

**ATLANTIC OCEAN**

## HIGHLAND CATTLE
These shaggy-coated cows may look fierce with their long horns, but they are actually very friendly.

## OUTDOOR CAPITAL
Fort William is the outdoor capital of the UK with skiing, snowboarding, mountain biking, climbing and walking along the West Highland Way.

**FORT WILLIAM**

## GLENCOE MASSACRE
On 13 February 1692, 38 men of the MacDonald clan were murdered by their guests, and 40 women and children died of exposure; there is a memorial in Glencoe.

## BIGGEST PARK
Wrap up warm for a visit to the enormous Cairngorms National Park – the UK's coldest temperature, -27.2°C, has twice been recorded here, and you can even go husky-racing.

**ARGYLL AND BUTE**

URSO

JOHN O' GROATS

LANDS END 874    PENTLAND SKERRIES 6

## NORTH POLE
John O'Groats is the most northerly inhabited point of mainland Great Britain; from here you can walk, run or cycle 1,407km to Land's End in Cornwall, the most southerly point.

WICK

## Come North to Climb the Cairngorms!

Fort William in the Highlands is close to Ben Nevis, Britain's highest mountain, and is a centre for hillwalking and climbing. You can go skiing at one of the five ski centres in the region, canoe along the Great Glen Way, go surfing in Thurso and even try husky-racing. Look out for the legendary Loch Ness Monster, and go to find Rudolph and friends at the Cairngorm Reindeer Centre. The biggest town is Inverness, which is near the Moray Firth, one of the best places to see dolphins in Europe. The Highlands is also home to rare wildlife, including wildcats, pine martens and golden eagles as well as ride the Hogwarts Express on the West Highland Line – a truly magical day out!

NORTH SEA

## DOLPHIN-WATCHING
The Moray Firth is one of the best places in Europe to see bottlenose dolphins – about 130 live there, and Chanonry Point is the best place to watch them playing.

MORAY FRITH

AIRN

MORAY

### ALI SMITH
#### B.1962
The award-winning novelist was born in Inverness; her books include *The Accidental* and *How to be Both*.

### MACBETH
#### C.1005-1057
The King of Scotland from 1040 until his death inspired Shakespeare's tragedy of the same name.

### MARGARET LORIMER
#### 1866-1954
The mountaineer and headmistress who climbed Mount Cook, New Zealand's highest mountain, in 1918 was born in Inverness.

### ROBERT MENLI LYON
#### 1789-1874
This Western Australian advocate for Indigenous Australian rights was born in Inverness.

## MEET RUDOLPH
The Cairngorm Reindeer Centre is home to Britain's only herd of free-range reindeer – you can follow a herder up the mountain to stroke and feed them.

## TAKE THE BISCUIT
Shortbread is a delicious Scottish biscuit made from a simple recipe: one part white sugar, two parts butter, and three parts flour.

ABERDEENSHIRE

### YVETTE COOPER
#### B.1969
The member of parliament, born in Inverness, is a prominent Labour politician and became the first woman to serve as Chief Secretary to the Treasury.

### BONNIE PRINCE CHARLIE
#### 1720-1788
Charles Edward Stuart led the Jacobite uprising of 1745 and was defeated at the Battle of Culloden, although he managed to escape.

### KAREN GILLAN
#### B.1987
The actor from Inverness played Amelia Pond in *Doctor Who* and has starred in the Guardians of the Galaxy films.

## CALEDONIAN FOREST
The Highlands is the only place in Britain where ancient Scots pines grow, descended from the first trees to appear after the last ice age, 9,000 years ago.

## MUNRO-BAGGING
Try "Munro-bagging": climbing all the mountains in the Highlands higher than 914m. There are 282 of them!

PERTH AND KINROSS

FORTH OF FRITH

# THE HIGHLANDS

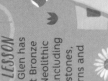
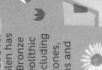

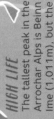

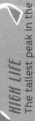
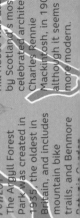
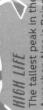
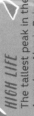

## STIRLING

**HISTORIC HOUSE**
Hill House was designed by Scotland's most celebrated architect, Charles Rennie Mackintosh, in 1902, although it seems much more modern.

**HIGH LIFE**
The tallest peak in the Arrochar Alps is Beinn Ime (1,011m), but the most well-known is the Cobbler, thanks to its strange shape.

**HISTORY LESSON**
Kilmartin Glen has important Bronze Age and Neolithic remains, including standing stones, burial cairns and hillforts.

**ENCHANTED FOREST**
The Argyll Forest Park was created in 1935, the oldest in Britain, and includes mountain bike trails, and Benmore Botanic Garden.

**CASTLE & COURTROOM**
In Inveraray, visit the castle, still home to the Duke of Argyll and the 19th-century jail, now a museum.

## PERTH AND KINROSS

**EMMA RICHARDS B.1975**
The sailor grew up in Helensburgh and became the first British woman and youngest ever person to complete the Around Alone, a round-the-world yacht race.

## HIGHLANDS

**BONE PADDLING**
The 150km Argyll Sea Kayak Trail runs from Ganavan Sands near Oban to Helensburgh. It is split into eight sections, so you don't have to do it all in one go!

## OBAN

**TOP TOWN**
Oban is known as the Gateway to the Isles and the Seafood Capital of Scotland.

**HIDDEN TREASURE**
A wrecked Spanish galleon laden with gold is said to lurk beneath the waters of the colourful fishing port of Tobermory.

**ANIMAL MAGIC**
Beavers were reintroduced to Knapdale Forest, more than 400 years after they were hunted to extinction.

**SHEINA MARSHALL 1896-1977**
The scientist was born in Rothesay. She became a leading marine biologist and a fellow of the Royal Society of Edinburgh in 1949.

**MAIRI HEDDERWICK B.1939**
The author and illustrator was born in Gourock and moved to Coll – she is best known for the Katie Morag children's books.

**SIR WILLIAM MACEWEN 1848-1924**
The revered doctor, who pioneered modern brain surgery, bone grafts and lung surgery, was born near Port Bannatyne on the Isle of Bute.

**DEBORAH KERR 1921-2007**
The actor lived in Helensburgh until she was three. She was nominated for six Oscars – her most famous film is the musical The King and I.

**COLL CALLING**
Coll is one of the best places in the UK to see basking sharks and corncrakes; it is also a Dark Sky island, which means it's a great spot for stargazing.

**HORSING AROUND**
Trek along the beautiful beaches and check out the spectacular scenery on horseback!

**CAVES & COLUMNS**
Staffa is famous for Fingal's Cave, which inspired Mendelssohn's The Hebrides overture.

## THE INNER HEBRIDES

**PUFFIN WATCH**
Lunga is the biggest of the eight principal Treshnish Isles – you can visit on a summer daytrip to see the thousands of breeding puffins and other seabirds.

**HOLY ISLAND**
Iona Abbey was founded in AD 563 by St Columba. It's believed that 48 kings of Scotland are buried on Iona, including Macbeth.

**EAGLE ISLAND**
Mull is one of the best places to see golden eagles and white-tailed sea eagles.

**SLATE ISLANDS**
The seven Slate Islands include Easdale, which hosts the World Stone Skimming Championships; Seil, which has a "Bridge over the Atlantic"; and Luing, home of the Atlantic Islands Centre.

**ATLANTIC OCEAN**

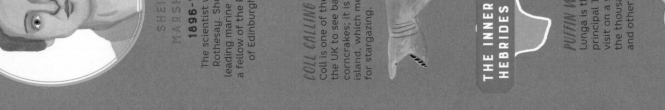

# ARGYLL & BUTE AND THE INNER HEBRIDES

## ARGYLL & BUTE

## Explore miles of isles – and wildlife galore!

"Island-hopping" might make you think of a holiday in Greece – but you can do it right here in Scotland! There are 35 inhabited islands and 44 uninhabited islands in the Inner Hebrides, an archipelago off the west coast of mainland Scotland. Many of them are connected by ferry, so they are easy to explore, with Islay, Jura and Mull being some of the largest of the southern islands. The islands are paradise for animals as well as people, from the eagles on Mull to the puffins on Lunga. Argyle and Bute has wonderful wildlife, too. Beavers now roam Knapdale Forest again, as they did hundreds of years ago, while Argyll Forest Park teems with red squirrels, pine martens and red deer.

### HELENSBURGH

### DUNOON

### ROTHESAY

### FUN & GAMES
Dunoon is the main town on the Cowal peninsula – it hosts the Cowal Highland Gathering, one of the biggest Highland Games in the world, each August.

### NEO-GOTHIC GEEKERY
Neo-gothic mansion Mount Stuart was one of the most technologically advanced houses of the 19th century, with the first telephone, underfloor heating and a heated pool!

### LOTS OF YACHTS
Tarbert hosts the Scottish Series, Scotland's top yachting event, on Loch Fyne; climb up to the ruins of Tarbert Castle for great views.

### WHAT A BUTE
Visit the seals at Scalpsie Bay; a tranquil, secluded spot which was used for military purposes in the Second World War.

### OH DEER
Jura is home to 200 people – and over 5,000 wild red deer! Hike up the Paps of Jura and take a boat trip to the Corryvreckan Whirlpool.

### SURFS UP
Islay is one of the best places in Britain to surf with white sandy beaches, beautiful clear waters and consistent waves.

### FILM STAR
Campbeltown is the main town on the Kintyre peninsula – its Wee Picture House, built in 1913, is believed to be the oldest purpose-built cinema in Scotland.

### A WEE DRAM
Islay, the Queen of the Hebrides, has eight whisky distilleries (once it had 23!); Bowmore, the main town, has a round church so that evil spirits have nowhere to hide.

### COME TO COLONSAY
Colonsay has a beautiful sandy beach, Kiloran Bay, lots of wild goats and rabbits, and a tiny book festival in April; you can walk to neighbouring Oronsay at low tide.

### CAMPELTOWN

### LOOKOUT POINT
There has been a lighthouse at the Mull of Kintyre since 1788; the spot was made famous by a song co-written by Paul McCartney for his post-Beatles band Wings.

### FIRTH OF CLYDE

### 1903-1950
The British writer was born in India – he lived in Barnhill farmhouse on Jura from 1946-48, where he wrote one of his best-known novels, *Nineteen Eighty-Four*.

### 1888-1946
The inventor was born in Helensburgh and is most famous for inventing television – he demonstrated the first working TV on 26 January 1926.

### 1858-1923
The politician was born in New Brunswick (now in Canada) and moved to Helensburgh as a child – he was prime minister for just 211 days.

# SOUTHERN SCOTLAND

**MARY SOMERVILLE 1780-1872**
The scientist was born in Jedburgh – she helped discover Neptune, was the joint first woman to join the Royal Astronomical Society, and is on the Scottish £10 note.

**DOUGLAS HAIG 1861-1928**
The controversial army officer was British commander on the Western Front for most of the First World War, including the Battle of the Somme – he is buried at Dryburgh Abbey.

**CATHERINE HELEN SPENCE 1825-1910**
The "Grand Old Woman of Australia" was born in Melrose and emigrated to Adelaide as a teenager – she became a writer and a campaigner for women's rights.

EAST AYRSHIRE

SOUTH LANARKSHIRE

*SPACE AGE*
Crawick Multiverse, on the site of a former coal mine, is a land art project by Charles Jencks: paths lead to landforms representing the sun, comets and black holes.

*STRIDING ARCHES*
The hilltop arches near Cairnhead are by the artist Andy Goldsworthy – there are others in Canada, the US and New Zealand that represent Scottish emigration.

*TIBETAN RETREAT*
The Kagyu Samye Ling monastery was founded in 1967 as the first Tibetan Buddhist centre in the UK.

*NATIONAL POET*
Robert Burns lived at Ellisland Farm and then in Dumfries from 1788 until his death – his houses are now museums. A Big Burns Supper takes place in January.

**KIRSTY WARK B.1955**
The TV journalist was born in Dumfries and has presented *Newsnight* since 1993.

SOUTH AYRSHIRE

*ENCHANTED FOREST*
Galloway Forest Park, the "highlands of the lowlands", is great for fishing, and spotting red deer and birds of prey.

*READ ALL ABOUT IT*
Wigtown is Scotland's national book town – it has the biggest second-hand bookshop in the country, and holds a literary festival in September.

*QUEEN OF THE SOUTH*
Dumfries sights include one of Scotland's oldest bridges, the 13th-century Devorgilla, and Greyfriars Church, where Robert the Bruce murdered John Comyn in 1306.

DUMFRIES

STRANRAER

*PORT OF CALL*
Stranraer is a ferry port on Loch Ryan – its landmarks include the Castle of St John (a towerhouse built c.1500) and the museum in the 18th-century town hall.

DUMFRIES & GALLOWAY

*LOCH OUT*
There are lots of watersports activities on Loch Ken, while St Mary's Loch is the biggest natural loch in the Scottish Borders.

*BUCKETS & SPADES*
The Solway coast has lots of sandy coves and has been dubbed the Scottish Riviera; other beautiful beaches include Luce Bay and Coldingham Bay.

*BACK TO NATURE*
At the Mull of Galloway, Scotland's most southerly point, you can climb the lighthouse and visit the RSPB nature reserve.

*DESERT ISLANDS*
At low tide, you can walk to the bird sanctuary on Rough Island or to Hestan Island, which has caves and a lighthouse.

ATLANTIC OCEAN

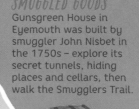

## SMUGGLED GOODS
Gunsgreen House in Eyemouth was built by smuggler John Nisbet in the 1750s – explore its secret tunnels, hiding places and cellars, then walk the Smugglers Trail.

## ON GUARD
The Coldstream Guards, founded in 1650, is the oldest regiment in the British Army in continuous active service – the Coldstream Museum tells the story.

**SCOTTISH BORDERS**

## ON YOUR BIKE
The 7stanes are seven mountain-biking centres across south Scotland, including Glentress, the flagship centre.

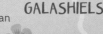

GALASHIELS

## THIRTY-NINE STEPS
The writer John Buchan lived in Peebles – visit the John Buchan Story museum or walk the 22km John Buchan Way to Broughton.

## DOG DAYS
Kelso hosts the Scottish Borders Dog Show in June, where you can see local Border Terriers and Border Collies, and other Scottish breeds such as Golden Retrievers.

NORTH SEA

## SPORTS REPORT
St Ronan's Border Games in Innerleithen began in 1827, making it the oldest sports meeting in Scotland – it culminates in the Cleikum Ceremonies to banish the devil!

## STATELY HOMES
The writer Sir Walter Scott lived at Abbotsford House; other historic houses include Floors Castle, Traquair and Thirlestane Castle.

## ALMIGHTY ABBEYS
King David I founded lots of monasteries in the 12th century – visit Melrose, Dryburgh, Jedburgh and Kelso on the 109km circular Border Abbeys Way.

## LOCAL FOOD
The Selkirk bannock is a rich fruit bread – Queen Victoria sampled it on a visit in 1867.

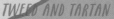

## TWEED AND TARTAN
Hawick is the cashmere capital of Scotland and is on the Textile Trail, which includes ten mills and museums, such as the Borders Textile Towerhouse.

## RETURN TO THE RIDINGS
Eleven towns stage the Common Ridings every summer – Hawick, Selkirk, Langholm and Lauder are the oldest.

HAWICK

**WALTER SCOTT**
**1771-1832**
The writer is best known for his historical novels *Rob Roy*, *Ivanhoe* and *Waverley* – he died at Abbotsford House and is buried at Dryburgh Abbey.

**JIM CLARK**
**1936-1968**
The racing driver grew up near Duns – he won two Formula One world championships and the Indianapolis 500, and was killed in a racing accident aged 32.

## CASTLE COUNT
Hermitage Castle is said to be the most sinister-looking castle in Scotland; others include Drumlanrig, Caerlaverock, MacLellan's, Threave and Duns.

## LOCKERBIE DISASTER
In 1988, 270 people were killed in the Lockerbie disaster – there are tributes at the Dryfesdale Lodge visitor centre and nearby memorial garden.

ANNAN

**GRETNA GREEN**

## WEDDING BELLS
Young couples have eloped to Gretna Green to get married since 1754 – 5,000 people still tie the knot here every year!

## MUSEUM TIME
The Devil's Porridge Museum tells the story of a first world war munitions factory; at Robert Smail's Printing Works in Innerleithen, you can try Victorian typesetting and printing.

ENGLAND

**CALVIN HARRIS**
**B.1984**
The singer, DJ and record producer was born in Dumfries – he was the first British solo artist to get more than a billion streams on Spotify.

## Cross the border for a big adventure!
The Scottish Borders' bloodthirsty past saw many fierce battles between Scotland and England, including the Wars of Scottish Independence in the late 13th and early 14th centuries, and generations of armed raids by Border Reivers. History has left its mark, with ruined abbeys and mighty castles to explore, including Hermitage Castle, said to be the most sinister in Scotland! In several border towns, history comes to life each summer during the Common Ridings, equestrian festivals that commemorate the men who once risked their lives to protect their townsfolk from invaders. Dumfries & Galloway is a more peaceful place, with rolling green hills, beautiful beaches along the Solway Coast and the wildlife-rich Galloway Forest Park. Hire a mountain bike and hit the trails!

# WALES

## Linger in the land of song!

Wales, or Cymru, is a proud Celtic nation, with its own unique identity and traditions. This Celtic culture dates back to the 5th century – cross the border from England and you'll spot that it remains a bilingual country to this day, with road signs in Welsh as well as English. The Welsh flag is emblazoned with revered medieval leader King Cadwalader's red dragon; other national symbols are the leek and the daffodil, which are worn on St. David's Day. Wales is perhaps best-known as the musical heart of the UK, world-famous for its male voice choirs, harpists and solo artists. You can hear rousing songs at rugby union matches and haunting music at festivals called eisteddfodau. The country is also treasured for its beautiful beaches, mighty mountains and more than 600 castles, plus exciting cities such as the capital, Cardiff, and second city Swansea. No wonder that whenever they leave, Welsh people long for the green, green grass of home!

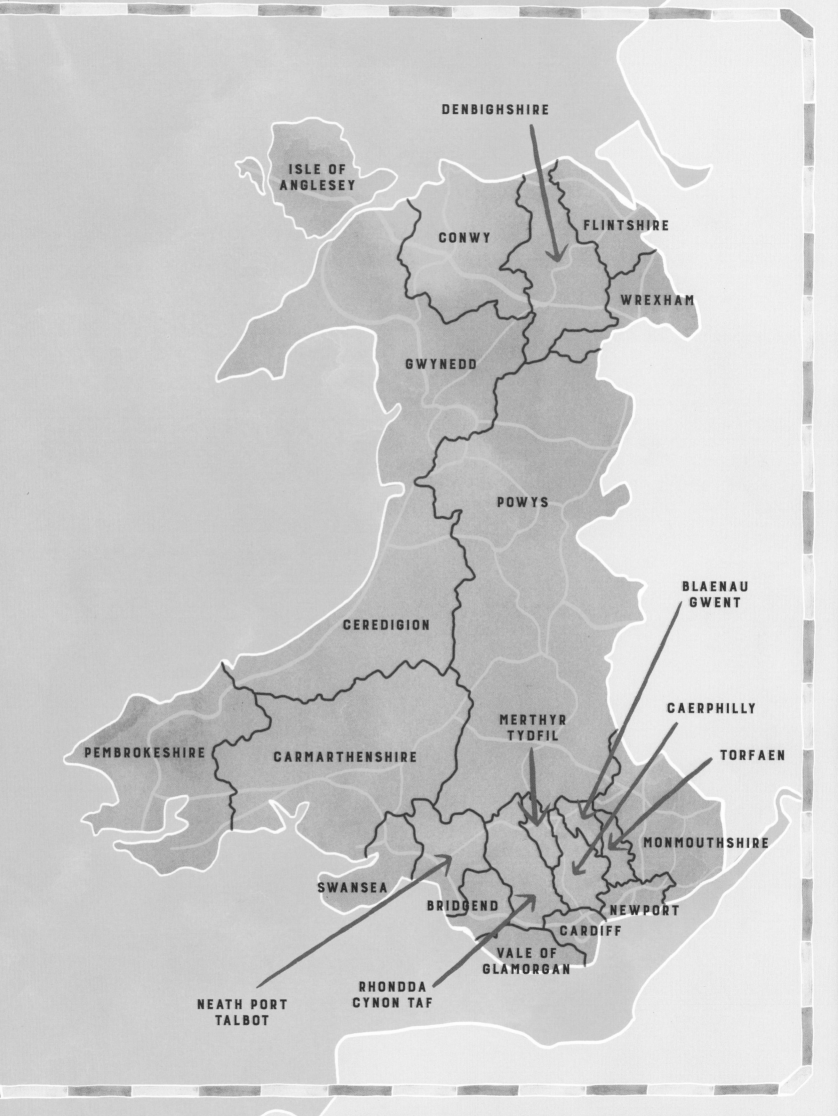

**HOLY ISLAND**
So-called because of its standing stones and religious sites, you can cross a bridge to tiny South Stack and climb its lighthouse.

**CLIFF CAMPING**
Anglesey is one of the few places in the world where you can go cliff camping: daredevils sleep on a portaledge on the side of a cliff.

**VILLAGE SPELLING TEST**
The longest place name in Europe means "Saint Mary's Church in a hollow of white hazel near the swirling whirlpool and the church of Saint Tysilio with a red cave".

**TOP TOWN**
Catch a ferry to Ireland from Holyhead or visit its Admiralty Arch (built early 1800s), which is linked to Marble Arch in London by the A5.

HOLYHEAD

ANGLESEY

LLANGEFNI

**NO KIDS ALLOWED**
In 2012, Bangor, the oldest city in Wales, banned under-16s from the city centre between 9pm and 6am, unless accompanied by an adult.

CONWY

**BUILDING BRIDGES**
The Menai Suspension Bridge, completed in 1826, joins the isle of Anglesey to mainland Wales.

CAERNARFON

BANGOR

**ELECTRIC ATTRACTION**
Visit the National Slate Museum and Electric Mountain – a tour inside a former power station – in Llanberis, at the foot of Mount Snowdon.

**LOVERS' ISLAND**
Llanddwyn Island is named after St Dwynwen, the Welsh equivalent of St Valentine – people send cards and flowers on her feast day, 25 January.

**CASTLE COUNT**
Wales has more castles per square kilometre than anywhere else in the world. They include: Caernarfon, Beaumaris and Harlech castles.

IRISH SEA

**ROYAL PARTY**
King Edward I held a jousting tournament in Nefyn in 1284.

**PREHISTORIC VILLAGE**
Tre'r Ceiri is one of the best-preserved prehistoric villages in the UK.

**PEAK PARK**
Snowdonia National Park contains all 15 Welsh mountains over 914 metres, including Mount Snowdon, the highest at 1,085m.

**SQUEAKY SANDS**
Porthor Beach is known as Whistling Sands because it squeaks or whistles when you walk on it.

**SHAGGY DOG STORY**
According to legend, Beddgelert is named after Prince Llewelyn's faithful hound Gelert.

**GETTING UP STEAM**
The Ffestiniog and Welsh Highland Railways have 65km of steam powered track through Snowdonia; you can even take a train to the top of Snowdon mountain.

GWYNEDD

**FANTASY VILLAGE**
The village of Portmeirion, built by architect Clough William-Ellis in the Italianate style, has been the setting for many films.

**BRILLIANT BIKING**
Coed-y-Brenin and Antur Stiniog are two of the best places to go mountain biking in Wales.

PWLLHELI

**SEA CHANGE**
When Harlech Castle was completed in 1289, it was on the coast, but the sea has since retreated, leaving room for Royal St David's golf course in between.

**KNIGHT STORY**
King Arthur's Labyrinth in Corris is an underground adventure – take a boat trip through a waterfall into a time of dragons and giants.

**BARDSEY ISLAND**
"The Island of 20,000 Saints" (said to be buried there) is also a nature reserve.

CARDIGAN BAY

**HISTORIC REGATTA**
Abersoch summer regatta has been going since 1881, with raft races, crab-catching and sandcastle-building competitions.

**SHELL ISLAND**
During winter storms, 200 different kinds of shells wash up on the beach at Shell Island.

**STARRY NIGHT**
Snowdonia is an International Dark Sky Reserve, which means it's a great place to go stargazing.

**GOING GREEN**
The Centre for Alternative Technology in Machynlleth teaches people how to look after the environment and live more sustainably.

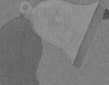

**LOST KINGDOM**
Cantre'r Gwaelod is a legendary sunken kingdom in Cardigan Bay – it is said that you can hear the bells ringing beneath the waves at Aberdyfi beach.

**FIRST WORDS**
The Cadfan Stone in Tywyn is inscribed with the earliest known Welsh writing, thought to be from the 9th century.

CEREDIGION

# NORTH-WEST WALES

## Set Your Sights On Snowdonia

There are lots of activities to try in Snowdonia. You can climb Mount Snowdon, the highest Welsh peak – or cheat and take a train to the top. There are mountain-biking and kayaking centres and huge underground caverns where you can whiz down zip lines and bounce on trampolines. Anglesey is the biggest island in Wales, and daredevils camp on the side of its cliffs! Anglesey's largest town is Holyhead, which is actually on Holy Island. There are many beaches along the beautiful Llyn Peninsular, including one that seems to whistle. Bardsey Island is just off the coast, and is a good place to see seals. See if you can spell the longest place name in Europe – it is 58 characters long!

**DENBIGHSHIRE**

### SNOWDON ADVENTURES
"Zip" across a former slate quarry at Zip World Velocity; Bounce Below at the underground trampoline park or Go Below in the underground caves.

### RIVER RACES
Plunge over rapids on the River Tryweryn with such scary names as the 'Ski Jump' and the 'Graveyard' at the National White Water Centre, near Bala.

### LARGEST LAKE
Llyn Tegid lake (Bala Lake) is the biggest natural lake in Wales and is the only place on Earth where the gwyniad, a white fish, can be found.

**DAVID LLOYD GEORGE**
**1863-1945**
Britain's only Welsh prime minister (1916-1922) grew up in Llanystumdwy and died there – the village now has a museum dedicated to him.

**LLYWELYN THE GREAT**
**C.1172-1240**
The Prince of Gwynedd is thought to have been born in Dolwyddelan and ruled most of Wales for 40 years.

**NAOMI WATTS**
**B.1968**
The actress lived in Llangefni and Llanfairpwllgwyngyll on Anglesey as a child, and went to a Welsh-language school.

**POWYS**

### PASSAGE TO PATAGONIA
In 1865, 153 colonists, left Wales for Patagonia. A pocket of the Welsh language and culture still exists there in Argentina today.

**DAWN FRENCH**
**B.1957**
The actor, writer and comedian was born in Holyhead and is best known for her sketch show *French and Saunders*, and playing Geraldine Granger in *The Vicar of Dibley*.

**PRINCE MADOC**
**C.1145-UNKNOWN**
According to folklore, the Welsh prince sailed to America in 1170, more than 300 years before Christopher Columbus's famed voyage in 1492.

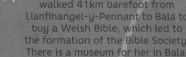

**MARY JONES**
**1784-1864**
In 1800, the 15-year-old walked 41km barefoot from Llanfihangel-y-Pennant to Bala to buy a Welsh Bible, which led to the formation of the Bible Society. There is a museum for her in Bala.

**ALED JONES**
**B.1970**
The singer was born in Bangor and grew up in Llandegfan, Anglesey – he became famous for his cover version of "Walking in the Air", the song from *The Snowman* film.

### MINI MOUNTAIN

You can ascend the Great Orme by tram or cable car – the headland is home to wild Kashmiri goats, and the site of a Bronze Age mine, a ski slope and a toboggan run.

### ALICE'S ADVENTURES

Follow the rabbit footprints along the Alice in Wonderland trail in Llandudno, where the real-life Alice Liddell spent her holidays.

### ROYAL RESORT

Llandudno is known as the Queen of the Welsh Resorts and has the world's longest-running Punch and Judy show (since 1860).

### BRILL RHYL

Rhyl has Britain's oldest miniature railway, which has been taking passengers around Marine Lake since 1911.

COLWYN BAY

IRISH SEA

### SYLVIA SLEIGH
1916-2010

The artist and feminist was born in Llandudno and emigrated to the US – she painted male nudes and founded an all-female gallery in New York.

### BAY WATCH

In Colwyn Bay, you can visit the animals at the Welsh Mountain Zoo or try all kinds of watersports at Porth Eirias.

### CASTLE COUNT

Rhuddlan Castle was built by England's King Edward I in 1277; other castles include Chirk, Hawarden, Flint, Ruthin, Castell Dinas Bran and Bodelwyddan.

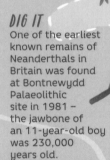

### MUSEUM TIME

More than 4kg of pearls were found in Conwy mussels every week in the 19th century – today the Mussel Museum tells the story of pearl fishing.

### HOUSE PROUD

Conwy's Quay House is the smallest house in Britain; the town also has a 14th-century merchants house, Aberconwy House.

### WALLED TOWN

You can climb Conwy Castle's eight towers and walk along the walls that enclose the town – people born within them are called Jackdaws after the birds that nest there.

### TITCHY CITY

St Asaph is one of Britain's smallest cities with one of the smallest cathedrals, which hosts the North Wales International Music Festival in September.

### INLAND SURFING

Surf Snowdonia is the world's first inland surfing lagoon. Surf the waves or tackle the Splash & Crash watery assault course.

### TERRY JONES
B.1942

The actor and writer was born in Colwyn Bay – he is a member of the Monty Python comedy troupe and has also written lots of children's books.

### TOP MAN

Sir Edmund Hillary trained on Tryfan before he and Tenzing Norgay made the first successful assent of Mount Everest in 1953.

### OUT & ABOUT

Betws-y-Coed is a village in Snowdonia and has lots of outdoor activities such as climbing, mountain biking and horse riding, plus the Conwy Valley Railway Museum.

### DIG IT

One of the earliest known remains of Neanderthals in Britain was found at Bontnewydd Palaeolithic site in 1981 – the jawbone of an 11-year-old boy was 230,000 years old.

CONWY

GWYNEDD

## Try a traditional seaside holiday!

Ever since the railway arrived on the north Wales coast in the mid-19th century, holidaymakers from Liverpool and Manchester have been flocking to its lovely seaside resorts. The Victorians called Llandudno the Queen of the Welsh Resorts, and today you can see the same Punch and Judy show that children watched 150 years ago! On rainy days you can visit the Welsh Mountain Zoo in Colwyn Bay or the SeaQuarium in Rhyl. Another coastal attraction is 13th-century Conwy Castle, a world heritage site. You'll have to head inland for an equally spectacular sight: the 1805 Pontcysyllte Aqueduct, known as the Stream in the Sky, is the oldest and longest navigable aqueduct in Britain, and the highest in the world. Take a canal boat across, and look down if you dare!

### ELEANOR BUTLER AND SARAH PONSONBY
1739-1829 AND 1755-1831

The Ladies of Llangollen were from Ireland and moved to Llangollen to live together, which caused a scandal – their house is now a museum.

### BILLY HUGHES
1862-1952

William Morris Hughes grew up in Llandudno and emigrated to Australia, where he became prime minister (1915-1923), and served in parliament for almost 52 years.

# NORTH-EAST WALES

## FALLING WATER
Take a waterfall walk to the 20m Dyserth falls or the three-tier Nant-y-Ffrith waterfall.

## ANCIENT ABBEYS
The remains of Basingwerk Abbey are in Greenfield Valley Heritage Park, which also has a museum and farm.

## PET CEMETERY
The Pet Cemetery in Holywell has peaceful gardens with memorials to much-loved pets.

## KEYS TO THE CASTLE
You can borrow a key from the library to explore Denbigh's 13th-century castle and town walls; there are free weekend guided tours.

## MOST HAUNTED
Meet ghosts, including Nora the Nun, a pack of dogs and a phantom army at the ruins of Ewloe Castle.

### FLINTSHIRE

### BUCKLEY

## MIGHTY MOLD
Theatr Clwyd in Mold is one of the top drama centres in Wales; Mold is also known for its markets and food festivals.

## READ ALL ABOUT IT
Gladstone's Library was founded in 1889 by the former prime minister and today has more than 250,000 books.

## TIMOTHY DALTON
### B.1946
The actor was born in Colwyn Bay and is best known for playing James Bond in *The Living Daylights* and *Licence to Kill*.

## IAN RUSH
### B.1961
The footballer was born in St Asaph – he is still Liverpool's leading goalscorer with 346 goals, and Wales's record goalscorer with 28 goals!

## TRAIL RUNNING
Ruthin's art trail starts at the Craft Centre and involves ten spy holes and 22 hidden figures; you can also visit the Old Gaol and the oldest timber-framed building in Wales.

## HEAD FOR THE HILLS
The Clwydian mountain range runs from Llandegla to Prestatyn – the highest point is Moel Famau (555m), which is surrounded by Iron Age hill forts.

### WREXHAM

## HISTORIC HOUSE
Erddig, a 17th-century stately home, is unusual for having lots of information about the servants who worked "below stairs", rather than just the rich Yorke family who owned it.

### DENBIGHSHIRE

## FULL STEAM AHEAD
The Llangollen Railway chugs 16km through the Dee Valley from Llangollen's Dee Bridge (built in 1345) to Corwen.

## CAROL VORDERMAN
### B.1960
The TV presenter grew up in Prestatyn and co-hosted the gameshow *Countdown* for 26 years – she has also written lots of school maths textbooks.

### WREXHAM

## LOST IN MUSIC
Llangollen is known for its festivals, including the International Musical Eisteddfod, established in 1947, and the Llangollen Fringe Festival, in July.

## COUNTING SHEEP
Search for Lady Baa Baa, Baabra and others on the Wrexham sheep trail, over 20 colourful sheep sculptures sit outside attractions in and around the town.

## SUPERNATURAL SIGHT
The Berwyn mountain range is south of Corwen – the highest peak is Cadair Berwyn (832m), the supposed site of a UFO crash in 1974.

## WORLD HERITAGE SITE
The 38m-high Pontcysyllte Aqueduct, which was designed by Thomas Telford and opened in 1805, is a world heritage site – walk or take a canal boat across.

### POWYS

### ENGLAND

# MID WALES

## Reach for the stars in the Brecon Beacons!

The Brecon Beacons National Park officially has some of the darkest skies in the UK – in 2012, it became the first International Dark Sky Reserve in Wales. Join a stargazing event or simply lie down and look up! Astronomy is just one of the activities you can try here – you can also go caving, climb a mountain (Pen y Fan and Corn Du are the highest) or scramble through waterfalls. Towns within the park include Hay-on-Wye, the best place in Britain to buy a book!
Head for the coast and you'll reach Cardigan Bay, the biggest bay in Wales, which is home to Britain's largest pod of dolphins. Watch the bottlenose dolphins and harbour porpoises from the sea wall in New Quay, or embark on a dolphin-spotting seafari!

### FRANK LLOYD WRIGHT
**1867-1959**
The US architect was born in Wisconsin but his mother, Anna Lloyd Jones, was from Llandysul – Fallingwater in Pennsylvania is one of his most famous buildings.

### ROBERT OWEN
**1771-1858**
The social reformer was born in Newtown and was a pioneer of childcare, education and the co-operative movement – you can visit his museum in Newtown.

**CARDIGAN BAY**

**IRISH SEA**

### WILDLIFE WATCH
About 300 bottlenose dolphins live in Cardigan Bay – the best place to spot them is New Quay, where you can also take boat trips and visit the Marine Wildlife Centre.

### TARON EGERTON
**B.1989**
The actor grew up in Aberystwyth and has starred in the Kingsman films, as Eddie the Eagle and as Robin Hood.

### CATRIN FINCH
**B.1980**
The musician was born in Llanon and was the Official Harpist to the Prince of Wales from 2000 to 2004, the first since John Thomas held the post in 1871.

### SECRET BEACH
Cardigan Bay's sandy beaches include hidden Mwnt; Tresaith, with rock pools and a waterfall; Penbryn, which starred in a James Bond film; and Llangrannog, for surfing.

### HORSING AROUND
Aberaeron hosts an annual Welsh Ponies and Cobs festival, devoted to four Welsh horse breeds – it includes a Welsh Mountain Pony grand national!

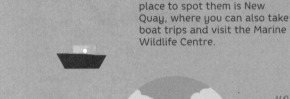

**CEREDIGION**

### TWM SIÔN CATI
**C.1530-1609**
The Welsh Robin Hood stole from the rich – but forgot to give to the poor! He was born in Tregaron and is celebrated on 17 May, and you can visit his cave hideout on Dinas Hill.

### FRANCES HOGGAN
**1843-1927**
The doctor was born in Brecon and was the first British woman to get a medical degree, plus she campaigned for equal education for women and girls.

### GEORGE MELLY
**1926-2007**
The jazz and blues singer had a country retreat called the Tower in Scethrog, near Brecon, and often performed at the Brecon jazz festival.

**PEMBROKESHIRE**

### STAR GAZING
The Brecon Beacons is the first International Dark Sky Reserve in Wales – on a clear night you can see the Milky Way, major constellations, nebulas and meteor showers.

**CARMARTHENSHIRE**

## CULTURE VULTURE
Machynlleth is home to Moma, Wales's Museum of Modern Art and the Owain Glyndwr Centre, devoted to a Welsh national hero.

## CASTLE COUNT
Powis Castle was built c.1200 and has famous gardens and a museum of Indian artefacts; other castles include Cardigan, and ruined Cilgerran.

## MIGHTY FALLS
Pistyll Rhaeadr is the highest single-drop waterfall in Wales; other falls include Sgwd Yr Eira, which means "Falling of the snow".

## BIOSPHERE RESERVE
Dyfi is the first UNESCO biosphere reserve in Wales – worldwide, others include the Amazon rainforest and Niagara Falls.

**POWYS**

WELSHPOOL

## BORDER WALK
Offa's Dyke, built by King Offa along the border of England and Wales in the 8th century, is now a 283km footpath – there is a visitor centre in Knighton.

## FULL STEAM AHEAD
The Vale of Rheidol steam railway runs from Aberystwyth to Devil's Bridge (three bridges built on top of each other).

## DESERT OF WALES
The Cambrian Mountains have been known as the Desert of Wales since the 19th century, because they are so sparsely populated.

NEWTOWN

ENGLAND

## TOP TOWN
In Aberystwyth, you can take the Cliff Railway up Constitution Hill and look at the view through a camera obscura, and visit the ruined castle and the National Library of Wales.

## MUSEUM TIME
The Judge's Lodging is a Victorian museum in Presteigne, and the Internal Fire Museum of Power in Tanygroes displays impressive engines.

## FEATHERED FRIENDS
See wild red kites at Llanddeusant and Bwlch Nant yr Arian feeding centres, and birds galore at the Ynys-hir RSPB reserve.

## PEDAL POWER
The National Cycle Museum in Llandrindod Wells has more than 260 bikes, including 19th-century hobby horses, bone shakers and penny farthings.

ABERYSTWYTH

## ON YOUR BIKE
Cycle along the shores of the Elan Valley's chain of reservoirs on the 13km Elan Valley Trail, an old railway line.

## SPORTS REPORT
Harness racing is a popular sport in Ceredigion – there are race weekends over the summer and Tregaron hosts an annual festival.

## COUNTRY LIFE
The Royal Welsh Show in Llanelwedd is one of the biggest agricultural shows in Europe, with pet shows, sheepdog trials and sheep-shearing contests.

## TOWN OF BOOKS
Hay-on-Wye has more than 20 bookshops – the annual Hay literary festival has a children's strand, Haydays, with visiting authors such as Jacqueline Wilson and Michael Morpurgo.

## ARTS & CRAFTS
Visit the Welsh Quilt Centre in Lampeter, and try chocolate-making and candle dipping at the Corris Craft Centre.

## ON YOUR MARKS
Llanwrtyd Wells, the smallest town in Wales, hosts the World Alternative Games with wacky contests such as bog snorkelling and a man versus horse race!

## ACTION STATIONS
Activities in the Brecon Beacons range from gorge walking and rafting at Black Mountain Activities to climbing and horse-riding at Llangorse Multi Activity Centre.

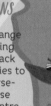

## BRECON BEACONS
The 1,340 sq km Brecon Beacons national park has four mountain ranges, caves and forests.

## WATER WORLD
Llangorse Lake is a top spot for watersports, such as kayaking and windsurfing, and has the only crannog (artificial island) in Wales.

## GOING UNDERGROUND
There are ten attractions at the National Showcaves Centre for Wales, including three caves, 200 dinosaur models, a Shire Horse Centre and an Iron-Age Farm.

## HIGH POINT
Pen y Fan is the highest peak in the Brecon Beacons at 886m – you can climb it while walking the 152km Beacons Way.

BRECON

MONMOUTHSHIRE

## FESTIVAL FEVER
Green Man is a family-friendly music festival near Crickhowell with an area for under-13s called Little Folk, and an adventure zone for teenagers.

NEATH PORT TALBOT

YSTRADGYNLAIS

RHONDDA CYNON TAF

MERTHYR TYDFIL

CAERPHILLY

BLAENAU GWENT

91

# PEMBROKESHI

## Welcome to the coast with the most!

The spectacular coastline of Pembrokeshire, in south-west Wales, is Britain's only coastal national park. You can walk the 300km Coast Path, stopping at some of the 50 beaches. Tiny St Davids is the only city – with population of 2,000, it is smaller than the village of Saundersfoot (population 2,500). Haverfordwest is the county town, and Tenby is one of the main seaside resorts. There are several small islands, including Skomer, where you can see puffins, and Grassholm, which is covered in bird poo! If you're lucky, you will spot whales and dolphins off the coast. You'd better practise your Welsh if you cross the Landsker Line – in the south, most people speak English, but north Pembrokeshire is mainly Welsh-speaking.

### MIGRATION WATCH
Strumble Head is one of the best places in Wales to see migrating seabirds such as skuas, petrels, terns, gulls and shearwaters.

### OFF TO IRELAND
Ferries to Rosslare in Ireland set sail from Fishguard Harbour in Goodwick.

MERCHED CYMREIG YN YMDEITHO O AMGYLCH Y [...]

THE MYTH

WELSH WOMEN MARCH AROUND THE BIG [...]

### BLACK BEACH
Abereiddy has a black sand beach that is full of tiny fossils, and a Blue Lagoon where you can practise coasteering.

### LAST INVASION
A 30-m tapestry in Fishguard Town Hall tells the story of the last invasion of mainland Britain in 1797; it took 70 women two years to make.

### LAND AHOY
Alfred Johnson landed at Abercastle harbour in 1876 after 57 days at sea; he was the first person to cross the Atlantic singlehanded, from west to east.

**PEMBROKESHIRE**

### WALK THIS WAY
The 300-km Pembrokeshire Coast Path takes 12 or more days to walk; the ascents and descents are the equivalent of climbing Mount Everest: 9,000 metres!

### HAVERFORDWEST

### RAMSEY ISLAND
The island's cliffs house birds of prey and nesting seabirds, while seal pups are born on the beaches.

### BISHOP'S PALACES
In Lamphey and St Davids, what look like ruined castles are actually the remains of Bishop's Palaces.

### QUEEN'S CORGIS
Queen Elizabeth II's favourite dog is the Pembroke Welsh corgi, a cattle-herding breed; she has owned more than 30!

### HENRY TUDOR
**1457-1509**
King Henry VII was born at Pembroke Castle and ruled England from 1485 after defeating Richard III at the Battle of Bosworth Field in the War of the Roses.

**ST BRIDES BAY**

### DEEP BLUE SEA
Milford Haven has one of the deepest natural harbours in the world, which has been used by everyone from Vikings to whalers.

### WHALE WATCHING
On a boat trip to the Celtic Deep, you can see whales, sharks, dolphins and porpoises.

### SKOMER ISLAND
Famous for its puffins, Manx shearwaters and the Skomer vole – you can stay overnight and witness the noisy shearwaters returning to their burrows in the dark.

### LOCK IN
The Old Point House Inn in Angle is so close to the sea, drinkers can be cut off by the spring tide.

**MILFORD HAVEN**

**PEMBROKE DOCK**

### GWEN AND AUGUSTUS JOHN
**1876-1939 AND 1878-1961**
These artist siblings are most famous for their portraits; Gwen was born in Haverfordwest and Augustus in Tenby.

### GRASSHOLM ISLAND
This island looks white from a distance because it is covered with 39,000 breeding pairs of gannets... and their guano (poo)!

**CELTIC SEA**

### AIM HIGH
Bosherton is a mecca for rock climbers, with 1,000 routes in the surrounding limestone cliffs, including the legendary Huntsman's Leap.

### SKOKHOLM ISLAND
Britain's first bird observatory was founded here in 1933; today only 26 people are allowed on the island at a time to make room for the birds.

### EXPERIENCED SURFERS ONLY
Freshwater West beach has some of the biggest and best surf in Wales.

# RE

CEREDIGION

## ON YOUR BIKE
Pembrokeshire has some great traffic-free cycle routes along disused railway lines, including Cardi Bach, the Tramway and the Brunel Cycleway.

## ROCK ON
Go rockpooling at Cwm yr Eglwys, in the Pembrokeshire Coast National Park, and climb over rocks at the west end to find a secret beach, only revealed at low tide.

## GENTLE GIANTS
At the Dyfed Shire Horse Farm in Eglwyswrw – pronounced "egg-lis-oo-roo" – you can meet the huge horses and have a ride.

## BOAT RACE
Coracles are small boats that look like half a walnut shell – race one on the River Teifi near Cilgerran and visit the Coracle Museum at Cenarth Falls.

## BOUNCING BOMB
A tunnel outside Maenclochog was used to test Barnes Wallis's bouncing bomb during the Second World War.

## BLEEDING TREE
There is a 700-year-old 'bleeding' yew tree in Nevern churchyard – some people say it will bleed until there is world peace.

## SPECIAL SPUDS
Pembrokeshire early potatos have protected status: they must be planted in February and harvested by July, and they can't be grown anywhere else in the world.

## OLD NEW YEAR
Pontfaen and Llanychaer still celebrate New Year, or Hen Galan, on 13 January, according to the old Julian calendar, which was abolished in 1752.

## TIME TRAVEL
Castell Henllys is a reconstructed Iron Age village where you can live like a Celtic warrior.

### SARAH WATERS
### B.1966
The novelist was born in Neyland and is best known for her books set in Victorian times.

## HOT STUFF
The eco-friendly Blue Lagoon Water Park near Canaston Bridge is thought to be the first water park to be heated by biomass.

## PARK AND RIDE
Oakwood Theme Park in Canaston Bridge has more than 30 rides including scary rollercoasters and a Neverland area.

CARMARTHENSHIRE

Welcome to Wales
Croeso i Gymru

### RHYS IFANS
### B.1967
Born in Haverfordwest, he has appeared in films including *The Amazing Spider-Man*, and *Harry Potter and the Deathly Hallows*.

### CHRISTIAN BALE
### B.1974
The actor from Haverfordwest starred as Batman in *Batman Begins*, *The Dark Knight* and *The Dark Knight Rises*.

## WATERWORLD
Four rivers meet at the Daugleddau estuary – the Western and Eastern Cleddau, Carew and Cresswell. Explore the hidden creeks by kayak.

## SHOPPING CENTRE
The market town of Narberth is one of the best places for souvenir shopping – you can buy Pembrokeshire pottery, paintings and sculpture.

## LANGUAGE BARRIER
The Landsker Line divides Pembrokeshire into English and Welsh speakers; the south of the county is English-speaking.

## DROWNED FOREST
There is a submerged forest at Amroth beach – tree stumps dating back to the last ice age poke through the sand when the tide is very low.

## FUN AND GAMES
Head to St Florence and take in Manor House Wildlife Park, Heatherton Activity Park and Tenby Dinosaur Park.

## LIFE SAVERS
There are six RNLI lifeboat stations along the coast, the earliest of which was set up in 1822. Watch the boats being launched at Tenby.

RNLI

EMBROKE

TENBY

## AN ABUNDANCE OF BEACHES
Pembrokeshire has more than 50 beaches – Barafundle Bay is one of the best.

## CALDEY ISLAND
An order of Cistercian monks live here, farming and making chocolate and perfume to sell to visitors.

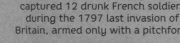

### JEMIMA NICHOLAS
### 1750-1832
A cobbler from Mathry who captured 12 drunk French soldiers during the 1797 last invasion of Britain, armed only with a pitchfork.

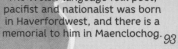

### WALDO WILLIAMS
### 1904-1971
The Welsh-language folk poet, pacifist and nationalist was born in Haverfordwest, and there is a memorial to him in Maenclochog.

## Swan around Swansea and the Gower Peninsula!

Swansea, the second city of Wales, is the birthplace of the country's most famous poet, Dylan Thomas. He is celebrated at the Dylan Thomas Centre in the city and the Boathouse in Laugharne. As well as being great for a city break, Swansea guards the entrance to the Gower Peninsula. This stunning area of cliffs and beaches was the very first place in Britain to be designated an Area of Outstanding Natural Beauty in 1956 (there are now 46 AONBs). After sunbathing and surfing here, call in at the old fishing village of Mumbles for a scrumptious ice-cream. But Swansea is only the tip of the iceberg – this area also boasts Carmarthen, reputedly the oldest town in Wales, and the dramatic Vale of Neath, which is teeming with waterfalls.

**CEREDIGION**

### MARVELLOUS MUSEUMS
West Wales Museum of Childhood is full of toys; Kidwelly Industrial Museum is devoted to the tinplate industry; Swansea Museum is the oldest museum in Wales.

### GOING FOR GOLD
The Dolaucothi Gold Mines are the only known Roman gold mines in Britain – you can take an underground tour and try panning for gold.

### HISTORY LESSON
The Rebecca Riots were protests by poor farmers in rural Wales between 1839 and 1843 – men dressed as women attacked toll gates, such as the 12 gates surrounding Carmarthen.

**PEMBROKESHIRE**

### SPIN A YARN
The National Wool Museum tells the story of what was once Wales's most important industry – you can have a go a spinning, carding and sewing.

### GARDENERS' WORLD
The National Botanic Garden of Wales has the world's biggest glasshouse, filled with endangered plants; other garden attractions include Plantasia and Aberglasney House.

### DYLAN THOMAS
**1914-1953**
The poet was born in Swansea and is buried in Laugharne; he is best known for his poem "Do Not Go Gentle Into That Good Night", and his radio play *Under Milk Wood*.

### OLDEST TOWN
Carmarthen claims to be the oldest town in Wales – it was known by the Romans as Moridunum and has a Roman amphitheatre, plus a ruined medieval castle.

**CARMARTHEN**

**CARMARTHENSHIRE**

### LITERARY LEGEND
Wales's most famous poet is celebrated at the Dylan Thomas Boathouse in Laugharne, and at the Dylan Thomas Centre, his birthplace and a festival in Swansea.

### ADVENTURE PLAYGROUNDS
Pembrey Country Park has a sandy beach, a dry ski slope and a toboggan run; Margam Country Park has an adventure centre as well as a castle and deer park.

### PARK LIFE
The coastline along the Loughor estuary has been turned into the Millennium Coastal Park with nature reserves, cycle paths and beaches such as Llanelli.

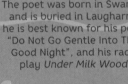

### DRIVE TIME
The Pendine Museum of Speed exhibits Babs, the car that broke the land speed record in 1926; the Swansea Bus Museum has a fleet of vintage vehicles.

### FIRST FLIGHT
Amelia Earhart, the first woman to fly across the Atlantic, landed at Burry Port in 1928 – a plaque in the harbour marks the spot.

**LLANELLI**

### BACK TO NATURE
At Llanelli Wetland Centre you can hand-feed geese and ducks, visit the flamingos, and go bug hunting or pond dipping.

### RUSSELL T DAVIES
**B.1963**
The screenwriter and TV producer from Swansea revived *Doctor Who* in 2005 – it is still going strong today, now with a female Doctor played by Jodie Whittaker.

### SURFS UP
Llangennith Beach is a popular surfing spot, as is Langland Bay, Caswell Bay and Aberavon Beach.

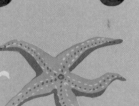

### BEAUTY SPOT
The Gower Peninsula became Britain's first Area of Outstanding Natural Beauty in 1956 – it is famous for its beaches, cliffs, caves and wild moors.

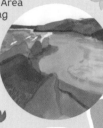

### CHAMPION SANDS
Rhossili Bay has been named the best beach in Europe; Bracelet Bay is great for rockpooling; other safe sandcastle spots include Oxwich Bay and Horton.

**ATLANTIC OCEAN**

**BRISTOL CHANN**

# SOUTH WALES

## LOCAL FOOD
This area is a good place to buy local delicacies such as Penclawdd cockles, laverbread (boiled seaweed), salt marsh lamb and Welsh black beef.

## HAUNTED HOUSE
Newton House in the grounds of Dinefwr Park is said to be one of the most haunted houses in Britain, with ghosts including Walter the Butler and Lady Elinor Cavendish.

## SEASON'S GREETINGS
There is a tiny village called Bethlehem in Carmarthenshire – people post Christmas cards from there so they have the postmark of Jesus's birthplace.

BETHLEHEM
WALES

## HIGH POINT
The Black Mountain is a mountain range on the border of Carmarthenshire and Powys – the highest peak is Fan Brycheiniog (802m).

POWYS

## CATHERINE ZETA-JONES
### B.1969
The actor was born in Swansea and appeared on TV in *The Darling Buds of May* before moving to Los Angeles and starring in films such as the musical *Chicago*.

## DISAPPEARING ACT
The Carmel National Nature Reserve contains the only known "turlough" in Britain: a seasonal lake that disappears every summer.

## CASTLE COUNT
The 13th-century Carreg Cennen Castle is in a spectacular spot on a hilltop; other castles include Kidwelly, Laugharne, Llansteffan and Newcastle Emlyn.

## MARY WYNNE WARNER
### 1932-1998
The mathematician was born in Carmarthen and was a pioneer in the field of fuzzy mathematics.

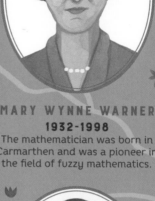

## ANCIENT MONUMENTS
Garn Goch is one of the biggest Iron Age hill forts in Wales; ruined 12th-century Talley Abbey is the only Welsh monastery of the Premonstratensians (or White Canons).

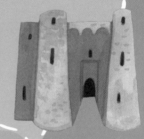

## BONNIE TYLER
### B.1951
The singer was born in Skewen – her songs include "It's a Heartache" and "Total Eclipse of the Heart", and she represented the UK at the Eurovision Song Contest in 2013.

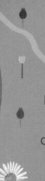

## SWANSEA

## COPPEROPOLIS
Swansea, the second-biggest city in Wales, was the centre of the copper industry in the 19th century.

## WATERFALL COUNTRY
The Vale of Neath is known as waterfall country because of its many falls, including Aberdulais, Pontneddfechan and Melincourt.

RHONDDA CYNON TAF

## ON YOUR BIKE
Afan Forest Park is a mountain-biking mecca with more than 100km of trails, plus a bike park; Brechfa Forest is another good mountain-biking site.

## DOROTHEA BATE
### 1878-1951
The palaeontologist was born in Carmarthen and discovered many extinct Mediterranean island species, such as a dwarf elephants and a mouse-goat.

NEATH
PORT TALBOT

NEATH

## ART ATTACK
The Glynn Vivian Art Gallery is Swansea's main art gallery, and runs workshops for families on Saturdays.

## DOG STAR
Swansea Jack (1930-37) was a black retriever who rescued 27 drowning people in Swansea over his lifetime.

## ANTHONY HOPKINS
### B.1937
The actor was born in Port Talbot – his most famous role is Hannibal Lecter in *The Silence of the Lambs*, for which he won an Oscar.

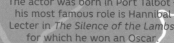

SWANSEA

PORT TALBOT

## ON THE WATERFRONT
The National Waterfront Museum is an industrial and maritime museum, and displays objects such as Corgi toys and Spectrum computers.

BRIDGEND

## BY THE SEASIDE
Mumbles, the gateway to the Gower Peninsula, has sights including Oystermouth Castle, a lighthouse from 1794, a Victorian pier and scrumptious ice-cream parlours.

## SHIRLEY BASSEY
### B.1937
The singer was born in the Tiger Bay area of Cardiff – she was the first Welsh person to have a No. 1 single, in 1959, and sang the theme songs to three James Bond films.

CITY CENTRE

### SEE THE SIGHTS
Explore the Centenary Walk's 41 landmarks and historic sites, including Animal Wall (with 15 animal sculptures) and a statue of Aneurin "Nye" Bevan.

### WIZARD WARES
Find Bertie Bott's Every Flavour Beans in the Room of Requirement, a Harry Potter-themed shop, at Castle Arcade!

### SET IN STONE
Cathays Park contains some of the grandest buildings in the city, including the City Hall, Crown Court, Glamorgan Building and Temple of Peace.

### TOILET TALK
The Wales Millennium Centre is one of the country's top arts complexes, showing musicals, dance, comedy and opera – and it often wins the Loo of the Year award!

CREU GWIR IN THESE STONES FEL GWYDR HORIZONS O FLWRNAIS AWEN SING

## RHONDDA CYNON TAF

### TAFF'S WELL FFYNNON TAF

### SPRING TIME
Taff's Well has the only thermal spring in Wales – the average temperature of the water in 21.6°C, compared with 11.3°C for groundwater in the rest of the country.

MORGANSTOWN

RADYR

### MODERN CASTLE
Castell Coch in Tongwynlais was built in the 19th century on the orders of John Crichton-Stuart, who was reportedly the richest man in the world.

PENTYRCH

Taff Trail

### ON YOUR BIKE
The Taff Trail is an 89km cycle route along the River Taff from Cardiff to Brecon – you can hire bikes at the Cardiff caravan and camping park.

## COLIN JACKSON
### B.1967
The athlete held the world record for the 110m hurdles for more than a decade – his record for the 60m hurdles, set in 1994, still stands today.

## TANNI GREY-THOMPSON
### B.1969
The former wheelchair racer is one of Britain's most successful disabled athletes, winning 16 Paralympic medals; she is now a peer in the House of Lords.

### LIVING HISTORY
St Fagans National Museum of History is an open-air museum in the grounds of a castle, with over 40 historical buildings, a farm and crafts such as Welsh clog-making.

### HOLY SITES
The Bishop's Palace, Llandaff, is a ruined medieval residence close to Llandaff Cathedra

CARDIFF

### ANCIENT CASTLE
Cardiff Castle was built in the late 11th century – today you can tour the underground tunnels, climb the Clock Tower and visit the Firing Line Museum about Welsh soldiers.

VALE OF GLAMORGAN

## Wander along the waterfront of the Welsh capital

Cardiff is the UK's youngest capital city. In 1801, it was only the 25th biggest town in Wales. It grew rapidly as a coal port from the 1830s and soon became the biggest Welsh town, and by 1905 it was officially a city. Finally, in 1955, it was named the capital of Wales. Today, it has all the hallmarks of a capital, from the parliament building to the national museum and sports stadium. One of the most exciting areas is the waterfront, Cardiff Bay – see if you can spot the connection to Roald Dahl!
From Cardiff, you can walk to the seaside at Penarth or take a boat to Flat Holm island. That's as far south as you can go and still be in Wales!

## RUTH HUNT
### B.1980
The charity worker is the CEO of Stonewall, the biggest LGBT rights organisation in Europe.

## CHARLOTTE CHURCH
### B.1986
The singer was born in Llandaff – she became a classical music star at the age of 11 before branching out into pop and TV presenting.

### WATER WORLD
Go white water rafting and kayaking at the Cardiff International Sports Village, which also has an ice rink and an Olympic-sized swimming pool.

LISVANE

## GARETH BALE
**B.1989**
The footballer plays for Real Madrid and Wales – he is currently the country's second-highest goalscorer of all time, after Ian Rush.

## ROALD DAHL
**1916-1990**
The writer was born in the Llandaff area of Cardiff – his books, including *Matilda*, *The BFG* and *Charlie and the Chocolate Factory*, have sold more than 250 million copies.

### ANIMAL MAGIC
At Cefn Mably Farm Park, you can hold the small animals, feed the bigger ones and ride on ponies, go-karts and diggers.

OLD ST MELLONS

NEWPORT

### LOCAL FOOD
Visit the city's farmers' markets and buy traditional food such as laverbread and Welsh cakes.

### FESTIVAL FEVER
The Children's Literature Festival runs over two weekends in spring and celebrates authors and illustrators with storytelling, performances and writing workshops.

### MULTICULTURAL CITY
Cardiff has one of the longest-standing Muslim populations in the UK, started by Yemeni sailors in the 19th century arriving at the city's port.

### VINTAGE VINYL
Spillers Records is the oldest record shop in the world – it opened in Queens Arcade in 1894, and can now be found on Morgan Arcade.

### MUSEUM TIME
Exhibits at the National Museum Cardiff include the world's biggest leatherback turtle and a humpback whale skeleton; the National Museum of Art is in the same building.

### PARK LIFE
Bute Park is one of the biggest urban parks in Wales, with an arboretum containing more than 3,000 trees.

### SPORTS REPORT
Welsh sport might be most associated with its national rugby team – and its supporters, whose rousing rendition of the National Anthem can be heard around the city on match day!

BRISTOL CHANNEL

Yr Hen Lyfrgell

### STORY TIME
Learn to speak Welsh at Yr Hen Lyfrgell (the Old Library) and visit the Cardiff Story museum.

### CULTURE VULTURE
St David's Hall hosts the Welsh Proms, while the New Theatre has been putting on shows since 1906.

**THE DOCKS**

### SCIENCE LESSON
Techniquest is a science centre with 120 hands-on exhibits plus a planetarium, laboratory and theatre.

### BABY BIG BEN
The clock on the terracotta Pierhead Building is known as Baby Big Ben – the building now houses a museum of Welsh history.

### CAPITAL CITY
Cardiff is the capital of Wales and the country's laws are debated at the Senedd, the Welsh Assembly building.

### BIG BUCKS
The first ever million-pound deal was done at the Coal Exchange in 1904 – today the building is a hotel.

### DESERT ISLAND
You can take a boat from Cardiff Bay to Flat Holm island, the southernmost part of Wales, which has an 18th-century lighthouse.

### SCANDI SPIRES
Roald Dahl was baptised in the Norwegian Church, which was built in 1868 for visiting sailors – Roald Dahl day is celebrated in September and Norwegian Day on 17 May.

### TIME LORD
*Doctor Who* is produced at the Roath Lock TV studios, and you can go on a guided walking tour.

### BY THE SEASIDE
Penarth, a seaside resort, has run a summer festival since 1965, with a Downhill Derby race and a carnival.

# CARDIFF

# THE VALLEYS

## Head for the heart and soul of Wales

The South Wales Valleys are the cradle of Welsh culture, with lots of native speakers, rugby union teams and male voice choirs. The landscape, too, is distinctive: mountainous terrain with towns and villages built in the narrow channels between the peaks. The Valleys were once a centre of the coal mining industry – visit the Big Pit museum at Blaenavon, go on a guided mine tour at Rhondda Heritage Park and meet Sultan the Pit Pony at Penallta Colliery.

You'll find Caerphilly at the southern end of the Rymney Valley. This town has two claims to fame: the biggest castle in Wales and the tastiest cheese! They come together at the Big Cheese festival, where competitors race around the castle carrying a truckle of Caerphilly. The losers get really cheesed off …

**ANEURIN BEVAN**
**1897-1960**
Nye Bevan was born in Tredegar and was MP for Ebbw Vale for 31 years – he was the chief architect of the National Health Service and is still considered a Welsh hero.

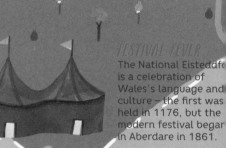

POWYS

**FESTIVAL FEVER**
The National Eisteddfod is a celebration of Wales's language and culture – the first was held in 1176, but the modern festival began in Aberdare in 1861.

**SING ALONG**
South Wales has a tradition of male voice choirs – two of the best-known are from Treorchy and Aberdare.

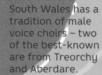

NEATH PORT TALBOT

BRIDGEND

**ON YOUR BIKE**
BikePark Wales in Gethin Woods is probably the best mountain biking park in the UK – its "uplift" takes you to the summit, so you can focus on coming dow[n]

**W.H. DAVIES**
**1871-1940**
The poet was born in Newport and spent part of his life as a tramp in the United States – his best-known couplet is, "What is this life if, full of care / We have no time to stand and stare".

**RUTH JONES**
**B.1966**
The actor and writer was born in Bridgend – she co-wrote and starred in the TV series *Gavin & Stacey* and *Stella*, both set in south Wales.

**BACK TO NATURE**
Kenfig National Nature Reserve is an important wildlife habitat of sand dunes and a lake, where you can see rare fen orchid flowers.

**FOLK CUSTOM**
The Mari Lwyd is a spooky New Year tradition where townsfolk follow a man holding a horse's skull on a pole – it is still celebrated in Llangynwyd.

RHONDDA CYNON TAF

**FIREMAN SAM**
Fireman Sam lives in the fictional Welsh village of Pontypandy – his home is a blend of two real towns, Pontypridd and Tonypandy, which are about 8km apart.

**VALLEYWOOD**
The Dragon International Film Studios in Llanharan are nicknamed Valleywood after the more famous studios in Hollywood.

BRIDGEND

VALLEYWOOD

**LOADSA MONEY**
The Royal Mint, where all UK coins are made, is in Llantrisant – you can visit the Royal Mint Experience and strike your own coin to take home.

**TOM JONES**
**B.1940**
The singer was born in Treforest, Pontypridd – his big hits include "Delilah" and "It's Not Unusual", and he is now a coach on the talent show The Voice.

**ANNEKA RICE**
**B.1958**
The presenter was born in Cowbridge – she is best known for the TV show Challenge Anneka, and now presents a show on BBC Radio 2.

**BUCKETS & SPADES**
Porthcawl is a seaside resort with seven beaches and a pleasure park – it also hosts the biggest Elvis Presley festival in Europe, when thousands of fans pay tribute to the King!

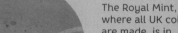

**VALE OF GLAMORGAN**

## LAURA ASHLEY
### 1925-1985
The designer was born in Dowlais, Merthyr Tydfil – she made home furnishings and clothes inspired by the countryside.

**ENGLAND**

## CASTLE COUNT
Follow the 31km Three Castles Walk to Skenfrith, Grosmont and Whitecastle; other mighty castles include Raglan, Cyfarthfa, St Donat's, Caldicot and Usk.

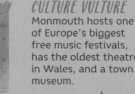

## SPORTS REPORT
Rugby union is Wales's national sport and is most strongly associated with the Valleys; Newport Gwent Dragons are one of the four top teams.

## TASTE OF WALES
Abergavenny, known as the Gateway to Wales, holds the country's biggest food festival, with kids' cooking classes, a farmyard and a Young Chef of the Year contest.

## CULTURE VULTURE
Monmouth hosts one of Europe's biggest free music festivals, has the oldest theatre in Wales, and a town museum.

**MERTHYR TYDFIL**

**MERTHYR TYDFIL**

**BLAENAU GWENT**

**MONMOUTHSHIRE**

**TORFAEN**

## PIT STOP
Iron and coal were huge industries in the Valleys: Blaenavon is now a world heritage site, home to the Big Pit National Coal Museum, and the Rhondda Heritage Park has guided mine tours.

## PIT PONY
Former Penallta Colliery is now a park – you can't miss Sultan the Pit Pony, a 200m-long earth sculpture by artist Mick Petts.

## ROMAN WALES
Caerleon was one of the most important military sites in Roman Britain – today you can visit the National Roman Legion Museum, plus the amphitheatre, baths and barracks.

## ROMANTIC RUINS
Tintern Abbey was the first Cistercian monastery in Wales (founded 1131) and today is a beautiful ruin, painted by J.M.W. Turner and immortalised in poetry by William Wordsworth.

**CAERPHILLY**

**CWMBRAN**

## KING OF THE CASTLE
Caerphilly Castle, built c.1268, is the biggest in Wales, and the second biggest in the UK after Windsor – it has a leaning tower, perhaps a result of past attacks.

## SECRET GARDEN
Dewstow Gardens were buried for over 50 years, then rediscovered in 2000 – today they are a labyrinth of underground grottoes, tunnels, ponds and sunken ferneries.

## HISTORY & HORSES
Chepstow's racecourse hosts the Welsh Grand National, has the oldest stone castle in Britain (built 1067), a 13th-century Port Wall and 16th-century Town Gate.

## LOCAL FOOD
White, crumbly Caerphilly is celebrated at the town's Big Cheese festival, and can be used in two classic dishes: Welsh rarebit (cheese on toast) and Glamorgan sausages (cheese and leek veggie sausages).

**NEWPORT**

**NEWPORT**

## MAKE A SPLASH
Pontypridd is home to the national lido of Wales – Lido Ponty was built in 1927 and reopened in 2015 with a main pool, an activity pool and a splash pool.

**BRISTOL CHANNEL**

## BUILDING BRIDGES
Newport, the third-biggest city in Wales, has one of only three surviving transporter bridges in the UK – you can climb the 74m-high towers and walk across the upper deck.

**CARDIFF**

## FUN & GAMES
Barry found fame in the sitcom *Gavin and Stacey* – Barry Island, now a peninsular rather than an island, has a beach and a Pleasure Park.

## VILLAGE LIFE
Cosmeston Medieval Village recreates life for Welsh peasants in the year 1350 – you might meet the swineherd, the reeve, the apothecary or the priest.

**BARRY**

## KING HENRY V
### 1386-1422
Henry of Monmouth was born in Monmouth Castle and ruled England from 1413 until his death – he famously won the Battle of Agincourt in 1415.

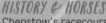

# NORTHERN IRELAND

## Walk in the footsteps of giants!

Northern Ireland is the smallest part of the UK, and the newest – it was created in 1921. Decades of conflict followed, which erupted into violence known as the Troubles, but since the peace process of the 1990s, including the Good Friday Agreement in 1998, it has become a safe and welcoming place to visit. Come here, and you'll be wowed by the lakes, mountains and glens and the cities of Belfast, Derry and Armagh; perhaps most impressive, though, is the spectacular scenery of the Causeway Coast, which legend says was hewn by giants. The nation isn't short on literary giants, either: Seamus Heaney and C.S. Lewis are just two of the writers who loom large on the nation's cultural heritage. Many people come for the "craic", a special Irish form of fun, which you'll find here in abundance, especially on St. Patrick's Day!

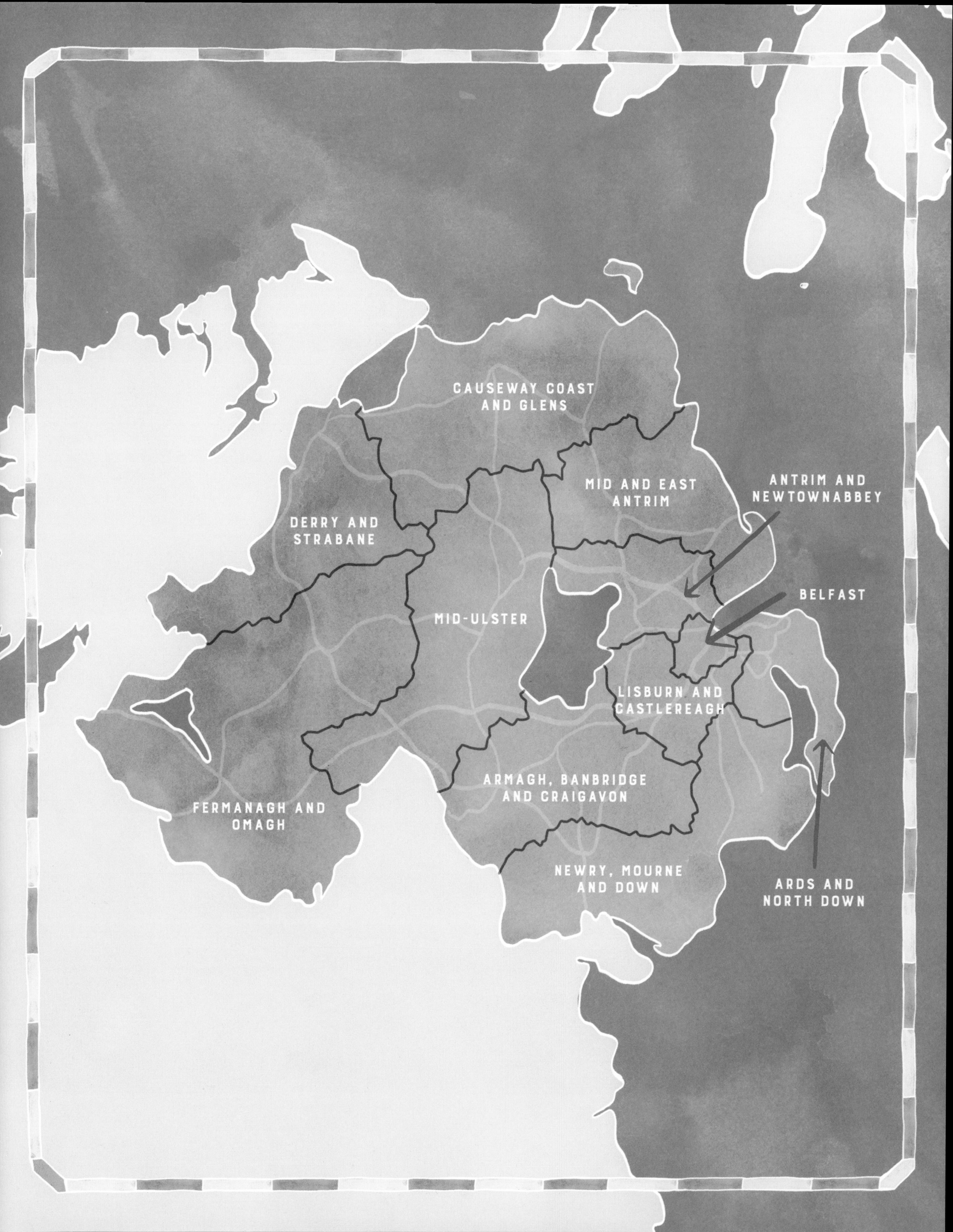
CAUSEWAY COAST AND GLENS
MID AND EAST ANTRIM
ANTRIM AND NEWTOWNABBEY
DERRY AND STRABANE
BELFAST
MID-ULSTER
LISBURN AND CASTLEREAGH
ARMAGH, BANBRIDGE AND CRAIGAVON
FERMANAGH AND OMAGH
NEWRY, MOURNE AND DOWN
ARDS AND NORTH DOWN

**SEAMUS HEANEY**
**1939-2013**
The poet and Nobel laureate was born near Castledawson and grew up in Bellaghy – find out about his life at the Heaney HomePlace museum.

*FLYING HIGH*
The 18th-century Mussenden Temple is perched on a clifftop above the Atlantic Ocean – there is a kite festival at this dramatic location in August.

*BIRD WATCHING*
Lough Foyle is a wetland and RSPB nature reserve – its mudflats and salt marshes teem with thousands of migrating birds.

*BEAUTIFUL BEACHES*
Pack your bucket and spade for Benone beach, one of Ireland's longest, plus the sandy beaches of Portstewart Strand, Downhill, Ballycastle and Castlerock.

*HOME VISIT*
Downhill Demesne is a ruined 18th-century mansion, and neighbouring Hezlett House is a thatched cottage and one of the oldest buildings in Northern Ireland (built 1690).

*GET ACTIVE*
You can fly a hovercraft at Foylehov Activity Centre and try other adrenalin sports at The Jungle NI and Carrowmena Activity Centre.

**DERRY AND STRABANE**

*LOOKOUT POINT*
Climb Binevenagh Mountain to Gortmore Viewpoint to see a sculpture of a Celtic sea god and views all the way to the islands of Islay and Jura in Scotland.

**KATIE MELUA**
**B.1984**
The singer was born in Georgia and moved to Belfast when she was eight – she holds the world record for the deepest underwater concert, 303m below sea level!

**MARY PETERS**
**B.1939**
The athlete grew up in Ballymena and now lives in Lisburn – she won a gold medal at the 1972 Olympics, in the pentathlon.

**C.S. LEWIS**
**1898-1963**
The writer was born in Belfast and is best known for The Chronicles of Narnia – there is a statue of him outside Holywood Arches Library in east Belfast.

**CAUSEWAY COAST AND GLENS**

*DUNGIVEN CASTLE PARK*
Behind the castle lies a woodland and wetland habitat open to explore; look out for dragonflies, birds and the native speckled wood butterfly.

## Have a big adventure in the land of giants

Belfast is the capital of Northern Ireland – and the birthplace of RMS Titanic! At Titanic Belfast, you can witness the doomed ocean liner's construction, maiden voyage and sinking in 1912, when more than 1,500 people died. Pay your respects at the Titanic Memorial, and spend a night in the Titanic Hotel. You can also climb aboard HMS Caroline and SS Nomadic, Titanic-era ships that are now museums.

But Titanic isn't the only gigantic attraction in these parts – the Giant's Causeway on the north coast is a legendary landscape, said to have been built by giant Finn McCool, and is Northern Ireland's only World Heritage Site. Clamber over the hexagonal stone columns to the Giant's Boot (size 93.5!) and find his Camel, then make a wish in the Wishing Chair.

**LIAM NEESON**
**B.1952**
The actor was born in Ballymena and has starred in films including Star Wars and Batman, and voiced Aslan in the Narnia films.

**MARY MCALEESE**
**B.1951**
The politician was born in Ardoyne, north Belfast, and was president of Ireland from 1997-2001 – she was the first president from Northern Ireland.

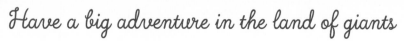

**MID-ULSTER**

# BELFAST AND THE NORTH-EASTERN DISTRICTS

## WHISKEY GALORE

Old Bushmills Distillery has been making whiskey since 1608 – from here you can ride the heritage Bushmills Railway to the Giant's Causeway.

## A BRIDGE TOO FAR

The Carrick-a-Rede rope bridge was first built in 1755 – it is 20m long and 30m high, and so scary that lots of people can't face the return crossing and have to be rescued by boat!

## ISLAND ESCAPE

Get a ferry from Ballycastle to Rathlin Island, the northernmost point of Northern Ireland, where you can see puffins and an upside-down lighthouse.

## GIANT STEPS

The Giant's Causeway's 40,000 basalt columns form stepping stones into the sea. Said to be built by a giant, it is really the result of a volcanic eruption.

## GO OUTDOORS

Fair Head is one of the best spots for rock-climbing and Whiterocks Beach is great for surfing.

## COLERAINE

## FOOTBALL FACT

SuperCupNI is one of the world's best international youth football tournaments. Founded in 1983, Wayne Rooney played in it in 2000.

## MIND THE COWPATS

You can sunbathe with cows at White Park Bay – cattle roam freely on the dunes and often lie down on the sand for a rest.

## FAIR PLAY

Auld Lammas Fair has been held in Ballycastle every August for 300 years – it is the best place to try dulse, a seaweed snack, and yellowman, a kind of honeycomb.

## FIRST HUMANS

Mountsandel Fort is the site of the oldest human settlement in Ireland, dating to between 7600 and 7900 BC – 5,000 years older than the Egyptian Pyramids!

## HOLY HILL

Climb Slemish Mountain, the first-known Irish home of St Patrick, for views of the Glens of Antrim and the Causeway Coast.

**GEORGE BEST**
**1946–2005**
The footballer from Cregagh played for Manchester United and Northern Ireland. He was one of the first celebrity footballers and considered one of the best players of all time.

## GAME OF THRONES

There are over 25 Game of Thrones filming locations to visit in Northern Ireland, plus GoT-themed sea safaris and helicopter tours.

## GALGORM CASTLE FAIRY TRAIL

Ever wondered where the Tooth Fairy lives? Take a tour of the miniature fairy village in the magical setting of Galgorm Castle.

## THE GLENS

The nine Glens of Antrim are an area of outstanding natural beauty – the Heart of the Glens festival takes place in Cushendall in August.

## BALLYMENA

**MID AND EAST ANTRIM**

## BIG BREAKFAST

The Ulster fry includes soda bread and potato farls alongside bacon, sausages, egg and tomato.

## THE PEOPLE'S PARK BALLYMENA

Visit this popular park to explore its pavilion, playground and pond. In the summer, its Art in the Park means there are even more surprises to discover!

## CASTLE COUNT

Medieval structures here include Glenarm and the ruins of Dunluce, Olderfleet and Shane's. Carrickfergus Castle is one of the best.

## PRESIDENTIAL PAST

Andrew Jackson Cottage is the ancestral home of the seventh US president, while the US Rangers Centre tells the story of the Americans in Carrickfergus during the Second World War.

## CARRICKFERGUS

## CITY CENTRE

## DAYS OUT

Attractions in Belfast include the Ulster Museum, Belfast Zoo, Crumlin Road Gaol, the W5 science centre and Linen Hall library.

## GARDEN PARTY

Destroyed by fire in 1922, Antrim Castle's beautiful 400-year-old gardens have been brought back to life.

## NEWTOWNABBEY

## GAELIC GAMES

Gaelic games comprise football, hurling, handball and rounders for men, and camogie and football for women.

## IRISH SEA

**ANTRIM AND NEWTOWNABBEY**

## TITANIC QUARTER

Titanic Belfast tells the story of the world's most famous ship, which was built in Belfast. You can also climb aboard the SS Nomadic and HMS Caroline.

## CLEMENTSMOUNT FUN FARM

Take a tour with Mia the cat and meet native farm breeds at this hands-on family farm – milk a cow the traditional way and feed the lambs yourself!

**BELFAST**

**ARDS AND NORTH DOWN**

**BELFAST**

## CAPITAL CITY

Belfast is the capital of Northern Ireland and its landmarks include City Hall and Stormont Parliament Buildings.

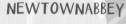

# THE SOUTH-EASTERN DISTRICTS

## Meet St Patrick, the patron saint of Ireland

There are lots of amazing legends about St Patrick – one claims that he chased all the snakes out of Ireland, while another says that his walking stick turned into a tree! The historic counties of Down and Armagh, which together make up the Southeastern Districts, have strong links with the saint. Follow in his footsteps to his colossal statue in Saul, where he founded his first church; to Armagh, whose two cathedrals are both named after him; and to Downpatrick, where he is thought to be buried – and which has one of the best St Patrick's Day parades. Saints aside, this region also boasts the heavenly Mourne Mountains, where you can climb Slieve Donard, Northern Ireland's highest peak. Truly, a blessed country!

**ELIZABETH BELL**
**1862-1934**
The physician was born in Newry and became the first woman to qualify as a doctor in Ireland; she was also a leading suffragette.

**BACK TO NATURE**
Oxford Island Nature Reserve is surrounded by water on three sides, and has bird-watching hides, picnic spots and play areas.

**MID-ULSTER**

**SAINTLY CITY**
Armagh is the religious capital of Ireland, with two cathedrals named after St Patrick.

**WATER SPORTS**
At Craigavon Watersports Centre you can try banana boating and wakeboarding, and over-12s can tackle the inflatable aqua park.

**PORTADOWN**

**SAINT PATRICK**
**C.385-461**
The patron saint of Ireland is said to have banished all snakes from the country – there is a huge statue of him near Saul, and a Saint Patrick Centre in Downpatrick.

**CHRISTINE LAMPARD (NEE BLEAKLEY)**
**B.1979**
The TV presenter was born in Newtownards and fronts Loose Women and travel documentaries – she once waterskied across the English Channel!

**STAR GAZING**
The Armagh Astropark contains the Observatory and Planetarium, where you can watch a space show and touch a 4.6-billion-year-old meteorite!

**ARMAGH, BANBRIDGE AND CRAIGAVON**

**PAGAN PILGRIMAGE**
The Navan Fort was the prehistoric capital of the Kings of Ulster – learn about Celtic life, and celebrate the sun god Lugh at the Wickerman Gathering in August.

**FESTIVAL FEVER**
Get arty in Newry with Sticky Fingers, a charity that runs an Art Cafe, an Imaginarium and an annual International Children's Festival in October.

**NEWRY**

**ANCIENT MONUMENTS**
There are 20 neolithic tombs in the Ring of Gullion, including Ballymacdermot Court Tomb, and Ballykeel Dolmen.

**NEWRY, MOURNE AND DOWN**

**EDDIE IZZARD**
**B. 1962**
The stand-up comedian and political activist spent much of his childhood in Bangor. In 2009, he ran 43 marathons in 51 days for charity, which took him across most of the British Isles... on foot!

**LOCAL FOOD**
Local specialities include Lough Neagh eels, Comber potatoes and Armagh bramley apples.

Into the Woods
586 Footsteps

**RING OF GULLION**
Climb Slieve Gullion (576m), the highest mountain in the Ring of Gullion, follow the Giant's Lair story trail or whiz down the Adventure Playpark's zipwires.

**REPUBLIC OF IRELAND**

## ANTRIM AND NEWTOWNABBEY

## IRISH SEA

### BY THE SEASIDE
Bangor is a Victorian seaside town with lots of attractions – the best is the Pickie Fun Park.

### DESERT ISLANDS
The three Copeland Islands (called Lighthouse, Mew and Copeland) are home to seals and birds such as Arctic terns – you can visit them by boat from Donaghadee.

### PAST LIVES
Lisburn's Irish Linen Centre has spinning and weaving demonstrations, while the Foyle Valley Railway museum brings the disused Derry to Donegal line to life.

## ARDS AND NORTH DOWN

BANGOR

## BELFAST

NEWTOWNARDS

### MUSEUM TIME
The Ulster Folk and Transport Museum is set in 170 acres of countryside, and has farm animals, horse-drawn carriages and a Titanic exhibition.

### LOOKOUT POINT
Climb 160m-high Scrabo Tower, built on a hill above Newtownards in 1857, for views as far as Scotland.

### SOMME MUSEUM
Explore the reconstructed trenches in Newtownards to see what life was like in the First World War.

## LISBURN AND CASTLEREAGH

LISBURN

### ROYAL CONNECTION
Hillsborough Castle is the Queen's official residence when she is in Northern Ireland, and is open to commoners at other times.

### FOWL PLAY
WWT Castle Espie has the biggest collection of waterbirds in Ireland, plus a Secret Swamp play space.

### LOTS OF LOUGHS
Strangford Lough is the largest inlet in the British Isles, covering 150 sq km.

### ST PATRICK'S DAY
The 17th March is celebrated all around the world – a huge parade is held in Downpatrick, where the saint is said to be buried.

### ART ATTACK
F.E. McWilliam was a surrealist sculptor – visit his gallery in Banbridge and take part in an art workshop.

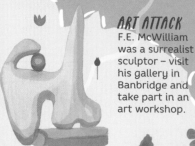

### MODEL VILLAGE
Kearney Village is a traditional fishing village now owned by the National Trust.

### GO TO JAIL
Explore the cells of the Down County Museum in Downpatrick where convicts waited to be transported to Australia.

### INTO THE WOODS
Castlewellan Forest Park contains Northern Ireland's national arboretum. It has giant sequoias, a peace maze and a play area.

### WATER WORLD
Exploris, an aquarium in Portaferry, has both tropical and native fish, an African Nile crocodile and rescued baby seals.

### FULL STEAM AHEAD
The Downpatrick and County Down heritage railway links Inch Abbey and Viking King Magnus's Grave.

### CASTLE COUNT
Try archery at Castle Ward, which doubled as Winterfell in Game of Thrones; or visit nearby Dundrum or Gosford.

**BRIAN BORU**
**C.941-1014**
The High King of Ireland reigned from 1002-1014 and fell at the Battle of Clontarf – his tomb is said to be in St Patrick's Cathedral, Armagh.

### ANCIENT CITY
Newry, known as the Gateway to the North, was founded in 1144, although there is evidence of human settlement from 4000BC.

### ENCHANTED FOREST
Tollymore Forest Park became Northern Ireland's first state forest park in 1955, and has follies, grottoes and caves.

### SPORTS REPORT
Royal County Down has been voted the best golf course in the world; it has hosted the Irish Open and the Walker Cup.

### INTO NARNIA
Enter the Narnia Trail through a wardrobe in Kilbroney Park, and visit the Tree People, the Beavers' House and the Citadels.

### MIGHTY MOUNTAINS
Slieve Donard in the Mourne Mountains is the highest peak in Northern Island at 850m; the 35km drystone Mourne Wall crosses it and 14 other summits.

**BEAR GRYLLS**
**B.1974**
The adventurer, TV presenter and Chief Scout was born in Donaghadee – his expeditions include circumnavigating the UK on jet skis.

**RORY MCILROY**
**B.1989**
The golfer was born in Holywood and had won three majors by the age of 25 – he has twice won RTE Sports Person of the Year.

### SEA LIFE
You can see baby lobsters at Seascope, a lobster hatchery and marine research centre, and learn about fishing at the nearby Nautilus Centre.

## OSCAR WILDE
### 1854-1900
The writer was born in Dublin but went to Portora Royal School in Enniskillen – he was sent to prison for "gross indecency" in 1895 and finally pardoned in 2017.

## TYPHOID MARY
### 1869-1938
Mary Mallon, from Cookstown, emigrated to the US in 1883 – she was the first carrier of typhoid, infecting about 51 people, although she never had the disease herself.

## FRIGHT NIGHT
Everyone wears fancy dress in Derry, aka the City of Bones, for the biggest Halloween parade in Europe.

DERRY

## WALK THE WALLS
Derry has the only intact city walls in Ireland – they are 8m tall and 9m wide, have four original gates and 24 cannons.

## GO OUTDOORS
You can go canoeing in Gortin Glen lakes, and cycle, horse ride, orienteer and camp in the forest park.

## CATCH YOUR DINNER
The River Mourne is a top spot for salmon fishing – the season runs from April to October.

STRABANE

## PRESIDENTIAL PAST
Visit US president Woodrow Wilson's ancestral home near Strabane, and Ulysses S Grant's ancestral home in Ballygawley.

## LOCAL FOOD
Boxty is a potato pancake made with mashed and raw grated potato – try it with Fermanagh black bacon.

## BUCKETS AND SPADES
County Fermanagh is landlocked, but you can still build a sandcastle here – Mullans Bay on Lough Erne has a small sandy beach.

## CASTLE COUNT
Harry Avery's Castle is a rare example of a stone castle built by a Gaelic Irish chief (Henry Aimhréidh O'Neill); other castles include Tully, Monea and Belle Isle.

## LEAVING HOME
The Ulster American Folk Park tells the story of Irish emigration to America, and hosts a huge bluegrass music festival each September.

## STARRY NIGHT
You can sleep in a transparent bubble dome in the forest at Finn Lough – perfect for stargazing!

OMAGH

## THE LAKELANDS
Go island-hopping in Lough Erne, where there are 154 islands – including Inish Corkish, which is populated by pigs!

## STRANGE STONES
White Island is famous for its six stone figures that are thought to be over 1,000 years old.

## FUN AND GAMES
Todds Leap activity centre has ziplines, a giant swing, a bungee trampoline and zorbing.

## COUNTY TOWN
Omagh is the county town of Co. Tyrone – it tragically made headlines worldwide after the Omagh bombing in 1998, when 29 people were killed.

## LOOKOUT POINT
The 11km walk through Lough Navar Forest includes a viewpoint over Lough Erne - try to spy the coast of Donegal and Sperrin Mountains.

## MOVERS AND SHAKERS
The G8 summit of world leaders was held at Lough Erne Resort in 2013 – guests today can use the same gym as Barack Obama!

## ISLAND TOWN
Enniskillen is is built between the upper and lower sections of Lough Erne, and has a 16th century castle.

ENNISKILLEN

## STATELY HOME
The parkland of 18th-century Castle Coole is full of ancient trees that are home to rare rhinoceros beetles, barkflies and digger wasps.

## SCHOOL DAYS
Famous pupils from Portora Royal School (now Enniskillen Royal Grammar School) include Oscar Wilde, Samuel Beckett and singer Neil Hannon.

## TREE OF LIFE
Florence Court is a Georgian mansion with a water-powered sawmill, an ice house and a 250-year-old yew tree – it is the "parent" of all yew trees in Ireland.

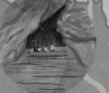

## GOING UNDERGROUND
The 11.5km Marble Arch caves are a network of underground chambers, passages and rivers – you can explore them on foot and by boat.

## ANIMAL MAGIC
The Crom Estate is a nature reserve with a ruined castle, and is a haven for rare pine martens – there may be as few as 320 left in all of Northern Ireland.

## CAUSEWAY COAST AND GLENS

### CITY SIGHTS
Derry's landmarks include the Guildhall and the Peace Bridge, and its museums include the Tower Museum, the Siege Museum and the Museum of Free Derry.

### HIGH LIFE
The Sperrins are a mountain range in Co. Tyrone and Co. Londonderry – the highest peak is Sawel Mountain at 678m.

### ON YOUR BIKE
Davagh Forest has mountain biking trails, from a 3km green run for beginners to a 16km red route for experienced riders.

### ANCIENT MONUMENTS
There are seven Bronze Age stone circles at Beaghmore, plus twelve cairns and ten stone rows.

**MID ULSTER**

### COSTUME COLLECTION
Springhill House is a 17th-century mansion with a library of rare books, a costume collection and a resident ghost called Olivia.

DUNGANNON

### FOOTBALL FACT
Tyrone has won three Gaelic football All-Ireland Championships, in 2003, 2005 and 2008.

### CAPITAL OF ULSTER
Dungannon was the capital of the O'Neill dynasty, which ruled Ulster for more than 300 years – learn more at Ranfurly House, then climb the viewing tower on Castle Hill.

**ARMAGH, BANBRIDGE AND CRAIGAVON**

### MUSEUM TIME
Check out the Blessingbourne Carriage and Costume Museum and the Sheelin Lace Museum or get a haircut and learn about steam trains at the Headhunters Barbers & Railway Museum near Enniskillen.

**ARLENE FOSTER**
**B.1970**
The politician was born in Enniskillen – she became the leader of the Democratic Unionist Party.

**MID AND EAST ANTRIM**

**ANTRIM AND NEWTOWNABBEY**

### CANOE CAMP
Follow the Blackwater Canoe Trail downstream of Blackwatertown and camp wild on Coney Island.

**SAMUEL BECKETT**
**1906-1989**
The writer was born in Dublin, but went to school in Enniskillen. He is the only person to have won a Nobel prize and played first-class cricket.

**DENNIS TAYLOR**
**B.1949**
The snooker player was born in Coalisland – he beat Steve Davis in the 1985 world championships, and is now a commentator.

**SAM NEILL**
**B.1947**
The actor was born in Omagh and moved to New Zealand as a chid – he played Dr Alan Grant in the Jurassic Park films.

**NEIL HANNON**
**B.1970**
The Divine Comedy singer was born in Derry but grew up in Fivemiletown – he wrote the theme tunes for *Father Ted* and *The IT Crowd*.

### Splash around in the Lakelands

Where are you landlocked but surrounded by water? In the historic county of Fermanagh – it is covered in lakes and rivers! You can hire a kayak or cruiser to explore the Lakelands, which are centred on Lough Erne. Why not moor up and spend the night on your own private island, or take an underground boat trip at nearby Marble Arch caves?
This region is famed for walls as well as water – Derry, Northern Ireland's second city, is one of the finest walled cities in all of Europe. The walls were built as defences in the 17th century, and they worked: the city withstood several sieges, including one in 1689 that lasted for 105 days. Walk around the walls today, and imagine how it would feel to be trapped inside …

# THE WESTERLY DISTRICTS

# INDEX

Brimming with creative inspiration, how-to projects, and useful information to enrich your everyday life, Quarto Knows is a favourite destination for those pursuing their interests and passions. Visit our site and dig deeper with our books into your area of interest: Quarto Creates, Quarto Cooks, Quarto Homes, Quarto Lives, Quarto Drives, Quarto Explores, Quarto Gifts, or Quarto Kids.

Maps of the U.K. © 2018 Quarto Publishing plc.
Text © 2018 Rachel Dixon. Illustrations © 2018 Livi Gosling.

First Published in 2018 by Wide Eyed Editions, an imprint of The Quarto Group.
The Old Brewery, 6 Blundell Street, London N7 9BH, United Kingdom.
T (0)20 7700 6700  F (0)20 7700 8066  www.QuartoKnows.com

A catalogue record for this book is available from the British Library.

ISBN 978-1-78603-025-2

The illustrations were created in watercolours
Set in Burford and Core Rhino

Published by Jenny Broom and Rachel Williams
Designed by Nicola Price  •  Design assistance from Sasha Moxon
Manufactured in Dongguan, China TL0718

9 8 7 6 5 4 3 2 1